DON LUIGI STURZO:
THE FATHER OF
SOCIAL DEMOCRACY

DON LUIGI STURZO:
THE FATHER OF
SOCIAL DEMOCRACY

John Molony

Connor Court Publishing
Ballarat

Published in 2016 by Connor Court Publishing Pty Ltd

Copyright © John Molony 2016

First published in 1977 by Croom Helm, London

ALL RIGHTS RESERVED

This book contains material protected under International and Federal Copyright Laws and Treaties. Any unauthorised reprint or use of this material is prohibited. No part of this book may be reproduced or transmitted in any form or by any means, electronic or mechanical, including photocopying, recording, or by any information storage and retrieval system without express written permission from the publisher.

Connor Court Publishing Pty Ltd
PO Box 7257
Redland Bay, QLD,
Australia 4165
sales@connorcourt.com
Phone: 0497-900-685

www.connorcourt.com

ISBN: 9781925138955 (pbk.)

Cover design by Ian James

Printed in Australia

CONTENTS

Acknowledgements	vii
Preface	ix
Introduction	1
1 The Emergence of Political Catholicism in Italy	9
2 The Dream Takes Shape	47
3 Democracy without Direction	83
4 Democracy in Decline	111
5 The Search for a Leader	141
6 The Stick and the Carrot	169
7 The Voice of the Watchman	193
8 Enter the Night	219
Bibliography	247
Index	267

For Lello and Anna

ACKNOWLEDGEMENTS

I am indebted to the assistance provided for me by the Italian Government during my study leave in Rome in 1974. Dr Paolo Canali, Italian ambassador to Australia gave me valuable advice while Professors Francesco Malgeri, Francesco Piva, Pietro Scoppola, Ignazio Ughi, Father Beria, Elizabetta Cucchia and Dr Carlo Danè all assisted me in my research work in Rome. The leading Italian historian of the Partito Popolare, Professor Gabriele De Rosa, not only encouraged me to write my own history of the party but he also shared his unrivalled knowledge with me. In particular he assured me that his and other historians use of the State Archives was such as to obviate the necessity of traversing that ground in my work as it could add but little to any further reinterpretation of the period insofar as it concerns the Partito Popolare. As a consequence I restricted my own archival research to the Istituto Sturzo and only used the State Archives to check some of the more important material available.

While a special word of gratitude must go to the secretaries at the Istituto Sturzo I also wish to thank the staff of the following libraries, institutes and newspapers for their unfailing courtesy and help: Archivio Capitolino; *Avanti*; Biblioteca Apostolica Vaticana; Biblioteca Di Storia Moderna e Contemporanea; Biblioteca Universitaria Alessandrina; Direzione Centrale D.C.; Istituto Gramsci; *Osservatore Romano*; Senato Della Repubblica.

Without the help in Rome of Mrs Gabriella Marcucci-Fanello and Senator Giuseppe Spataro, my work would not have begun nor would it have been successfully concluded. To Paddy Maughan and Barbara Gow, who typed a manuscript and checked a bibliography which I had almost lost in shipwreck off the west coast of Africa, I express my deep gratitude.

ABBREVIATIONS

A.L.S. Archives of the Sturzo Institute, Rome

O.R. *Osservatore Romano*

PPI Partito Popolare Italiano

PREFACE

Luigi Sturzo was an old man of 81 when I met him in Rome in 1952. It was just prior to his nomination as senator by the President of the Italian Republic, Luigi Einaudi. Seated in a large armchair and wrapped in a warm rug Sturzo talked to me of Italy and Australia. To my intense surprise he knew more about Australia and its political system than I had anticipated or indeed dared to hope. I put to him the question 'Do you think a Catholic political party would have a future in Australia?' His negative reply was immediate, direct and decisive. He went on to explain that in a society where the democratic process worked satisfactorily and where the people differed in their religious convictions it was much more reasonable and positive for everyone to work within the already established party system. I then asked him 'Why did you yourself found a Catholic party in Italy?' Again he was quick to answer, 'I did not found a Catholic party. It was a party of Christian inspiration with no direct ties with the Church.' He paused and said, it seemed to me sadly, 'But that is another story of another time and another place'. A nun came in quietly and the interview was over. I resolved then that I would go back to that time and place and, if possible, live again that story.

Twenty-one years later I returned to Rome to pick up the threads of the past and it was as well that those years had elapsed before I attempted my task. Old passions had cooled, Sturzo was a memory with a piazza named in his honour, King and Duce were only a troubled dream and many historians had worked on the rise of fascism to power, while men who had been young in the early 1920s felt free to talk of those distant days. Above all, the years of which I write could be seen in perspective even though the Vatican still stood in solemn grandeur across the Tiber and those who ruled the destiny of the Italian Republic were ever mindful of its power. Thus it was possible to probe the ideals, the fears, the hopes, the frustrations of Sturzo and the party he had founded and to understand in some measure the deeper meaning of that attempt to bring a new element into Italian life. That Sturzo's party died in its infancy is a matter of record but the reason, the manner and the purpose of that demise has perhaps been obscured by time and apathy.

Essentially this is not merely a story about politics. It is a story of an ancient people who had come relatively late to democracy and who failed to respond to its ideals. The men of the Risorgimento had bequeathed to Italy all the outward forms of a modern democracy but the one basic thing they were unable to impart was its spirit. Thus in a land weakened by war, ravaged by ideological ardours, embittered by poverty and rendered aimless in its search for national identity, democracy went to the wall. It comes as no surprise that those political expressions which scorned the outward form of democracy were amongst the first victims of dictatorship. Thus the old Italian socialist movement was rent asunder with disunity and all its forms dissolved before the Duce. Yet it is a surprise that Sturzo's party, which formally at least was dedicated to both the form and spirit of democracy, was so quickly smitten with the rest. To some it would come as an even greater surprise that the Italian fascist state and the Vatican worked hand in hand to help destroy the Partito Popolare.

No simple explanation for such a complex event is possible and to try to fit the facts to a theoretical model is a betrayal of the craft of the historian. This present book is an attempt to understand what happened and if it appears harsh in its analysis it is because the facts themselves are harsh. It ill behoves the outsider to find fault with the house of another and what is said here of Italy and its people, its institutions and its leaders is to speak in part of what I have known and loved because I grew to manhood in the city on the Tiber.

One facet of the difficulty an historian strikes when he begins to write about the Partito Popolare stems from the bewildering variety of opinions on it held by contemporary Italians. Even those who were firmly committed to the party such as Luigi La Rosa, a member of the parliamentary party who stayed faithful to the end, were unable at times to judge its efficacy. La Rosa wrote to Sturzo in 1925, 'Our party will go down in history as the most typical manifestation of byzantism in that extreme Byzantium which is called Italy.'[1] The Partito Popolare was essentially a centre party and it was neither sufficiently anti-fascist for the left nor pro-fascist for the right. It was of Christian inspiration but the Vatican suspected its commitment to its Christian ideals while others thought of it as a creature of the Vatican. It fought for the rights of the workers and the farm labourers and thus it was feared by the industrialists and the land owners, but because it did not accept the concept of class warfare it was despised by the socialists who were uneasy at its power base in the working class. Even outside of Italy Sturzo and the party he founded were badly misrepresented by some Catholics. Francesco Saverio Nitti who had been Prime Minister of Italy in 1919–20 and, like so many other notable Italians, had to flee Italy after 1924, wrote to Sturzo from Zurich in March 1925, 'Who is this journalist Belloc who has written so many stupidities about you, about freedom and about fascism? He must be an ignorant swindler or at the very least a person of repugnant cynicism.'[2]

It is not difficult to understand the Vatican's attitude to the Partito Popolare because the basis of all Sturzo's political thought was a concept of democracy which, as a civic and human ideal, was neither appreciated nor accepted in the Vatican. The political aims of the Vatican as distinguished from those of the Catholic Church, of which the Vatican is the central, administrative unit, were twofold.[3] Generally the Vatican wanted to retain the *status quo* in Italy by the bolstering of a mildly progressive, moderate capitalist state that would at the worst be neutral or at the best favourable to the position of the Church in Italian society. More specifically the Vatican aimed at a solution to the Roman Question and it had done so for some years prior to the advent of Mussolini. Both aims were thwarted by the Partito Popolare in that, while it showed no interest in the Roman Question which it regarded as a matter which time and patience would solve, it upset the balance of power by rejecting the outworn framework of liberal Italy and worked for a new form of society with its basis in social justice.

The more positive element in Italian society which concerned the Vatican was the triumphant growth of socialism. The socialists had grasped their opportunity with the rapid breakdown of the post Risorgimento state apparatus after 1918 and it did not seem improbable that socialism might come to power in the peninsula. Such a prospect was anathema in the Vatican and especially so to Pius XI who had an almost pathological fear of both communism and socialism and to whom it was unthinkable that an organized body of Italian Catholics, such as the Partito Popolare, could even contemplate concerted action with the socialists. The brutality of fascism, even the murder of Matteotti, was a minor irritant in Vatican eyes because Mussolini and his regime had met socialist violence with even worse and more effective fascist violence, had promised to solve the Roman Question and bade fair to restore to the Church some of the departed glory of the medieval or even of the pre-1848 period.

Thus the Partito Popolare was not only expendable to the Vatican but more positively it had to be dismantled. Fascism itself with its threats against the Church was not decisive in helping Pius XI and Cardinal Gasparri to make up their minds about Sturzo and his party although they offered a suitable rationale for a decision which would ultimately have been taken without the presence of fascism. Sturzo had a concept of freedom which lies at the very core of democracy because with freedom democracy begins and its end is human dignity and human development. To fascism, to the Vatican and indeed to all forms of totalitarianism freedom was the reward which one achieved by submission to the model imposed from above. That Sturzo's concept at length prevailed with Vatican II and John XXIII speaks volumes on the development of man since the time of Sturzo.

Nonetheless it is more important to understand the position taken up by the Vatican than to attenuate or denigrate it. By the early 1920s the loss of temporal sovereignty had reduced the papacy to a minor position in international affairs as instanced by Benedict XV's fruitless appeals for peace. Vatican finances were in a shambles due to losses sustained in the First World War; liberalism and freemasonry had well-nigh spent themselves in a welter of anti-clericalism; socialism threatened the very fabric of established religion and civil society; the fear of modernism had stifled the development of theology; the bulwarks of European Catholicism in France and Germany had been ravaged and the nascent Christian social movement had almost died in suspicion, division and recrimination.

It is in this context that the rejection of the Partito Popolare by Pius XI and Gasparri must be seen because by 1922 the men who ruled the Vatican had become inward looking, hesitant and uneasy about all that was not within their own authoritative grasp and which did not conform to their understanding of theology. Hence the impetus they gave to Catholic Action which was centralized, reliant upon ecclesiastical authority and directed fundamentally at the spiritual rather than the civic or political. Pius XI hoped that from its womb a renewed Church would be born which would unite clergy and laity in a common work of transformation of all society. In the broad sweep of human history it is just possible that Mussolini and fascism can be seen as an impetus to change in the Church because it was from Catholic Action in its purest forms that the Church of Vatican II was shaped. To some extent Luigi Sturzo and the Partito Popolare can be seen in that light — not in darkness but in splendour because he and his party were a witness to integrity in the face of all forms of human weakness and human aberration.

Some people may be tempted to argue that the phenomenon of

fascism is a mere fragment of human history and that its infamy, even in Italy, was such that no repetition is possible in the modern democratic states. In counterbalance it can also be argued that there is always in man the urge to impose his own system on others and that the faint hearted or the unthinking, by choice or by default, can allow themselves to be put in bondage. In that context it is worth recalling an episode that took place in Paris. That frail embodiment of the Mediterranean spirit, Francesco Luigi Ferrari, was living there in exile and he represented what remained of the Partito Popolare at an international conference of Christian Democrats held in 1931. Ferrari rose to speak in a debate on the formulation of political tactics and he warned the German delegates not to follow a weak line in regard to Nazism in their country. A German replied brusquely, 'Doctor Ferrari, you are forgetting that we are Germans; we are not Italians.' Prophecy blended with wisdom in Ferrari's reply: 'No I have deliberately not forgotten that very thing and it is precisely because you are Germans that your destruction will be more complete and more humiliating than that of Italy.'

Notes

1. La Rosa to Sturzo, 15 June 1925, A.L.S., f. 114A, c. 8.
2. Nitti to Sturzo, 21 March 1925, ibid., f. 116A, c. 74.
3. While it is clearly intended to distinguish between the Vatican and the Catholic Church by the use of precise terminology there is no implication that the Vatican itself was a monolithic structure in which every member of the Roman Curia or the papal household held identical views on matters such as the Roman Question, fascism or the Partito Popolare. It is the public, official stance of the Vatican, expressed either by the pope himself or by his official spokesmen that is of relevance.
4. C. Sforza, *L'Italia dal 1914 al 1944 quale io la vidi* (Rome, 1944), p. 159.

Introduction

When, on 9 November 1926, Benito Mussolini decreed the dissolution of the Partito Popolare Italiano together with the other anti-fascist parties, his own creation, the Partito Nazionale Fascista, reigned triumphantly in Italy. His totalitarian regime mocked itself by masquerading as a government and, year by year, it ignominiously betrayed the conscience of a whole people. The fascist party unrelentingly devalued every form of personal individuality and foisted on the nation alien and barbaric values, including racism. It identified fascism with the very nation itself, as if the veins of an ancient and honourable people now coursed with venom. All of this had been based on the major premise of an immense and almost unbelievable rejection of the inviolable dignity of the human person.

Yet the immortal words of Leo XIII in his encyclical of 1891, *Rerum Novarum*, remained unheeded in the Vatican and Pius XI refused to condemn fascism. Leo wrote, 'No one may outrage with impunity that human dignity which God Himself treats *with great reverence.*' He stressed furthermore that 'man himself can never renounce his right to be treated according to his nature or to surrender himself to any form of slavery of the spirit'. Those words were never heard in fascist Italy.

It is an undeniable fact that, on the temporal level, the Catholic Church in Italy gained some benefits under the fascist regime. In particular the solution to the long vexed Roman Question, by virtue of which a sovereign Vatican state came into being, was looked upon with much satisfaction by the pope and the Catholic world generally. Furthermore, Catholic Action in Italy managed to retain its independence from the state and thereby saved a multitude of young Italians from wallowing in the ideological idiocy peddled by the fascist youth movement. Finally freedom of cult, whether in the churches or the schools, was preserved.

At the same time democracy in Italy was throttled and the trade union movement became an agent of the state. In the dying stages of the regime, Jews were persecuted but, throughout its existence since 1922, Italian citizens innocent of all but their rejection of fascism, were killed, imprisoned or forced into exile. Finally, Italy was impoverished, her institutions were debauched and the whole nation was forced to its knees in a shameful alliance with the evil of National Socialism under Hitler.

On the night of Mussolini's deposition from power, 24–5 July 1943, those who had acted in the name of the ruling class of Italy, which included its intelligentsia, writers, artists, press and other creative elements, as well as trade unions, industrialists and capitalists failed to recognize, much less acknowledge, that either by direct involvement, supine abstention from opposition or mere lack of interest in anything but their own personal advantage, had contributed to the long endurance of their own serfdom.

On a day of abject national shame, Vittorio Emanuale III and his newly appointed prime minister, Pietro Badaglio, fled from Rome on 8 September 1943. Renamed the Partito Fascista Repubblicano the fascist party had been reduced to nothingness in spirit and structure. Well before its creator was shot dead on 28 April 1945 by Italian partisans, fascism in the north of Italy based at Salò, and disguised as a meaningless Social Republic, stumbled on amidst hatred, murder and violence, as well as economic and military failure.

Some have argued that, with the foundation of the Movimento Sociale Italiano in late 1946, the former fascist party was reborn. They were wrong. Fascism had no transcendent existence. Its essence was rooted in the here and now. Its day lay in the past because it offered nothing for the future except final destruction. By 1946 fascism had nowhere to live except in the unhealthy minds of a miserable minority.

It had left no lasting seeds among the Italian people because in their core they had remained supremely human.

A political party, once its essence is lost, rarely revives. Although the Partito Popolare Italiano, founded by Luigi Sturzo in 1919, had been dissolved brutally by Benito Mussolini in 1926, but its essence had neither been squandered nor dissipated. Sturzo had summed it up in early 1926.

> The Partito Popolare did not come into being for a passing moment, a transitory situation or a particular problem. It was given life to express on the political landscape a vast, coherent and realistic platform destined to be of immense value to Italy. The ideal motives that lay behind this platform have not been weakened, rather they have been strengthened, and the same applies even more pointedly to the moral incentives. No one in good faith can contemplate without sadness and deep concern the attempt by the Government to involve the Church with the fascist regime and ensure its loyalty by virtue of favours and benefits.
>
> The Partito Popolare knows well the limits of its practical actions because it has no competence or responsibility in the matter of religion. Yet it has the right and duty to refuse approval to a political system which wants to make religion an instrument of its dominance. This is especially so when such a system tends towards the deification of the Nation-State, to identify the State with the Government, the Government with a political party and the party with a person. Than this concept there can scarcely be another one which is more pagan and more repugnant to the spirit of civilization and to the principles of Christianity.
>
> In all our actions we must be guided by our determination to do our duty without being preoccupied by political gains, personal satisfaction or the hope of a favourable outcome. The rest lies in the hands of Providence. *It is better to place our trust in God than in the rulers of the world.*

After the suppression of the Partito Popolare, Italian Catholic

Action shaped many of the leaders in the next two decades who would become the mainstay of a new political party. In January 1939 Giorgio La Pira (1903–77) founded the review *Principî* at Florence where he later became mayor. A formidable critic of fascism, he exposed the false gods of race, state and proletariat which were then crucifying the nations of Europe and Russia. His ideas gave a spiritual and intellectual basis for a movement that would proclaim human rights and especially the right of all citizens to a role in making the democracies of the future. By 1943 Alcide de Gasperi was the acknowledged leader of a group of younger men formed in Catholic Action, especially the university group, FUCI, as well as former members of the Partito Popolare. Among them were Mario Scelba, Stefano Jacini, Giuseppe Spataro, Giovanni Gronchi, Achille Grandi, Giorgio Tupini, Amintore Fanfani and Aldo Moro. In 1943 the new party was founded and called *Democrazia Cristiana* with De Gasperi as its leader.

By its very name *Democrazia Cristiana* differed from that of the old PPI in that it had taken a first step away from aconfessionalism. In essence it looked to the democratic state to safeguard morality, protect the integrity of the family and help parents to give a Christian education to their children. To some discernible degree therefore the state would act as guarantee for, and a defender of, religion. The generation reared under fascism had become accustomed to expect the state to play that role and with De Gasperi, who realized that without the approval of the Church his party could never come to power in Italy, they prevailed over the old popolari to whom the state was a separate and secular entity from which one was entitled to demand justice and equity for all citizens and to respect religion but not to show favour to any particular form of it.

Unsurprisingly, when added to the threat of Italy passing into a subservient role as a mere satellite of Soviet communism, it was almost inevitable that the state as represented by a *Democrazia Cristiana* government would be aligned with the Church in a concerted, and successful effort, to maintain Italy's freedom. That prolonged relationship was in stark contrast to the lack of any approval by the Church of the opposition to the fascist regime adopted by those elements of the Partito Popolare who remained loyal to Sturzo and to his concept of the role the Partito Popolare ought to undertake in society.

Indeed Sturzo in the early 1920s resolutely refused to contemplate establishing any form of a direct alignment with the Catholic Church. At the same time he was positively inclined to working with the Socialist Party in opposing fascism. The ruling elements in the Vatican remained steadfastly opposed to any such alignment. In short, Sturzo remained true to the original concept of the Partito Popolare which he spelt out when he said, 'It is superfluous to explain why we are not called a "Catholic party." The two words are antithetical. Catholicism is a religion, it is universal. A party is political; it creates division. From the very beginning we have rejected the idea that our characteristic should be religion and we have wanted to place ourselves clearly on the specific terrain of a party that has as its direct objective the public life of the nation.'

In Rome on 18 January 1919 Sturzo had launched an appeal to his countrymen in which he said that the 'political parties of every nation must contribute to, and strengthen, every tendency and principle that gives promise of banishing the danger of any future war, of putting all nations on a firm footing, of activating the ideals of social justice, of uplifting the general conditions of work and of energizing the spiritual and material strength of all those countries which are united in the solemn bond of "a community of nations." ' He foreshadowed that new community as having a legal and binding aspect which would include arbitration between them when desirable, the abolition of secret treaties and the rejection of military conscription. Finally, he called for universal disarmament.

To foster that end Sturzo decided in 1921 to make personal

contact with other political parties in Europe which had their base in the Catholic masses. With De Gasperi in September of that year he visited Germany, spoke extensively with the leaders of the Centre Party and met Konrad Adenauer who was then mayor of Cologne. Developments in fascist Italy combined with World War II to impede progress towards international collaboration but, unsurprisingly, De Gasperi never forgot the initial step and the reasons behind it. After he formed his own Christian Democrat government in late 1945, which remained in office until 1953, he began to assume a role as an outspoken supporter of the drive to form a federation of democratic European states. He helped to organize the **Council of Europe** and the **European Coal and Steel Community** in 1951, which were lapidary steps in the vast work of developing an integrated Europe to replace the constantly divided and often warring nation states that made it up.

The demands of post-war Italian politics forced the Christian Democrats into sketchy alliances, including with the socialists and communists, until 1947 when De Gasperi excluded them. At the same time he and his government looked to the Vatican for approval and support in its gaining and retaining political power which it received in full measure. Various Christian Democrat governments made up of center coalitions with left and right wings followed until 1963 when Aldo Moro formed a government in coalition with the socialists, which alliance endured well into the 1970s. Buffeted by scandals and corrupt political and financial behaviour the Christian Democrat Party finally succumbed to the inevitable in 1994. After almost 50 years in power in one shape or another it collapsed in 1994. One cannot estimate how Luigi Sturzo would have reacted when the party clothed its remnants with the name given to it over 75 years before — the Partito Popolare Italiano. In more recent times the legacy of Luigi Sturzo was revived by Romano Prodi who became prime minister of Italy twice (1996–8 and 2006–8) as well as president of the European Commission from 1999 to 2004 while Mario Monti, prime minister since 2011, is a son of that same tradition.

It is not enough to conclude on a note of desperation when speaking of the Partito Popolare in either of its manifestations in Italy from 1919 until 1994. Together with the socialists, communists and a few minor, but courageous, groups, its unfailing opposition to Mussolini and his government will stand upright with honour into the future. Christian Democracy as an enduring political force in Italy for two generations must not be remembered merely for its ignominious demise. Who but the deluded would now wish to have witnessed Italy, that seedbed of western civilization, suffer the prolonged agony of Poland, Czechoslovakia, Hungary, East Germany and the other satellite states as they groveled beneath the heel of Soviet imperialism? And if Italy had fallen, who will assert with confidence that Spain, Portugal, Greece, perhaps even France, would not have followed it into darkness? The unique bulwark in Italy which prevented that initial disaster was the Christian Democrat Party.

It is not within the direct ambit of this work to trace the development and centrality of parties based on Christian and democrat principles in other European states since World War II. Such governments held office in many countries and their representatives met formally and informally but regularly, which resulted in fruitful developments of both the relations between them and the decisions they made locally. They accepted fully a profound commitment to democracy and did not hesitate to break free from forms of confessionalism in respect of the Catholic Church. While upholding the independent existence of each state, to them the supranationality of Europe in its essential elements, whether geographically, spiritually or intellectually was a given as were its Christian roots. Nonetheless, how that unity would operate on an economic level remained, and remains, uncertain except that a welfare state was accepted as desirable by all. While the fundamental teachings of Leo XIII's *Rerum Novarum* were a cornerstone of much Christian Democrat thinking, the one contribution of Pius XI accepted by them was the principle of subsidiarity which implied the recognition of the necessary role of regions in the development of a healthy nation.

In 1976 a transnational European People's Party was formed which now groups 38 national states and has 265 representatives in the European Parliament. In October 2012, sixty one years after Sturzo founded his party in Rome, the Nobel Peace Prize was awarded to the European Union for 'the advancement of peace and reconciliation, democracy and human rights in Europe.' Luigi Sturzo and his Partito Popolare Italiano might not have been foremost in the minds of those who united Europe. Yet, while Benedict of Nursia will remain recognized as a founder of the old Europe, the day will surely come when Luigi Sturzo of Caltagirone will stand with Robert Schuman, Konrad Adenauer and Alcide De Gasperi as a founder of the new Europe.

1
THE EMERGENCE OF POLITICAL CATHOLICISM IN ITALY

Darkness had already fallen across the Tiber on that late December evening of 1918 when Luigi Sturzo was called before Cardinal Pietro Gasparri. Italy had come out of the First World War victorious, yet in the corridors of the Vatican prelates walked with measured and hesitant steps. Some had pinned their hopes on a German victory and watched their castles fall in ruins. Others had longed and prayed for peace, as indeed had Pope Benedict XV, to see all papal initiative spurned by the great powers. Gasparri himself had brought his work as a canon lawyer to fruition with the *Codex Iuris Canonici* in 1917, but more pressing matters were now at hand. The finances of the Vatican were a shambles, the Church in Eastern Europe was trembling before the threat of an enemy seemingly more dangerous than the barbarians of old, and in Italy itself no real progress had been made towards healing the rift between Church and state. It was no time to trouble a Vatican Secretary of State, but here was a slight Sicilian priest who wanted to found a new political party. Perhaps the curial cardinal saw some faint glimmer of hope ahead. Perhaps this would be the party to reconcile both sides of the Tiber and restore to the Church her role in Italian society. It was worth a try at any rate — there was so much to be gained and little enough to lose. Political parties could come and go while the Church remained. That was the lesson of the past and both priest and prelate knew it.

Sturzo later recounted the story of his interview. Gasparri had already discussed the matter with the pope and he told Sturzo that as far as the Vatican was concerned he could go ahead and set up his party despite the fact that it was to be independent of the Church in that it was simply to be founded by Catholics, rather than a Catholic party with a religious basis. Gasparri even accepted the theoretical possibility of some form of eventual alliance with the socialists in preference to the liberals, but he stressed the need for Sturzo and his followers to recognize that responsibility for their actions lay with themselves and that the Church and Catholic Action must never be involved. With needless irony Gasparri warned the priest that if mistakes were made they would lie at Sturzo's door — as if both men were unaware that it was not the wont of the Vatican to acknowledge the sins of the Church's children. Sturzo plucked up the courage to allude to the lifting of the *non expedit* and Gasparri replied that the pope would see to that when and how he pleased.[1] Less than a month later, 18 January 1919, the Partito Popolare Italiano was founded and on 10 November of that year, a few days before the Italian general elections, the pope lifted the *non expedit*.[2] After almost 60 years, during which Catholics in Italy had hovered on the fringes of public life, the time had come for them to play their role in a nation that had been born despite them. It is of some interest that their withdrawal was the fruit of papal disapproval and their later participation rested upon papal approval.

The formation of an expression of political unity amongst Catholics had been rendered inevitable by the step taken by Pius IX in 1868 when, in the aftermath of Italian unity, he had instructed the Sacred Penitentiary to send a reply to those Italian bishops who were asking whether Italian Catholics ought to be permitted to vote or participate in elections. The reply was simple, so simple indeed that it was frequently misunderstood. 'Considering all the circumstances, it is not expedient' — *non expedit*.[3] The interpretation that an absolute veto was to be imposed and that 'all the circumstances' were a fixed norm was too readily assumed, with a consequent strengthening of intransigent, conservative and ultramontane attitudes in the Church. Indeed by 1886 The Holy Office had decreed that it was no longer a case of inexpediency, but that the participation of Catholics in public life on the electoral level was prohibited.

As a result, when the day had come for them to enter into political life, it was inevitable that they should do so as Catholics rather than simply as citizens for the precise reason that over two generations the Vatican had insisted that as Catholics they differed from their fellow citizens. The reason for the difference was never fully elucidated, but it had a great deal to do with the fact that the Italian state had made Rome its centre and thus deprived the papacy of its temporal possessions. The Roman Question had thus assumed dimensions which involved the very consciences of a considerable number of Italian citizens in that not to be dedicated to its solution in a manner acceptable to the Vatican was to be axiomatically a Catholic lacking the fullness of faith. To what extent the generality of Italian Catholics took the Roman Question seriously will never be known. Nevertheless it is clear that on the political level Catholics in Italy did not become a cohesive force until the founding of the PPI. The years that elapsed between 1870 and 1919, however, saw other developments in Italian Catholic life that in some senses paved the way for the formation of the PPI. During that time Italian Catholic Action was formed, a version of Christian Democracy took shape and from the 1890s onwards Luigi Sturzo and many other Italian Catholics were experimenting with ideas and movements that saw their fruition with the development of the PPI.[4]

Sturzo was born at Caltagirone in Sicily on 26 November 1871 and his early life thereby coincided with the period in which Italy was seeking to consolidate the work of her unification. His childhood was happy and secure and the sensitivity of his nature was heightened by his close, lifelong bonds with his twin sister, Emmanuela. Music, art, religion and politics were part of the fabric of the Sturzo household.

They were all ingredients that could be smoothly combined with an ecclesiastical vocation and in the case of both Luigi and his elder brother Mario such proved to be the case. Luigi studied at the seminaries of Acireale, Noto and Caltagirone but his interests in those early years were primarily literary with Horace, Dante and, later, Machiavelli as their basis.[5] Through his intellectual and moral formation he easily fitted the pattern of clerical life as a seminary teacher. He was studious, gifted and devoted and it was to the seminary at Caltagirone that his bishop sent him in 1890 even before his ordination. There he joined his brother Mario, taught history and literature and showed the signs of a closed mentality that can so easily be part and parcel of such institutions. He displayed that mentality almost immediately when he wrote a long letter to his bishop arguing against seminarians being permitted to take outside examinations. To the zealous young cleric such behaviour could cause a loss of vocations, introduce worldly ideas into the seminary and weaken discipline there.[6] But other factors were at work which drove him to assume an attitude and a role which eventually gave 'the fascists a hundred and one reasons to hate Luigi Sturzo'.[7] His bishop had decided to send him to further his studies in Rome and it was in that city that the path of his life was set.

In November 1894, after his ordination to the priesthood in May of that year, Sturzo arrived in Rome. It was a big step for the young Sicilian because it gave him a chance to move in another world; a world of learning, idealism, intrigue, ambition and rapid change. He lived in the same college as Nicola Monterisi, went to the Jesuit run Gregorian University where he was a contemporary of the young Eugenio Pacelli, later to become Pius XII, and of Emmanuel Suhard who became cardinal archbishop of Paris and the inspirational figure of the Catholic revival in France. He met and talked frequently with Giacomo Radini Tedeschi who was also a major influence in the life of Angelo Roncalli, later Pope John XXIII. He tried to divide his life, without much success, between his Roman studies and his dedication to the development of a social and political apostolate in Sicily to which his whole being had begun to call him given the miserable condition of the people of the island. Thus he was happy when, from 1898 onwards, having gained an undistinguished doctorate, he was able to relinquish his studies and devote himself to Sicily. But Rome had left its mark on Sturzo and although he returned gladly to his diocese it was to the City that he returned for the decisive moments of his life.

The growth of Italian sentiment which ultimately gave birth to that movement of idealism, poetry, dedication and heroism, which we call the Risorgimento, had within it a fatal dualism. From those distant days of the sixth century when the Empire of the West had been allowed to meet its own fate before the barbarian invasions, a segment of the people who made up Italy had looked to the papacy as its protector, its provider and ultimately as its king. Within Italy itself they were the people who added to their political convictions others on a religious level that again spanned the centuries. In the wake of Gregory VII's *Dictatus papae*, the struggle over Investiture and clerical celibacy to the final formulation of spiritual absolutism with the definition of Infallibility, a chord was struck in the hearts of those who were the papal party. Even beyond the confines of Italy the same phenomenon was apparent in that those who most readily accepted the totality of papalism accepted both its spiritual and political overtones.[8] In Italy itself the Guelph party had its Ghibelline counterpart with its rejection of the papal political programme and frequently also the spiritual accompaniment. This duality reached its apogee with the Risorgimento in that the evident obstacle to Italian unity from within was the papacy and Pius IX was the figurehead upon whom Italian nationalists heaped their opprobrium when it was ultimately apparent that he was not with them in their struggle to make a nation. The division caused in Italian society was a source of rejoicing to some and *L'Armonia* of Turin, amongst the most widely read clerical journals in the peninsula, summed it up. 'For us in these days it is a great advantage to have a clear and neat division between the component elements of Italy... There is no middle path — we are either for the Pope or against the Pope.'[9]

In the first years of his priesthood Sturzo apparently shared the views of the intransigent Catholic minority and with them he believed that the pope needed to be king of a 'free state, however small' because the temporal power was 'a natural truth joined to the truth of faith.'[10] Understandably, given his orthodoxy and his capabilities, he was quickly given a responsible position as a leading chaplain to the *Opera dei congressi* which had been founded in 1874 to unite in a monolithic form of Catholic Action all the elements of Italian Catholicism that were prepared to accept their disenfranchisement on a political level consequent upon the *non expedit*.[11] The purpose of the *Opera* was specifically religious in that it concerned itself with dogmatic instruction, church ceremonies, spiritual retreats and the diffusion of edifying literature. In his first public lecture on 6 October 1895 Sturzo spoke of the need to save youth from the perils brought upon society largely by freemasonry, and two months later he summarized Catholic Action as an auxiliary one to the 'salvific work of the priest.' Some slight indication of his future thought was contained however in the words by which he defined the purpose of Catholic Action as one of 'making the Christian spirit flower again in the family and in society'. Already he was firmly convinced that the only policy to follow was that of refusing involvement in politics and concentrating on the formation of a strong Catholic body committed to integral reform, but he knew that the temptation to immediate political action was very strong and that Catholics felt an instinctive urge to become part of the total social fabric of Italian society.[12]

On the political level Sturzo saw the failure of the moderate elements amongst Catholics who had tried to bring about reconciliation between Church and state. Their defeat was symbolized by the forced public recantation of his views in his own cathedral by their leader, Bishop Geremia Bonomelli, in 1889. With this act Leo XIII had finally made it clear that he was to be a suitable successor to Pius IX in rejecting any premature overtures that would lead to harmony between Church and state.[13] And it was a lesson that did not escape the attention of young clerics throughout Italy such as Sturzo, although he was probably unaware that Leo had been persuaded to renounce his hopes of a reconciliation by the Catholic powers — France and Spain — who did not want to see a strong Italy. Thus when, in 1897, he began a new publication called *La Croce di Costantino* as the voice of Catholic Action in the diocese of Caltagirone, Sturzo sounded as papal as the pope himself. In articles on such topics as 'Love for the Pope', 'Catholics and Liberals', 'Soldiers', and 'Solemn Protest', Sturzo proclaimed in unequivocal terms the position of the papacy in the Church and the inviolability of the pope's right to his temporal power. Catholics were told that if they didn't love the pope they forfeited their right to be called Catholic, Leo was proclaimed as 'our great captain' and all were asked to defend the temporal power and to remember the 'Old prisoner' in the Vatican.[14]

Nevertheless it was impossible for a man with the spirit of a Sturzo to live in Caltagirone and not face the pressing social problems that surrounded him. Despite the fact that his own background was aristocratic and his family was of ample means, Sturzo did not need to be told that it was difficult to reconcile belief in a benevolent God with the pressing problem of misery, especially when the Church seemed to have no message to offer the poor other than a humble resignation to their lot. In Sicily in particular that lot was a burdensome one and the brutal materialism which was increasingly the economic philosophy of European liberalism had aggravated the situation of the peasant. Sturzo said in 1903 that the south could be compared to Africa on a map he had seen in the Vatican where the latter was summed up with the words 'Here there are lions'. In the case of the south it would be sufficient to write 'Here there are southerners'. He went to the roots of the matter when he said that the distinction in Italy between the north and the south was not simply geographical, but one that went deep into all Italian life and touched 'the most complex psychological and historical causes'. To Sturzo there could be no simple solution to this problem and he especially rejected one that did not take into account the economic and social causes while merely emphasizing the spiritual. To do such was to make a mockery of Christianity because it was necessary to alleviate bodily misery in order to be able to do good for the souls of the people'.[15]

Despite the fact that the North had gradually become aware of the South since the Risorgimento such awareness did nothing to rectify absentee landlordism, the raping of an already impoverished soil for quick economic gain, the prevalence of malaria, the exorbitant interest on loans which sometimes reached more than 100 per cent and the general air of contempt with which the wealthy treated the poor.[16] All this Sturzo understood simply because he lived in a town of 45,000 inhabitants, 28,000 of whom were farm workers who often had to travel long distances on foot to their miserable farms, which in any case they did not own. In 1893-4 Sturzo also saw the brutal repression of the workers in Sicily by the liberal state when, led by zealous agitators, the peasants strove to remedy their situation, and he knew that to stand beside the poor in a fight for justice as well as charity was to risk alienation from the ruling class within the state and the Church. He was nevertheless convinced that any genuine work of social reconstruction depended upon the people because the aristocracy had proved a failure and the bourgeoisie 'conserved the double characteristics of irreligion and egoism'. At the same time he was cautious of the socialist movement because of its violence, its tendency to create unrest and its fatalistic cry to the workers to 'kill or be killed!'[17]

The element that gave impetus and meaning to Sturzo's work

was the birth in Italy of a new political philosophy that called itself Christian Democracy. It had its origins in France and Germany and in its Italian formulation on a theoretical level it was the work of a remarkable young priest, Romolo Murri.[18] A step towards a more open attitude to social questions on the part of Catholics had been taken with the publication of Leo XIII's encyclical *Rerum Novarum* in 1891. This proved a more fertile soil for the development of ideas involving the responsibility of Catholics for the wellbeing of the workers. Although tinged with paternalistic overtones, the concept nonetheless could lead to genuine development on the level of political and social thought and action.[19] Sturzo met Murri frequently in Rome in 1896 and grasped eagerly the fundamental concept whereby the laity as such were given a task to play in the world, complementary to but not essentially subordinate to the Church's salvific work in the spiritual order.[20] This development would be divisive in that it enhanced the dualism which the Church had always tried to ignore or suppress but that was not then evident to either Murri or Sturzo. One astute bystander, Napoleone Colajanni, saw the danger clearly when he remarked that, if put into practice, Murri's ideas would threaten the socialist left, but he added that the socialists need not worry, for Murri, if he persisted with his ideas, would be excommunicated.[21]

On his return to Sicily, Sturzo was quick to propagate the new idea embodied behind the words Christian Democracy. Faced as he was with the ever present problem of the oppressed he did not allow himself to enjoy the luxury of speculation or theoretical argumentation, nor did he ignore the fact that the bourgeois elements in society and those who preached moderation in the Catholic Church coalesced to worsen the lot of the peasants, oppressed in southern Italy as they were by 'capitalism and ruinous economic conditions'.[22] The Italian economic situation, even in the North, had worsened in the decades after the Risorgimento and the Catholic movement had given a lead there with the setting up of credit societies and societies of mutual aid.[23] Sturzo thus turned his attention to the formation of small rural banks based on the parishes in his diocese; he began a form of young workers' movement and he tried to interest the local clergy in the social problems that confronted the laity. Though he had a cooperative and sympathetic bishop, Sturzo realized that his greatest problem was to convince the clergy and the educated laity that the social problem was a matter to be taken seriously and that Christian Democracy involved 'the reconstruction of a Christian society in the fullest meaning of the word.'[24] By now history and literature were no longer his competence in the seminary where he had begun to teach sociology and economics and, clear indication that the intransigence of his youth was gone, he was quoting Ketteler to his students: 'If St Paul were alive today he would become a journalist.' The kind of activity he was engaged in and the unrest it caused led inevitably to denunciation by a priest for his 'subversive' activity. He was charged before the courts but escaped any penalty, yet the warning was clear that it was dangerous to continue along such a path.[25]

It was precisely on the level of its ultimate scope that the movement, or 'our party' as Sturzo thought of it, was called into question by Catholic conservatives and, finally, by ecclesiastical authority itself.[26] Leo XIII, who was sensitive to the need for change, overcame his aristocratic and curial background sufficiently to recognize that the Church faced a new world in which the question of the working masses could not be ignored. In some faint and tentative manner he understood that people everywhere would demand a role in the shaping of their own destiny and he was prepared to give his assent to that process, even when Catholics took part in it, provided it did not transgress doctrinal boundaries, did nothing to weaken the hierarchical nature of the Church or interfered with its own political role. Thus he 'baptized' the movement by himself using the words 'Christian Democracy' and recognizing that it ushered in 'a future of peace, prosperity and happiness' provided it remained Christian rather than socialist.[27]

What Leo, the cultivated humanist, did not understand was the impact of the centuries on the educated and wealthy members of the Catholic masses. Men who had been nurtured on dualistic concepts which placed a negative value on the temporal, and concentrated man's finality on the spiritual and on a transcendental concept of salvation, were unlikely to find much of an appeal in a movement that seemed to ignore these values. Murri and Sturzo could plead that Christian Democracy meant a genuinely profound application of the principles of the Gospel to the temporal order, but again they were unlikely to strike a chord in those whose mental torpidity or economic ease depended upon a strictly individualistic application of the Gospels. Furthermore, what were convinced papalists to make of a public Catholic programme that seemed to ignore the Roman Question so long dear to the hearts of the papacy and its loyal followers? Finally, what was to become of that manifestation of Catholic unity called the *Opera* if its members were to argue about matters such as a just wage, absentee landlordism, interest on loans, workers' unions and the like? The *Opera* had survived the struggle as to whether the Roman Question was to remain the major preoccupation of Italian Catholics, and it could likewise survive the arguments about teaching the catechism, helping the clergy, publishing healthy literature and promoting charitable ventures because all that was allegedly the stuff of Catholicism. But a concern for the social question was a new and uncharted area and, while Murri was soon to learn his lesson, it was a hard school in which Sturzo would spend his life.

Despite rumblings from the conservatives that the new youth of the *Opera*, turning more and more to Christian Democracy, were 'dangerous innovators' Sturzo continued to write about the need 'to form in the people, together with their religious conscience, a social conscience also, and to prepare the masses for the struggle and the triumph over socialism'.[28] When the movement was accused of smacking too much of socialism he did not accept the challenge except to ask for proof but he was not slow, perhaps unwisely given the nature of his argument, to answer the charge that the Christian Democrats did not give sufficient weight to the papal cause. He replied by citing the dedication to the papacy of some of the early fathers of the new movement — Toniolo, Albertario and Stanislao Medolago-Albani — but he was careful to omit Murri.[29] Then he went on

> however, in the platform of Christian Democracy, which has as its objective the social restoration of the people, in its economic, juridical and political content ... there can be no place for a direct plank on the condition to which the revolution has brought the Holy See, just as there could not be a place for a statute of the League against Blasphemy.

Finally he argued that the best way to combat the 'revolution' against the papacy was to observe rigorously the *non expedit*, 'the only thing we can and must do, leaving the rest to God and His Vicar'.[30]

On the broader political level the end of the century saw in Italy a development in the socialist movement that, by appealing to the deeper economic and social needs of the working and deprived masses, threatened to upset the equilibrium of the liberal, bourgeois state. The danger was felt by the authoritative power structures in both state and Church to the extent that Prime Minister Crispi called for common action with the Church, by which he meant electoral support for himself, together 'with God, with the King and for the Fatherland'.[31] Whether he thought that with such rhetoric, a tariff war with France and a humiliating military exercise in Ethiopia, he would compensate for crushing taxation, fiscal burdens and a costly state apparatus is uncertain, but the Vatican, seemingly undecided as yet whether liberalism or socialism was the greater danger, spurned his offer and the socialists doubled their vote in the elections of 1897.

The old liberal state reacted against both the Catholics and the Socialists, not because it saw them as equally 'subversive' and thus already objectively aligned,[32] but because anti-clericalism was part of its very nature and the Church was an enemy it knew how to combat with derision and suppression. Since 1870 it had pursued a systematic course in ecclesiastical affairs which was shameful, counterproductive and pointless and it saw no reason to deviate from that path until fear of a greater threat to its existence forced it to change its policy.[33] The Catholic movement, as distinguished from the Church itself, was another matter because it had assumed remarkable proportions by the late 1890s with 4,000 parish groups and 700 workers' societies backed by 24 daily papers and 155 periodicals so that repressive measures taken by the government, through which some groups were temporarily disbanded, were of little moment in its overall progress.[34]

During the latter years of his pontificate Leo XIII managed to steer an uneasy but steady course between the conservative and progressive elements within the *Opera*. Count Giovanni Battista Paganuzzi, as president, held fast to the old line, refused to use the words 'Christian Democracy' and deplored the divisions that the young activists caused within Catholic ranks, but Leo rejected his appeals to make a decision between the two camps. In Sicily, Sturzo was using language that was anathema to Paganuzzi by defining Christian Democracy as a system in which 'the interests of the people will be guaranteed and safeguarded by the people themselves', demanding the representation of every 'class' in Parliament and looking to the day when the Church would be in the vanguard in vindicating the rights of the 'proletariat'. The day would come when a proper solution could be found for the Roman Question because then the people would become truly Christian and Italian.[35]

Meanwhile, Murri was holding meetings in the very centre of Rome and preparing to launch an independent national paper as the voice of the movement called *Il Domani d'Italia* when Leo finally spoke in an encyclical, *Graves de Communi*, of 18 January 1901. The pope made it clear that he did not conceive of Christian Democracy as political action, but rather as a form of 'beneficial Christian action on behalf of the people'.[36] Murri simply interpreted the encyclical favourably given that it did not express categorically a condemnation of party political action and, with Leo's tacit approval, the new movement continued to grow although it remained tightly bound to the overall system of ecclesiastical authority that prevailed within the *Opera*.

Sturzo took a calm view of developments on the mainland. In any case he was overwhelmed with the very real problems of the day-to-day activity of the movement in Sicily where, since 1898, the fate of the working masses had grown steadily worse. In May of that year the state had engaged in bloody reprisals against the workers. They were people whose basic fault was that they were starving and it was increasingly difficult to convince them that only by coordinated action amongst themselves would it be possible to ameliorate their situation. Over and above the work of direct social action through cooperatives, rural banks and mutual aid societies, Sturzo had begun to direct the movement into political representation on the municipal and commune level throughout the island. In so doing he was forming the local cadres of what he increasingly called 'the Catholic party', gaining valuable experience himself in political action which culminated with his taking office as deputy mayor of Caltagirone, and curbing his own and his associates' instinctive desire for greater national development on the grounds that power was useless until it was based on 'the popular conscience and the activity of citizens'. To the innate dislike of state centralism that is normally part of the mental attitudes of provincial residents, Sturzo added convictions based on experience and, as early as 1902, he was claiming economic autonomy for the communes.[37]

Furthermore, the very fact that Sturzo was taking his place in councils and committees, on which level he had to make daily contact with socialists and radicals, meant a broadening and a reinforcing of his own democratic and civil convictions that marked him off in a unique manner from the generality of the Italian Catholic clergy. Luigi Sturzo was still Don Sturzo, said his Mass with devotion, kept close contact with his bishop and constantly proclaimed his loyalty to the pope. In his daily life, in his associations on a personal level, in the convictions that motivated a great deal of his activity he was rapidly moving away from that tightly knit, rigidly controlled concept of priestly vocation that prevailed throughout the Catholic Church.

Leo XIII, the 'venerable, august and beloved pope of Christian Democracy' died on 20 July 1903 and Sturzo was amongst the first to recognize the debt of the Catholic progressives to the old pastor who had done a great deal to lead the Church away from its identification with the worst elements in Italian and European society.[38] Leo had certainly condemned socialism and upheld the necessity of private property, but he had also condemned despotism and the *laissez-faire* attitude of wealthy industrialists. In fact he had warned them that 'to exploit the weakness of the poor was a crime crying to heaven for vengeance'.[39] Such things as a just wage, the right to associate in workers' unions and the betterment of working conditions all flowed from Leo's philosophy and awakened the conscience of many Christians in Europe. Professor Helleputte in Belgium, Leon Harmel in France and Murri and Sturzo in Italy had benefited from his lead and their work had helped to give birth to Christian Democracy on the continent.[40]

Leo had also come to appreciate the need for a solid intellectual basis upon which to build a new spirit in the Church. He realized the sterility and imitative nature of most Catholic thought in theology and philosophy, whether contemporary or over the succeeding centuries since the Reformation. Thus, when he upheld Thomas Aquinas as the prototype and exemplar for intellectual endeavour, he did not propose that the great medieval thinker was to be taken as a fixed norm to whose cathedral of thought no stone was to be added, but he hoped that, following the guidelines laid down by Thomas, other scholars would enrich and strengthen Catholic thought in the modern world. Leo could not foresee an immediate future in which his successor would stifle Catholic initiative and thought in practically every field other than the strictly spiritual, nor that Aquinas would be used as the basis for a reversal to a medieval concept of society with a consequent strengthening of conservative and reactionary elements in the Church.

Within a few months of the election on 3 August 1903 of the Patriarch of Venice, Cardinal Giuseppe Sarto, as Pius X, Sturzo noted that orthodoxy has become a preoccupation bordering on 'mania' amongst certain conservative elements in the Church in Italy.[41] He little realized that the same 'mania' would permeate right through the Church under Pius, with his anti-modernist campaign, and that, in its wake, 'Le Sillon' in France and Christian Democracy in Italy would be stifled and generous workers such as Marc Sangnier in France and Murri in Italy would be lost to the cause. In a recent study the apparently harsh statement is found that Pius 'transformed the Leonine garden of ideas into a desert and called it the kingdom of God'.[42] It is the kind of statement that Sturzo as a loyal papalist would never have agreed with publicly, preferring to place the blame for the pope's attitudes on his close advisers. In the light of history however it rings true and little can be said to counterbalance it until historians have worked through the Vatican archives for the period of Pius' papacy, at which time some deeper understanding of his motives at least may be gained.

A year of the new pontificate had scarcely elapsed before a marked change had taken place in Italian Catholic Action. In 1903 Count Giovanni Grosoli had succeeded Paganuzzi as president of the *Opera*. Paganuzzi was an old friend of the new pope and Grosoli, a moderate progressive, could never rightfully fill his shoes in the eyes of Pius X. It was Grosoli's unenviable lot to try to bridge the gap between the old conservative forces and the new guard of Christian Democracy but the first Congress at which he presided at Bologna in November 1903 was seen as too decisive in its leanings to the latter. The journalist observer for the moderate paper, *La Perseveranza*, summed up his wonderment when he said that he felt he was present 'at a workers' or socialist assembly.'[43] The point at issue was simple enough for the conservatives who saw their control of lay Italian Catholicism at stake. One side spoke of the rights of the papacy, the other of the rights of the people, especially the poor, and Sturzo even attempted to have the question of the South brought forward. Given the circumstances which had provoked a ferment of ideas and activity it was inevitable that the progressive elements would win and the fundamental question as to what the mission of the Church consisted in was never really asked.

Poor Grosoli, confident that unity was restored and proud of the trust Pius seemed to place in him despite the motions of no confidence in his leadership put up by the old guard, allowed himself the indiscretion of referring to 'dead questions in the national society' in a circular he sent to the directors of the *Opera* in July 1904.[44] In the Vatican the Roman Question was by no means dead and the circular was officially disowned. Grosoli's resignation was followed by those of Sturzo, Meda, Medolago and many others and within a few days Pius dissolved the *Opera* as a national movement of Catholics with the ringing phrase 'It is preferable that a work [opera] is not carried on at all rather than that it be done without or against the will of the bishop'.[45] It was an inevitable conclusion to an organization that had gone beyond the mission of the Church and one is entitled to observe that the purity and sagacity of Pius' motives, his evident distrust of Murri and his followers, would stand unchallenged were it not for the fact that his own and his close advisers' equally temporal interest in a question that since 1870 was fundamentally political had motivated much of their activity in the Italian peninsula.

Sturzo's reaction to the news that the *Opera* had been dissolved was characteristically forthright and penetrating. He recognized that the purpose of the *Opera* was exclusively religious and as a consequence political activity was an invasion into a field in which it had no role.

The Catholic movement on a national level being finished, Sturzo maintained that all had to support it on a diocesan level and he was especially pleased that the second group of the *Opera*'s activity had been left intact. The second group consisted in mutual aid societies, cooperatives and the professional unions, and Sturzo saw real hope there because the Holy See had given a degree of genuine autonomy to these activities and in Sicily they had been founded by, were inspired by and controlled by the Christian Democrats. It was time, while strengthening their activities, for all to concentrate on a genuine work of education through study circles and cultural activity so that the ideals of Christian Democracy might take firm root in Catholic minds.[46]

Unlike Joseph Cardijn in Belgium, Sturzo did not attempt to formulate a method for Catholic lay activity on an apostolic level precisely because in his own priestly work he had not experienced the effect of the industrial revolution on the working class.[47] Likewise he instinctively saw political activity as part of the solution to the problem of the Church in Italy, for the exact reason that the papacy had inculcated that solution into the minds of Italian Catholics since 1870, if not from time immemorial. Thus it was not very wide of the mark for Murri to write of the young Sturzo that 'for him the Church is the administration of souls, the State the administration of things'.[48] To Sturzo the loss of the *Opera* was not of any real consequence because he was already dedicated thoroughly to the invigoration and salvation of Italy as a social unit, rather than Italians as individuals or the Church as an organization within Italian life, and for that purpose a political movement with an ideal, a programme and a cohesive structure was necessary. Furthermore he had already seen that economic action, apart from political action, was no answer to the needs of the oppressed Sicilian because those who held political power also wielded economic sanctions through their control of finance. Thus they could control politics by denying finance to those who opposed them. It was a Gordian knot that could only be cut by striking at the political power structure from without and to do that he soon saw that a new party had to be built liberated 'from the old bonds of other parties'.[49]

In September 1904 a general strike was proclaimed consequent upon the brutal repressive measures taken by the government against unrest amongst the miners in Sardegna and farmers in the province of Trapani. The strike induced Prime Minister Giovanni Giolitti into calling a general election in the hope that the conservative forces would manifest greater unity in the face of mounting turmoil amongst the workers and poor classes. Hitherto the one element of significance that was lacking in the conservative ranks was the Catholic and to some, including Tommaso Tittoni, Giolitti's Minister of External Affairs, the time seemed ripe for an attempt to win Catholic support. Tittoni was an astute observer of the Vatican scene and he knew that, besides being much less committed to outright adhesion to the *non expedit* than his predecessors had been, Pius was concerned with establishing better relations with Italy, especially as France had become increasingly hostile to the Holy See since the advent of the Combes government and the breaking of diplomatic relations with the Vatican in June 1904. The resulting Italian elections in November saw a softening of Pius' attitude which fell short of the actual lifting of the *non expedit*. Thus a few clerical moderates backed by Catholic votes centred upon the Catholic stronghold of Bergamo participated in the elections and won seats.[50] It was proof that socialism and workers' unrest were feared more than continued hostility on the part of the liberals against the Holy See in Italy. It illustrated furthermore that the Church under Pius was still wedded to the concepts of the old political *status quo* with all its inherent limitations in the face of a changing social situation.

Sturzo was clearly taken aback by the turn of events. He had deplored the brutality of the measures taken by the government against the workers, while recognizing that a few workers were involved in 'organized revolutionary activity'. At the same time he manifested his increasing contempt for Giolitti and his government which he judged had done nothing in the way of reform for two years. The only clear way for Catholics to act was to observe the *non expedit*, break totally with the liberals and freemasons and 'acquire their own personality in public life' with the 'building of a national party on a solid base'. He recognized also that the electoral behaviour of the socialists who selected a single candidate or else abstained was a way 'to manifest the popular will' and that the only reason for which a majority of electors voted for Giolitti was his anti-socialism, hiding as he was behind the word 'freedom'.[51] After the election Sturzo recognized that the call to law and order had rallied the voters around the government which in itself was run down and lacking energy while the socialists were the party 'born from struggle and ideals and leavened by the common people'. He was scathing in his criticism of the Catholics who had helped an inimical government to power by prostituting their vote and engaging in the 'politics of eunuchs'. What was worse however was the fact that while he and the Christian Democrats were fighting

> against the socialists with our own strength and our own ideas which themselves have a social democratic value, it has been, on the other hand, a reactionary act [for the Catholic opportunists] to bolster up the moderates and the conservatives thus rejecting outright a network of hope and vitality, which responds to the needs of the proletariat and the future of the Christian social forces.[52]

All of this had postponed the formation of 'our party', created a political untruth in the nation with the continued existence of a *non expedit* in which no one any longer believed except the Christian Democrats, and gave strength to a government which was supported by some Catholics only, while the mass of their co-religionists did not accept it. He suggested that the Holy See might grant freedom to Catholics to break away from the conservative structure and achieve their own freedom and political physiognomy in their own party.[53] In 1905 Pius X decided to regroup the Catholic lay forces in a tripartite union of three branches — popular, electoral and economic. Despite the pretence of involving public opinion throughout the country in the formulation of the new type of Catholic Action, it was simply constructed on papal and curial fiat and no consideration seems to have been given to the fact that the electoral union in particular meant direct ecclesiastical involvement in the political sphere. Sturzo was unhappy with the new situation but did not react except with pointed written criticism in *La Croce*, in which he refused to be condemned to sterility because 'We need contact with reality and such contact is had on the level of life and its struggle'. Nonetheless he tried to curb Murri by telling him that 'If you believe that by way of conflict with ecclesiastical authority we will acquire freedom and strength you fool yourself because such conflict will weaken and paralyse us.'[54]

Murri and his followers rejected the papal creation out of hand and formed the National Democratic League in November 1905. It was made up of small groups of Catholic militants, especially in the Romagna, and although it lacked the specific nature of a political party it was aimed at the political awakening of young people and the proletariat. It affirmed its own independence from formal ecclesiastical subjection and like all such movements in a time of upheaval it attracted a radical element.[55] Political radicalism was an element the Vatican might have tolerated until it conflicted with the chosen political aims of the Curia, but theological radicalism was anathema. Justly or otherwise, Murri and the League were accused of modernist leanings and thus became involved in the unhealthy hysteria gripping Pius and his close associates who were conducting a campaign for orthodoxy which resulted in stifling intellectual activity in the Church of their period and for over a generation to come. In the ensuing emotional maelstrom the League was condemned, Murri was excommunicated and most Italian Catholics lapsed back into their customary state of passive acceptance.[56] Murri, with whom Sturzo had been expressly forbidden to maintain contact, was elected a deputy in the Italian Parliament on the day he was excommunicated, 19 March 1909, and Pius pronounced the ecclesiastical epitaph of the valiant apostle of Christian Democracy with the words 'he is better off out of the Church'.[57]

Perhaps because of his geographical isolation, certainly because of his political good sense and his refusal at any time to dabble in the clouded waters of theological speculation, Sturzo remained safe in Sicily.[58] He had his hands full with matters of immediate practical moment as mayor of Caltagirone as well as provincial councillor representing Catania.[59] Nonetheless he did not lose sight of his ultimate objective — 'a Christian Democrat party' — and he encapsulated his thoughts on its formulation in a speech that has since become famous in the folklore of modern Italian democracy on both the political and academic level. Sturzo's speech has been acclaimed as the 'magna charta' of both the Partito Popolare and the later Christian Democrat Party. As such it is worth some examination.[60]

After an analysis of the years 1897–1905, which he saw as a period of struggle between the old and the new currents of thought, Sturzo proclaimed that the time had come to transform Catholic civil energies into a national party. To him such a party could not depend on ecclesiastical authority for the very sound reason that the political aims of the papacy differed from those of a lay party of Catholics in Italian civil life to whom the Roman Question was no longer primary. Indeed it, together with the preconceptions of the old conservative party, was 'a museum piece'. Sturzo refused to believe that a lay party which set to one side the Roman Question would fail in its duty towards the Holy See because he thought that the freedom enjoyed presently by the papacy needed only its recognition by a judicial act which finally had to be the fruit of a 'new attitude on the part of the nation towards the Church'.

With his rejection of the Roman Question as an obstacle to the formation of a party, Sturzo linked the theoretical question of the future party's attitude to the monarchy. He accepted the present state of affairs, but said that there was no reason to adhere to a monarchical form of government. In fact neither the altar nor the throne were the organic coefficients of the Catholic party based as it would be on the fundamental grounds of an organism with free, constitutional rights and dependent for its existence upon the people. He did not think the title Catholic should be used by the party given its sacral tonality, nor was it appropriate to use Christian Democracy which now represented only a fraction of the Catholic masses 'rather than a programme of life', but he recognized that the party itself would always, of necessity, be both democratic and Catholic. To him 'the new Catholic party must have a social democrat content, inspired by Christian principles: outside of these limits it will never have the right to a life of its own, it will become an appendix of the moderate party'. Finally it was no time to waste energies in 'weak and miniscule initiatives' which was a clear reference to Murri's League, but to get on and consolidate. The hour would come because the power of an idea was with them; history and human progress itself would prove them right.[61]

It was a profoundly simple but equally perceptive and courageous analysis of the development of the Catholic movement that led Sturzo to his public proclamation of the need for an autonomous Catholic party in Italy. Murri had given birth to the idea, but on the practical level he saw it in outmoded terms to the extent that he wanted to pour his new wine into the old vessel of the Church, to make use of the structure and strength of the Church to convert the state into a Christian Democracy. Just as Giolitti hoped to use the Church to foster his concept of the liberal state and Mussolini later used it for a time to help construct the fascist state, so too Murri wished to use it, but in a far more honest and loyal way. Murri could not conceive of a Christian Democrat Italy without the Church's commitment to the task of transformation.[62] Sturzo recognized that such an objective, which was essentially political in that it involved on the civic level the practical application of principles which stemmed from a Christian inspiration, was not the work of the Church and could never be the work of the Church. The task of the Church to Sturzo was to formulate the principles of a just social order as Leo XIII had attempted in *Rerum Novarum*. It remained for citizens inspired by the principles to apply them in the secular sphere. Two questions however remained which only time could answer. The first was whether the task itself of crystallizing action within the framework of a party would stand the test of fissurization to which all party politics is exposed. The second was whether the persons who ruled the Church in Italy would tolerate political action by Catholics which was judged inimical or counterproductive to the political aims which they saw as essential for the wellbeing of the Church.

In the years between 1908 and the beginning of the First World War, Italian Catholic Action continued to develop on various levels.62 The Popular Union organized Social Weeks on the lines followed in France, and it managed to set up a group for Italian Catholic women which engaged in charitable activities. However the main area of activity was that of developing the 'white' or Catholic union movement. Based mainly in the north, especially in Lombardy and in the Veneto and drawing its membership from light industry and agricultural workers, the white unions made up about an eighth of Italy's organized work force. The class struggle had early been accepted as part of their driving force and Candeloro admits that charges levelled against the white unions by the socialist press of engaging in blackleg activity were false and inspired by the anti-clerical bent of the socialists.[63] The unions had their main cooperative and economic strength in a network of small banks that, particularly in rural areas, provided financial assistance to the members and their families. The major bank on which the smaller ones relied was the Banco di Roma founded in

Rome in 1880 and directed by two men who were very much at home in high ecclesiastical circles, Edoardo Soderini, friend of Leo XIII, and Ernesto Pacelli, uncle of the future Pius XII. The growth of the bank was remarkable both in and outside Italy from 1900 onwards, but during the war with the Ottoman Empire, called the Libyan War (1911–12), its foreign interests suffered with the loss of 50 million lire and it was in a parlous financial situation by the outbreak of the First World War. Nonetheless its foundation saw 'a gradual and progressive entry of clerical and Vatican elements into the Italian capitalist system, on the basis of activity that was in the main financial with political consequences also …'[64]

On the level of their involvement in Italian political life the prewar period spelt an effective but unofficial end to the *non expedit* and resulted eventually in the so called Gentiloni Pact by which, with papal approval, Catholics gave their votes to government candidates who were prepared to promise their support to fundamental Catholic policies such as anti-divorce laws and religious education.[65] Ottorino Gentiloni was president of the Electoral Union of Catholic Action and in the campaign of 1913, the first under adult male suffrage, he directed the Catholic campaign under Vatican surveillance. Short of the formation of a Catholic party it meant direct involvement in politics on the part of the Church for the precise reason that if Catholics could not take part in politics by founding a Catholic party — a step still forbidden by the Vatican — they could take part only when and in the form agreed upon by the Vatican. Thus Catholic Action was transformed into an 'electoral machine, devoted to selling votes' under the direction of the Vatican. Two prominent Catholic laymen, Filippo Meda and Giovanni Maria Longinotti, were aware of the grave dangers in such a policy because, with the involvement of Catholic Action, it seemed 'that the Pope had become the head of an electoral organization' which was a danger not apparently perceived in the Vatican itself.[66]

This concern and involvement of the Vatican was not related purely to minor issues of obtaining favours from the government, but was also closely linked to disquiet with the growth of the Italian socialist movement and the Vatican saw clearly that Catholics as such would be ineffective in opposition to the socialists. In the electoral sense the tactic was successful in that, while only 29 Catholic candidates were elected, Gentiloni and the *Osservatore Romano* could both claim that the 228 seats — sufficient for a resounding victory for Giovanni Giolitti — were won on Catholic votes. The Vatican newspaper called the Catholics a 'safety anchor' for the liberals who were thus enabled to defeat the socialists soundly.[67]

Although Sturzo had involved himself and the remnants of the Christian Democrat movement in Sicily in local administrative politics with some success, he achieved little on the level of national politics. The whole machinery of national politics was to Sturzo a mess of corruption stemming from Giolitti downwards. Backed by the Mafia, acquiesced in by the Church and suffered under by the people, national politicians simply used the South as a voting coffer and did nothing to alleviate its economic and social misery or to lift it from its semi-feudal state. Although he had been a member of the national council of the Electoral Union of Catholic Action in 1908, Sturzo had no faith in tactics which would not result in a breaking of ties with the old parties and he begged for a neutralist policy that would judge issues on their merits alone, irrespective of their political origins. To him it was especially deplorable that the priests led the youth of Catholic Action to accept any form of alliance with the old, discredited parties of the right, but he knew full well that in adopting such a line he was almost a lone figure and that he was an object of suspicion in that he seemed to favour the socialists.[68]

As a result of Sturzo's attitude Sicily was brought to acquiesce in the new Vatican tactic only by a visit there of Gentiloni who contrived to nullify the influence of Sturzo and his friends.[69] Sturzo recognized the advantage that could accrue to the South through the new electoral law of adult male suffrage, but for Catholic Action to organize that vote behind men who, though looked upon by Rome as faithful Catholics, were in fact known to Sturzo as corrupt and violent, was a betrayal of the workers and the poor.[70] He still tried to foster the candidature of worthwhile men despite Gentiloni but the election results, many of them the fruits of violence and intimidation, saw only one genuinely Catholic candidate successful. The papal line in Sicily was consequently a debacle and Sturzo himself had become an object of suspicion to many local bishops, but with his customary loyalty he remained faithful to the pope, blaming the mistaken politics on the Curia.[71] On a visit to Rome Pius X addressed him gently as 'Mister Mayor' and warned him that he was being denounced to the Vatican by his enemies but that he, Pius, would take no action against him. His own brother Mario, since 1903 bishop of Piazza Armerina in Sicily, had warned Luigi against confusing justice and charity, but it was easy for an honest priest to see the pinnacle of both virtues in the person of a pope and, in the circumstances, it was almost inevitable that the Vatican would adopt a political stance that bolstered up the old, conservative elements of society in the face of the new unbridled forces rising on the left.

In early 1914 Giolitti resigned from office in favour of another conservative, Antonio Salandra. It could be said that, despite the misgivings of Sturzo and, later, Salvemini, Giolitti had given almost ten years of stability to Italy, and the North at least had witnessed a degree of economic progress that enabled the country to stand with dignity on the lower rungs of the European powers. That Giolitti proved incapable of solving the problem of the South is scarcely surprising given the inability of anyone to solve it in the 50 years since unification. That he looked upon it as an area to be raped politically and economically does no more than rank him with his countless predecessors and at least some of the people of the South were able in his period to solve their own problem by emigrating in unprecedented numbers.[72] His one venture in colonial expansion, with the Libyan War, evoked a curiously positive response in Sturzo who thought that it would help Italy grow to 'greatness' and that the South would benefit with an agricultural and commercial outlet to Africa and the East, as well as providing a respectable alternative to America for emigration. Such hopes were unfounded and in the main the Libyan War did little more than provoke socialist–nationalist antagonism at home and sow the seeds of the imperialistic madness epitomised later by Gabriele d'Annunzio's poetry and Mussolini's pathetic maps along the Via dei Fori Imperiali.[73]

With the death of Pius X in August 1914 and the election of Benedict XV as his successor a month later it seemed for a time that the remaining elements of the old Christian Democrat movement would again prosper. Benedict was a quiet, cultured prelate who shared little of the passionate thirst for orthodoxy and uniformity so dear to Pius X. Yet circumstances he could neither temper nor control were to shape his short pontificate for his election took place when Europe was already at war. Italy remained neutral until May 1915 when, despite the inclinations of most Italians, the Salandra government entered the First World War.[74] Benedict himself remained firmly dedicated to peace despite the leanings towards the Triple Alliance in the Vatican where German–Austrian interests were regarded with greater favour than those of masonic and anti-clerical France in particular. Italian Catholics were divided on the issue of intervention, with the old guard being pro Germany and Austria; the white unions, with Guido Miglioli as their spokesman, strongly opposed, and the rest, comprising most of the Catholic movement, gradually in favour of intervention on the side of the England and her allied powers.[75] The story of Italy's tragic involvement in the war is epitomised by the pathetic letters addressed to King Vittorio Emanuele III begging him to call a halt to the 'useless slaughter' from which Italy emerged victorious, but with the greater struggle of adjusting to peace yet to be undertaken.[76]

By the outbreak of the war Sturzo had already assumed a pivotal role in Italian Catholic life. As secretary of the central committee of Catholic Action and as a member of the directorate of the Popular Union he was in a position to use his influence to foster Italian intervention in the war and he did not hesitate to do so. In spite of warnings from his old Sicilian friend, Emanuele Arezzo, that he was 'betraying both Italy and honour' he wrote and spoke about the 'civilizing mission' of Italy in the world, saw the war as a means of bringing to light the hidden moral reserves of the people, of creating 'a nation where previously there had been no more than a multitude' and praised it as 'the great test of our life as a young nation, the sacred and tragic moment of vitality and experience'.[77] Despite the flamboyance of his rhetoric, excusable no longer on the grounds of his youth but perhaps understandable in the light of a long tradition of Italian clerical belligerency stemming back to Julius II and well beyond, Sturzo judged the war as a means of uniting Italian Catholics, giving them a role in national life and sloughing off the political accretions and ties of the past.[78] To this end he spent the years 1915–18 in a fervid round of activity in which he organized meetings, made personal contacts, and supported Filippo Meda, his close companion of those days, who became the first of the Catholic deputies to take cabinet office as finance minister in 1916. Despite his rhetoric Sturzo also saw the war as a step towards a clarification of political issues and he outlined the shape of the Catholic programme for the post-war period when, based on universal suffrage, a vote for women and proportional representation, the true living organisms of Italian life would assert themselves.[79]

Finally Sturzo dimly understood as year followed bloody year that other and darker seeds were being sown in the chaos and misery of war. As an old man he said that the war was the crucible from which Italy emerged in 1918, turbulent, leaning to the left, discontented in its national life, weakened at its economic base and without a leader at its head.[80] Those very conditions of national anxiety, bred from distrust in the parliamentary process, disenchantment with the monarchy, suffering from economic hardship and sheer weariness with the brutality of war were already shaping dreams of greatness in the head of the leader to be. Benito Mussolini wrote from the front in 1915 that the war was not simply a struggle against external enemies but was also one of the poor of Italy against the greedy, Italy the ideal against Italy the parasite. He added that after the war the 'moral values' of Italy would have to be brought to light again.[81] What elements of morality Mussolini would bring to Italy lay still in the future. Meanwhile, however, Luigi Sturzo was to have his hour.

Notes

1. See Luigi Sturzo 'Christian Democracy in Italy', in *The Commonweal*, (New York, 28 January 1944) and in C. Sforza, *L'Italia*, p. 77.

2. Sturzo translated the name of his party as Italian Popular Party. As 'popolare' has not quite the same meaning in English as 'popular' it seems preferable to use the Italian name, or simply PPI as an abbreviation. Popolari will be used for the members of the party.

3. On the *non expedit* see G. Dalla Torre, *I cattolici e la vita pubblica italiana* (Rome, 1962); C.M. Buonaiuti, *Non expedit: storia di una politica (1866–1919)* (Milan, 1971); R. Aubert, *Le Pontificat de Pie IX (1846–1878)* (Paris 1952); G. Mollat, *La Question Romaine de Pie VI à Pie XI* (Paris, 1932).

4. Gabriele De Rosa in *Il movimento cattolico in Italia della restaurazione all'età giolittiana* (Bari, 2nd edn, 1972), has given a lucid account of those years. See also F. Magri, *La Democrazia Cristiana in Italia*, 2 vols (Milan, 1954); Dino Secco Suardo, *Da Leone XIII à Pio X* (Rome, 1967); G. Spadolini, *L'opposizione cattolica da Porta Pia al '98*, 3rd edn (Florence, 1955).

5. For Sturzo's early years see A.C. Gaudenti, *Luigi Sturzo: Il pensiero e le opere* (Rome, 1945); G. Petrocchi, *Don Luigi Sturzo note e ricordi* (Rome, 1945). The best biography is F. Piva and F. Malgeri, *Vita di Luigi Sturzo* (Rome, 1972).

6. Sturzo to Monsignor S. Gerbino, bishop of Caltagirone, 14 April 1890. A.L.S., f.s.

7. I. Giordani, *Rivolta cattolica* (Turin, 1925), p. 300.

8. The *Dictatus* of 1095 was a set of decrees which, among others, stated that the Roman Church was founded by God alone; the Roman pontiff alone can with right be called universal; the Roman Church has never erred, nor will it err to all eternity, the Scripture bearing witness and that he who is not at peace with the Roman Church

shall not be considered Catholic. For a discussion of the effects of papal absolutism on one country see J.N. Molony, *The Roman Mould of the Australian Catholic Church* (Melbourne, 1969).

9. *L'Armonia*, quoted in G. Candeloro, *Il movimento cattolico in Italia* (Rome, 1953), p. 109.

10. Speech given at Caltagirone 12 October 1895, 'Brevi considerazioni sul potere temporale dei papi'. A.L.S., f. 166, c. 20. To Sturzo the true source of power in Rome was Freemasonry. The King himself was a Freemason there were over 300 others in the Parliament. Ibid. Pius IX had made it clear that he considered the temporal possessions of the Church both 'necessary and indispensable' and when he set up Catholic Action for youth in 1868 he entitled his Papal Brief *'Dum filii Belial'* to indicate that those who did not accept him and his temporalities in the way he expected of his own 'children' were of another fraternity. See L. Bedeschi, *Le origini della Gioventù Cattolica* (Rocca San Casciano, 1959), pp. 57 and 67.

11. On the *Opera* see A. Gambasin, *Il movimento sociale nell'opera dei congressi (1874–1904)* (Rome, 1958).

12. Sturzo thought that, as late as 1897, few Sicilians knew of their 'grave duty' to abstain from voting and even less took any notice of it, but Candeloro admitted that in central and north Italy it had a marked effect on electoral returns which never ran higher than 60 per cent. See article by Sturzo, 'Cattolici e liberali', 11 April 1897 in *La Croce di Costantino*, ed. G. De Rosa, (Rome, 1958), p. 25 and G. Candeloro, *Il movimento*, p. 142.

13. On Leo XIII see V. Mangano, *Il pensiero sociale e politica di Leone XIII* (Rome, 1931); G. Rossini, *Aspetti della cultura cattolica nell'età di Leone XIII* (Rome, 1961); C. de T' Serclaes, *Le Pape Lèon XIII*, 3 vols. (Paris, 1894) and E. Soderini, *Il pontificato di Leone XIII*, 3 vols. (Milan, 1932 3).

14. L. Sturzo in *La Croce*, pp. 24, 26, 28 and 31.

15. See Sturzo's speech at Bologna, 13 November 1903, 'La Questione Meridionale' in A.L.S., f. 144, c. 4, and his speeches recommending the setting up of a Peoples' Bank at Caltagirone, 3 January 1899. Ibid., f. 115, c. 2; f. 126, c. 77.

16. See the speech of Sturzo at Caltagirone, 24 September 1896, A.L.S., f. 149, c. 14. See also on the period G. Are, *Economia e politica nell'Italia liberale (1890–1915)* (Bologna, 1974).

17. In 1901 Sturzo was lamenting that the 'great evil' of the island was the absenteeism of landlords. He also noted that 11.72 per cent of the population died of malaria at Caltagirone in 1900. See his 'Note sommarie sui contratti agrari e le cooperative agricole di lavoro in Sicilia', A.L.S., f. 115, c. 2. On socialism see his speech at Caltagirone, 3 January 1897, ibid., f. 149, c. 3 and on the bourgeoisie see the speech at Caltagirone, 24 September 1896, ibid., f. 149, c. 14.

18. On Murri see R. Murri, *Battaglie d'oggi*, 4 vols, (Rome, 1903–4); G. Maurilio, *Romolo Murri e il modernismo* (Rome, 1968); S. Zoppi, *Romolo Murri e la prima democrazia cristiana* (Florence, 1968) and Sturzo's radio talk in the 1950s 'Origine e sviluppi del movimento democratico e sociale cristiano in Italia' (Rome, n.d.), in which he praised Murri whom he recognized as the principal inspiratory figure of his youth.

19. See *Rerum Novarum* in Anne Fremantle, *The Papal Encyclicals in Their Historical Context* (New York, 1956), pp. 166–5. See the review of C. Brezzi, *Cristiani-sociali e intransigenti, L'opera di Medolago Albani* (Rome, 1971) in *Il Messaggero* of 30 May 1974 in which Roger Aubert is quoted as having said 'The encyclical is not only many decades behind the Manifesto of Marx, but it resorts to abstract argumentation, without analysis of the real situation created by the development of capitalism'. Sturzo himself thought highly of *Rerum Novarum*. See his speeches of 15 May 1905 and 21 May 1905, A.L.S. f. 145, c. 10; f. 145, c. 12. For a more recent analysis of the encyclical see John Molony, *The Worker Question: A new historical perspective on Rerum Novarum*, Melbourne, 1991.

20. Murri wrote to Sturzo on 3 April 1902 stressing the need to encourage the laity to join the economic and civil movement embraced by Christian Democracy. See letter in *La Croce*, p. 84. For further correspondence see L. Bedeschi, *La corrispondenza inedita fra Sturzo e Murri (1898–1906)* (Bologna, 1972).

21. See quote of Colajanni in G. Candeloro, *Il movimento*, p. 276.

22. Sturzo in *La Croce*, 7 May 1899, p. 36. On the south see R. Villari (ed.), *Il Sud nella storia d'Italia* (Bari, 1961), and F. Vötchting, *La questione meridionale* (Naples, 1955). Mazzini said, p. 52, that Italy was like a chain that could never be any stronger than its weakest link — the South.

23. Sturzo instanced Bergamo as a leading example of a diocese in which there were 43 cooperatives and 140 mutual aid societies. See *La Croce*, 25 December 1895, p. 18. See also Stanislao Medolago Albani, *Il movimento cattolico bergamasco, 1913–1921* (Bergamo, 1921). For economic conditions in the North of Italy at that time see the report to the Convegno di Studii di Vicenza, *O.R.*, 8 March 1974 and L. Cagagna (ed.), *Il Nord nella storia d'Italia* (Bari, 1962). Gramsci wrote that, by never allowing industry to spread to the South, the North had created a permanent hegemony for itself. See A. Gramsci, *Il Risorgimento* (Rome, 1971), p. 262.

24. Sturzo in 'Da Bologna a Note', 6 December 1903, in *La Croce*, p. 101.

25. See G. De Rosa's introduction to *La Croce*, pp. xvii–viii. The proceedings of the case are found in A.L.S., f. 115. See also Sturzo's speech, Caltagirone, 25 January 1902, A.L.S., f. 127, c. 16.

26. On the development of Christian democracy see L. Bedeschi, *I pionieri della D.C.* (Milan, 1966); G. Capelli, *La prima sinistra cattolica in Toscana* (Rome, 1962) and I.

Giordani, *Pionieri della democrazia cristiana* (Rome, 1945).

27. *La Croce*, p. xxxvi. These two quotes were used by Sturzo on the banner of *La Croce*.

28. Sturzo in 'Il papa e la democrazia cristiana', 6 November 1898, ibid., p. 34.

29. Sturzo had followed Toniolo's Roman conferences in 1897–8. Writing to Toniolo he called himself the 'warm admirer' of the old scholar who had laid the theoretical foundations of a school of Catholic sociology while retaining an essentially medieval view of the world. See Sturzo to Toniolo, Rome, May 1898, A.L.S., f. 145, c. 1. For Toniolo see C. Toniolo, *Opera omnia*, 16 vols (Vatican City, 1947–3). For Albertario see G. Pecora, *Don Davide Albertario campione del giornalismo cattolico* (Turin, 1934). Sturzo thought Albertario was an immoderate intransigent whose papalism was unbounded, but who in the end came over to the cause of the workers. See Sturzo in *Origine e sviluppi*, p. 12.

30. Sturzo in 'Perche si combatte', 2 July 1899, *La Croce*, p. 40.

31. Quoted in G. Candeloro, *Il movimento*, p. 25.

32. A. Gramsci, *Il Risorgimento*, (1949), p. 177.

33. For some of the areas in which 'the Church unquestionably suffered at the hands of the Italian state', see C. Seton Watson, *Italy from Liberalism to Fascism, 1870–1925* (London, 1967), p. 227 and passim.

34. For an account of the attempts to repress the Catholic movement see G. De Rosa, *Il movimento*, pp. 170–9. Sturzo gave the figures for the development of the movement in Sicily since 1895 in a talk given at Caltagirone 25 September 1901 entitled 'Note sommarie per l'organizzazione delle unioni professionali nell'interno della Sicilia'. A.L.S., f. 115, c. 1.

35. Sturzo in 'Il nostro programma. Ai Lavoratori Italiani', 16 December 1900 and 'La lotta fra Stato e Chiesa', 2 June 1901, both in *La Croce*, pp. 58–64, 70–7.

36. See the encyclical in Igino Gordani, *Le encicliche sociali dei papi* (Rome, 1956), pp. 223–34. In 1902 Sturzo, undaunted, gave a lecture later printed as *Lotta di classe come legge di progresso* (Milan, 1902). T. D'Ambrosio in his *Bibliografia Sturziana* (Naples, 1961), p. 13, remarks that the names of Marx, Hegel, Labriola and Croce were then triumphant and that 'no Catholic thinker of any worth was opposed to the materialistic theories of those philosophers' and that Sturzo already saw reality not '*sub specie aeternitatis*' but in its historical development.

37. Sturzo in 'Perche partito di centro', 8 December 1902 and 'Autonomie communali', 8 June 1902, *La Croce*, pp. 78–80 and 85–7. At a gathering of scholars held at Venice in September 1974 to exchange views on the official Catholic movement in the nineteenth century, Gabriele De Rosa said it was 'a movement more inclined to denunciation than to discussion, more to prophecy in a biblical tone than to reason'. See article by Paolo Alatri 'Alle origini dell' integralismo', in *Il Messaggero*, 2

October 1974. That this stricture was inapplicable to Murri and Sturzo's movement is apparent even though it still held true of the older elements of the *Opera*.

38. Sturzo in a lecture at Caltagirone, 2 August 1903, entitled 'Leone XIII e la civiltà moderna' in *La Croce*, pp. 217–32.

39. J. Desmond O'Hagan in John Molony, (ed.) *A New Age of the Human Person*, (Melbourne, 1963), p. 21.

40. For a detailed study in English of the development of the movement see Michael P. Fogarty, *Christian Democracy in Western Europe, 1820–1953*, (London, 1957).

41. Sturzo in 'Il programma del XIX Congresso Italiano', 11 November 1903, in *La Croce*, pp. 94–9. The background of Pius X and the Catholic movement in Venice is traced in B. Bertoli, *Le origini del movimento cattolico a Venezia* (Brescia, 1965).

42. The quote is from the excellent article by Sandor Agocs 'Christian Democracy and Social Modernism in Italy during the Papacy of Pius X' in *Church History*, vol. 42, no. 1, March 1973, pp. 73–88. See also P. Scoppola, *Crisi modernista e rinnovamento cattolico in Italia* (Bologna, 1961), where Buonaiuti is quoted, pp. 362–3, as remarking that the modernist scare drove priests away from their books into the safer waters of politics thereby bringing about the ruin of liberal Italy!

43. *La Perseveranza*, 11 November 1903, quoted in G. De Rosa, *Il movimento*, p. 213.

44. G. De Rosa, ibid., pp. 254–5. Pius X was certain that Murri was the true author of the circular and this irritated him even further. See R. Murri, *La Democrazia Cristiana Italiana* (Rome, n.d. probably 1945), pp. 61–2.

45. See G. De Rosa, *ibid. Il movimento*, p. 259. Pius X was echoing the words of Ignatius, bishop of Antioch in the early part of the second century, with whom he felt more affinity than with the young clerics of the twentieth century. Medolago once said 'In Italy our friends know as much about sociology and economics as I do about Arabic'. See *Il Messaggero*, 30 May 1974. To Pius sociology and economics and other such concerns with which the *Opera* was becoming involved were inevitable and perhaps harmful bypaths into which Catholics would stray if they lost sight of their hierarchical leadership.

46. Sturzo in 'Le nostre posizioni dopo gli ultimi avvenimenti', 14 August 1904 and 'Agli amici di Sicilia', 11 September 1904, in La Croce, pp. 121–5 and 126–30.

47. For an examination of Cardijn's methods see J.N. Molony, *Towards an Apostolic Laity* (Melbourne, 1960).

48. See the quote in G. Rossini (ed.), *Modernismo, fascismo, comunismo. Aspetti e figure della cultura e della politica dei cattolici nel 900* (Bologna, 1972), p. 153.

49. Letter of Sturzo, 1 June 1910, in F. Piva and F. Malgeri, *Vita*, p. 166.

50. See G. Candeloro, *Il movimento*, pp. 309–17 and G. De Rosa, *Il movimento*, pp. 262–9.

51. Sturzo in 'Lo sciopero generale', 25 September 1904; 'Le imminenti elezioni politiche e i cattolici', 16 October 1904; 'Le elezioni politiche e il programma del governo', 23 October 1904, in *La Croce*, pp. 131–3, 134–6, 136–40.

52. Sturzo in 'Le elezioni generali del 6 novembre in Italia. Il governo — I socialisti — I cattolici', 13 November 1904, in *ibid.*, pp. 144–8.

53. See previous source and 'Il presente e il futuro del partito cattolico nazionale', 20 November 1904, *ibid.*, pp. 149–52.

54. *Ibid.*, pp. 169–75 and Sturzo to Murri, May 1906, in L. Bedeschi, *La corrispondenza inedita*, p. 131.

55. For the League see C. Giovannini, *Politica e religione nel pensiero della Lega Democratica Nazionale (1905–1915)* (Rome, 1968) and P. Scoppola, 'Il modernismo politico in Italia; La Lega Democratica Nazionale' in *Rivista Storica Italiana*, no. 69 (Naples, 1957), pp. 61–109.

56. R. Murri, in his *Dalla democrazia cristiana al partito popolare italiano* (Florence, 1920), pp. 21 and 151, admitted that modernism was linked to Christian Democracy but denied categorically that either he, Loisy or Tyrell were ever guilty of heresy. De Rosa took the view that modernism 'permeated' the whole of Murri's work which was 'a laicist deformation of the ecclesiastical organism' and would, if successful, have resulted in 'a clericalist deformation of the State'. See G. De Rosa, *La crisi dello stato liberale in Italia* (Rome, 1955), pp. 17, 19; fn. pp. 48–9.

57. See M. Guasco, *Romolo Murri e il modernismo* (Rome, 1968), p. 362. P. Scoppola in his introduction to this work holds firmly that Murri was no modernist in the sense defined by *Pascendi*, the document with which Pius condemned the movement, see p. viii. Murri himself held that the great error he committed for which Pius would not allow him to remain in the Church was to maintain the right of Catholics to their own political autonomy. See R. Murri, *Dalla Democrazia*, p. 24.

58. Murri, *ibid.*, p. 151, said that Sturzo had no interest in modernism, but that by temperament he was a politician with a lack of feeling for the 'problems of the interior life'.

59. See Sturzo's manuscript 'Sedici mesi di amministrazione', 27 April 1907, A.L.S., f. 175, c. 33.

60. For the speech, given at Caltagirone, 24 December 1908, see *La Croce*, pp. 233–6, under the title 'I problemi della vita nazionale dei cattolici italiani'.

61. He spoke of democracy as 'a spiritual, religious movement'; of 'living democracy in a religious way' and of 'verifying in the democratic nation the spirit and the living tradition of Italian catholicism', R. Murri, *Dalla Democrazia*, pp. 43 and 51.

62. Candeloro gives a fairly full account of these developments in his *Il movimento*, pp. 328–40. See also V.C. Galati, *La Democrazia Cristiana* (Verona, 1955) and

L. Bedeschi, *Dal movimento di Murri all' appello di Sturzo* (Milan, 1969). Sturzo himself was of the opinion that during the period 1909–15 the Christian Democrat movement was in a long trough of inactivity. See his *Figure del movimento*, passim.

63. G. Candeloro, *Il movimento*, pp. 339–40.

64. From author's introduction, Innocenzo Cervelli, *I cattolici dall' unità alla fondazione dell' Partito Popolare* (Bologna 1969), p. 42. Considerable study has been done on the Banco di Roma. See Banco di Roma (ed.), *Dall' impero di Roma all impero fascista*, (Rome, 1940); *Relazione del consiglio d'amministrazione e dei sindicati* (Rome, 1891); L. Splendore (ed.), *Il Banco di Roma* (Rome, 1913); A. D'Alessandro, 'Il Banco di Roma e la guerra di Libia' in *Storia e politica* (Milan, July, September 1968), pp. 491–509. Alessandro asserts that the Bank forced the government to go to war in Libya to protect its interests there on the threat of passing them to Austrian German banking groups, p. 502–6. On this see also G. Delle Donne, 'Revista e dibattito politico' in *Nuova Antologia*, vol. 522, fasc. 2086 (Rome, 1974), pp. 275–84.

65. Murri summed up Pius X's politics as a continuation of the tactic that, as Patriarch of Venice, he had fostered successfully there by which an electoral alliance was achieved between the Catholics and the conservative or moderate elements. See R. Murri, *La Democrazia*, p. 71. Giolitti had the insight to realize that Pius X was a pope who appealed to the conservative and bourgeois elements in Italian society. See Giovanni Spadolini, *Giolitti e i cattolici 1901–1914* (Florence, 1960), p. 368. See also F. Aquilante, *Il patto Gentiloni. Gli eletti coi voti dei cattolici ella XXIV legislatura* (Rome, 1914).

66. See G. De Rosa, *Filippo Meda a l'età liberale* (Florence, 1959), pp. 161 and 158. De Rosa called Meda 'the Turati of the Catholic movement', p. x.

67. *O.R.*, 6 November 1913. For another view of these years see G. Spadolini, *L'opposizione*, appendix entitled 'Cattolicisimo e liberalisimo nell' Italia giolittiana', pp. 526–616. For the text of the seven points to be agreed upon by candidates as a prerequisite of Catholic support, see G. Della Torre, *I cattolici*, pp. 144–5,

68. Sturzo to the Catholic Electoral Committee of Valguarnera, Caltagirone, 27 May 1910, A.L.S., f. 103, c. 27; Sturzo to Ignazio Torregrossa, Caltagirone, 18 June 1910, *ibid.*, f. 103, c. 84; Sturzo to Faranna, Caltagirone, 8 December 1910, *ibid.*, f. 20, c. 23.

69. See F. Piva and F. Malgeri, *Vita*, pp. 178–80.

70. Sturzo had been concerned with the Mafia in Sicily for many years. In 1900 he wrote a play denouncing it which ran only once in Caltagirone. See 'La Mafia', A.L.S., f. 126, c. 85.

71. Ibid., pp. 151, 178. Some years later Sturzo said that he had always opposed the Gentiloni Pact as it was like a lance in the Achilles heel of Italian Catholicism in that it confused the social Catholics and cemented the rest to the old clerical moderate

stand. See preface to L. Sturzo, *Il Partito Popolare Italiano*, 3 vols, (Bologna, 1956), vol. 1, p. 5.

72. On Giolitti see the excellent study by W.A. Salomone, *Italy in the Giolittian Era. Italian Democracy in the Making, 1900–1914* (Philadelphia, 1960). Also Nino Valeri, *Giovanni Giolitti* (Turin, 1971) and G. Sotgiu, *L'Italia di Giolitti* (Cagliari, 1972).

73. On the Libyan War see G. Salvemini, *Come siamo andati in Libia* (Florence, 1912); L. Ganapini, *Il nazionalismo cattolico. I cattolici e la politica estera in Italia dal 1871 al 1914* (Bari, 1970); F. Malgeri, *La guerra libica, 1911–1912* (Rome, 1970). For Sturzo's attitude to the war in Libya see F. Piva and F. Malgeri, *Vita*, pp. 174–5.

74. B. Vigezzi, *L'Italia di fronte alla prima guerra mondiale*, vol. 1, *L'Italia neutrale* (Milan, 1966).

75. For the text of Miglioli's 'L'opposizione alla guerra' see I. Cervelli, *I cattolici*, pp. 197–200. See also G. Miglioli, *Con Roma e con Mosca. Quarant'anni di battaglie* (Cremona, 1945).

76. See R. Monteleone, *Lettere al re* (Rome, 1973). Benedict XV used the term 'useless slaughter' in reference to the war and was roundly condemned by Italian nationalists as a consequence. For the pope's appeal 'Ai capi dei governi belligerenti' see I. Cervelli, *I cattolici*, pp. 201–5. For the role of Italy in the war see P. Melograni, *Storia politica della grande guerra 1915–1918* (Bari, 1969) and I. Bonomi, *La politica italiana da Porta Pia a Vittorio Veneto, 1870–1918*, 3rd edn (Turin, 1966).

77. See the criticism of Arezzo and the speeches of Sturzo in F. Piva and F. Malgeri, *Vita*, pp. 191–3, 202.

78. For recognition of the part played by Catholics in the war effort see G. Colosimo, *Opera tratta dagli scritti di Gaspari Colosimo (1916–1919)* (Pompei, 1959), p. 168.

79. See speeches given by Sturzo at Rome, June 1917 and June 1918, 'La resistenza spirituale' and 'La riforma degli enti pubblici', A.L.S., f. 145, c. 20.

80. Sturzo in his preface to *Il Partito*, p. 5.

81. See letter from Benito Mussolini to Sergio Panunzio, summer 1915, in B. Ginnari, *Il mezzogiorno dopo la guerra* (Naples, 1918), p. 1–3.

2

THE DREAM TAKES SHAPE

During the half century that had elapsed from the foundation of the new Kingdom of Italy to the end of the Great War the Catholic Church in Italy had developed a relationship with the Italian nation that was far more consistent and mature than in any previous period. The end of the Papal States had attenuated the more violent forms of anti-clericalism that had so vexed Italian life for centuries. The participation of Catholics as loyal citizens in the war had helped otherwise reluctant Italians to accept their Catholic brothers as partners in the struggle of a single nation. Finally, on a political level, experience had seemed to indicate that Catholics were prepared to cooperate with the already accepted expressions of Italian political life and, hopefully, would work within them, and for them, in the name of the common good. However this hope overlooked the long period of maturity, hardship and idealism that had shaped the current of Christian Democracy which, despite the papal anathema hurled at Romolo Murri, lived on. Even more significantly it forgot Luigi Sturzo. He enjoyed favour with the lay heads of Italian Catholicism, perhaps more to the point he was their acknowledged leader. In the Vatican he was tolerated, but his activity engendered perplexed anxiety. As for Sturzo he was confident that something new was about to happen in Italy and he gave expression to that in Milan on 17 November 1918.

In a manner unique perhaps to clerics, to whom participation in its life is normally forbidden, Luigi Sturzo had an exalted concept of the function of parliament in the democratic system. To him parliament had to be above suspicion, had to work efficiently, had to abide inflexibly by the constitutional norms and, in short, had to do what its purpose implied — express and incarnate in law the will of the people. Despite his own years as a public figure holding office on a municipal level, despite his own contact with politicians, Sturzo had never waned in that idealism. Indeed he never was to wane from his inflexible ideals even when, as an old man 30 years later, he took his place as a senator at Palazzo Madama and conscientiously researched meticulously every word he spoke in that assembly. As a result, furthermore, of that idealism Sturzo was imbued with the conviction that a healthy parliament could achieve its aims. He was never naive or unaware of the power of extra parliamentary or anti-parliamentary bodies but he always hoped that, by its own integral activity, parliament would remain the supreme expression in the body politic and that, as a consequence, democracy would remain healthy.

As a result of these convictions it was not of a new party that Sturzo spoke at Milan on 17 November 1918, but rather of a new concept of parliament that would free the Italian state from the bonds of the past and open the way to a fuller, more vital expression of Italian democracy.[1] To that fundamental concept Sturzo always remained true and as a result others wondered when he took decisions that appeared to contradict either the best interests of governmental stability by his refusal of unhealthy alliances, or when he seemed to conflict with the instinct for survival of his own party. Alliances and party interests were secondary to the main purpose of Sturzo's activity which retained parliament as the expression of democracy at its apex. The one thing that Sturzo seemed to underestimate was the influence of his priesthood on his political role. By nature he belonged to democracy, by grace to the priesthood and by definition that was anything but a democratic institution. It was a lesson time would reveal.[2]

Yet if Sturzo was deliberately vague on the requisite steps to be taken for the regeneration of parliament there were those present, such as the Archbishop of Milan, Cardinal Andrea Ferrari, who fully understood the implications contained in the speech. As a consequence the archbishop advised Sturzo to seek an audience with the papal Secretary of State, Gasparri, in order to find out what view the Vatican held on the entry of Catholics into political life.[3] At the same time his speech called forth a prearranged public appeal by a leading Milanese layman, Stefano Cavazzoni, for the formation of a political party based on Catholic Action. In his reply to Cavazzoni on 22 November Sturzo affirmed the need for the new party, but he saw clearly that the historical development of the Catholic movement demanded that it take another path in its political fulfilment and, granted that requirement, it had to free itself from the ties to ecclesiastical authority which any organic connection with Catholic Action would necessarily imply. Thus he affirmed the aconfessional nature of the new party and eventually gave it form even in a nominal sense by calling it the Partito Popolare Italiano without any reference therefore to its religious motivations.[4]

It was inevitable that those who thought of Italian Catholicism as a monolithic structure directed in every aspect of its public life by the papacy would see the new party as simply another emanation of Vatican politics. Both the *Messaggero* and the *Giornale del Popolo* saw the hand of the Vatican behind it; most socialists dismissed it as a clever trick designed to fool the electorate while *L'Epoca* of 20 January 1919 said 'the clericals had put together a somewhat banal programme'.[5] On the other hand it comes as no surprise that Antonio Gramsci saw the new party in another light. In a long article in the socialist paper *Avanti*, Gramsci took the birth of the new party seriously and saw it as part of the 'inexorable process of the dissolution of Italian society of old'. The Italian liberal state had failed in its struggle with the Church, the war had destroyed the 'religious myth' and Catholics, aware of this, were becoming a lay party which, renouncing universality, would become the expression of the will of the bourgeois class. Although Gramsci remained convinced that the proletariat would opt ultimately for the 'idea of the Soviet' which would usher in the new international order, he nonetheless saw in the new party's formation 'the most important fact in Italian history since the Risorgimento'. With a prophetic note *Avanti* itself wrote 'Our party and their party are the genuine forces in the country, destined to a giant encounter when in a little while all the other parties are eliminated.'[6]

The main contributing historical factor to the formation of the PPI was undoubtedly the First World War. After a conflict in which Catholics had fought and died for their country it was not possible to deny them a role in its peace. They had won their freedom to be Italians and both Church and state realized this fact. Sturzo realized it before all others.[7] As a result Sturzo went to Gasparri not to ask his or the pope's permission to found a political party, but to ensure that the Vatican would not place any obstacle to its foundation. Even in the embryonic stages of its development Catholic social doctrine rejected the possibility of the existence of an official Catholic party because as such it would lie outside the competence of ecclesiastical authority. More importantly the long practice of Vatican diplomacy indicated the wisdom of keeping one's options open which resulted, at the very least, in an attitude of caution in regard to a new party. Finally the fact that Sturzo was a priest and as such bound by obedience to his ecclesiastical superiors enhanced, rather than diminished, Vatican uneasiness in regard to his party because to deal with Sturzo either benignly or otherwise would result in giving an impression of Vatican interference in political matters. All of this Gasparri summed up in a letter he wrote some years later to Carlo Santucci, his friend from boyhood, who had accompanied Sturzo to the audience with the cardinal. There is little doubt as to the veracity of the letter when one bears in mind the official attitude of the Vatican as ascertainable from contemporary public facts. Gasparri said that the Vatican had had nothing to do with the origins of the party and that as far as he was concerned it was no more than 'the least bad of all', that is to say when compared with the socialist, radical or liberal parties. His main objection to it was the fact that it had a priest as its 'president or director' and that it allowed men, Guido Miglioli for example, whose ideas were far too advanced, to be counted among its members.[8] Thus when Sturzo left the apartments of the Secretary of State on that night in December 1918 he carried neither refusal nor approval but the simple, official recognition of a fact. A new party was to be created and Sturzo had to go ahead and give it shape and life. It was not, as Mario Missiroli asserted in January 1919, a step by which Catholics 'liberated themselves permanently from Vatican subjection' but it was rather an assertion of lay independence in temporal matters.[9] The Vatican acknowledged this fact but, as time has proved in human affairs, it could afford to wait before judging the outcome.

During December Sturzo was busy gathering together a provisional executive committee which decided on the practical steps to be taken for the formation of the party and by 28 December the *Osservatore Romano* saw fit to refer publicly to such proceedings when, under the rubric 'Italian Affairs', it denied that the Holy See had given its consent to the formation of a Catholic party in the country.[10] Undaunted, or perhaps encouraged, the small group went ahead and despite the fact that Filippo Meda, still a parliamentary member, was not a participant, its composition illustrated the wealth of human experience, idealism and dedication to a purpose upon which the nascent party could draw. In a room of the Albergo Santa Chiara in Rome on the evening of 18 January 1919 Sturzo delineated, from the bed to which he was confined due to a minor indisposition, an appeal to 'all free and strong men'.[11] It was a decisive moment in the development of the modern Italian state not so much because a new and ultimately powerful political party was born, nor because it marked the entry into public life of an organized body of Catholics who, as a group, had hitherto been absent from the Italy that had been united without them. It was decisive because it marked the beginning of an experiment in the relations between

Church and state, between the sacred and the profane, between the layman and the cleric, which was unique. That very act meant the end of the theocratic dream — an end accepted reluctantly on both sides of the Tiber and one which would yet sound its death rattles because it was a dream that died so hard. It was the ancient dream of Empire itself when the gods and the caesars became one, it was the dream of Constantine, Charlemagne and Henry VIII, of Gregory the Great, Innocent III and Boniface VIII. Small wonder it died hard and small wonder too that in its death others would suffer and other hopes would be shattered.

The appeal was launched at a moment in which desperate psychological factors resulting from the war had predisposed many Italians to look for a new way ahead. Most people were convinced that war was a barbarism the nations could never revert to and that, in unity, Europe had to build anew. The ebullient words of Woodrow Wilson, then visiting Italy, seemed full of promise for the tired, older nations of the Continent, coming as they did from the leader of a powerful and victorious America, and they found an echo in the appeal of the Partito Popolare.[12] Nonetheless the appeal and the attached twelve point programme did enunciate a series of explicit principles and planks which concretized the thought and experience of Sturzo. Basically the central concept was the autonomy and freedom of the individual as a person within his natural groupings of family, class and commune. His position in those groupings was juxtaposed and harmonized with the state which itself had to genuinely express the will of the people. As such it was an expression of Thomistic doctrine applied to the demands of the modern state and its specific delineation in the programme, including a demand for a vote for women, was progressive, humane and reasonable. Yet it was inevitable that, because of the origins of the party, immediate attention would centre on Point VIII which stated:

> Freedom and independence of the Church in the full development

of its spiritual authority. Freedom and respect for the Christian conscience considered as the foundation and the safeguard of the life of the nation, of the liberties of the people and of the increasing development of civilization in the world.[13]

In itself such a statement would seem to suffice even in a country in which Catholicism was the major religion of the people. As Salvemini pointed out the census of 1911 showed that only 5 per cent of 35 million Italians registered themselves as being other than Catholic, but that the 95 per cent contained many whose adherence to the Church was minimal, indifferent or confused including the young man who said to Salvemini 'Let us hope that in purgatory the holy soul of Lenin prays for us.'[14] However Italy was basically a Catholic nation and its people acknowledged that Catholicism was the religion of the nation. For any other Catholic nation the plank of the new party's platform would probably have sufficed even though it contained no specific reference to such vexed questions as marriage and divorce. But since 1870 the Church had found itself in an unaccustomed situation in Italy and the longed for solution to the Roman Question which would set matters aright again was already under discussion at high levels. It is probable that Luigi Sturzo and the founders of the Partito Popolare were unaware of those discussions but a reading of their platform, in which no reference whatever was made to the Roman Question, brought little joy to the quickening hearts of the Vatican diplomats.

As early as 1915 Gasparri had said, in an interview with the *Corriere della Sera*, that the Holy See expected that the Roman Question would be answered by the feelings and sense of justice of the Italian people.[15]

This was at least a recognition that the Vatican no longer relied upon foreign intervention, diplomatic or otherwise, in its ambitions for the Holy See in Italy itself. On the other hand the hoped for maturity in the Italian people was long in germination and by 1919 the Vatican had turned to diplomacy as a more expedient means of solving the problem. The terms of reconciliation had not been specified but it was accepted that some form of territorial independence was regarded as a *sine qua non* in the Vatican.[16] Thus the formation of a political party, headed by a priest and based on Catholic support, but which omitted any reference to the Roman Question was already a source of disquiet to which Sturzo added when he was interviewed by *Il Messaggero* on 23 January 1919, a few days after the issue of the appeal and programme of the party.[17] His interview came to the attention of the prestigious Jesuit magazine *Civiltà Cattolica* whose editor was always appointed with papal consent and whose policies were taken as approved by the Vatican.

As *Civiltà Cattolica* put it, Sturzo 'with scant regard for accuracy of expression' had said that his party 'could not and did not fly under a religious flag' and that as a result it had 'amongst its pivotal points religious liberty' which 'we understand as religious freedom for all cults'. The magazine observed that the priest had not explained how his party thereby differed from the liberals who in their 'false' theory recognized the same right for truth as for error and in fact frequently favoured the latter even in countries which were fully Catholic, such as Italy. Nonetheless, and especially when theological weaknesses were so apparent, it was still necessary not to speak of a Catholic party or of Catholic representatives because 'it is all too evident that we are unable to recognize in them either the appropriate power or the proper mandate [requisite in an official Catholic body] nor, certainly do they desire such [power or mandate]'. Furthermore it was clear to the commentator that the Partito Popolare suffered from the defect of remaining aloof from matters for which Catholics demanded a solution. It recognized in its platform the spiritual authority of the Church, but what about the authority to teach and rule, as well as the legislative, executive and punitive functions of the Church? The modern atheistic states denied those powers and the implication was that the Partito Popolare denied them also.[18]

It was scarcely an auspicious beginning for a young party which claimed to be aconfessional, but nonetheless relied heavily upon support which was very sensitive to official Catholic opinion. Perhaps Romolo Murri was not far wrong when he wrote 'the autonomy which it [the Partito Popolare] enjoyed was a concession, not a conquest'.[19] In any case Father Enrico Rosa, editor of *Civiltà Cattolica* summed up official feeling gently when he said two years later that 'The Vatican was irritated above all by the fact that Don Sturzo didn't want to include in his programme the faintest suggestion that one could look forward to an accord between Church and State'.[20]

The *Osservatore Romano* was initially cautious in its approach to the party, and simply announced its official foundation without comment together with the appeal and platform but it was quickly apparent that behind the scenes there was considerable concern, especially within the top echelons of Catholic Action.[21] For 50 years it had been accepted that Catholics, in their public life on a political level, had some degree of dependence upon the papacy and the hierarchy and this dependence was carefully delineated within the framework of the old *Opera* or of Catholic Action in a more recent period. Now it seemed that Sturzo, himself a leading figure in Catholic Action, had side stepped the whole problem of the dependence of the Catholic laity upon the hierarchy by the simple expedient of setting up an aconfessional party. A contemporary, Mario Ferrara, wrote that by his act Sturzo had cleverly disposed of the heads of Catholic Action and destroyed 'a bulwark upon which the leaders of the so called liberal party and the large Catholic landlords relied'.[22] The papal nominee as president of Catholic Action was Count Dalla Torre with whom Sturzo had been in constant contact prior to the formation of the PPI and who formed a bridge between the new party and the Vatican. But when Dalla Torre saw the inevitable signs of a mass exodus from his own organization to the PPI he soon made it evident that he at least was not to be disposed of so easily and the field he chose to fight on was the role of Catholic Action as the chosen instrument of the papacy.

After a preliminary foray at the end of January involving an audience with the pope and an exchange of letters between Dalla Torre and Benedict on the activity of the Popular Union, Dalla Torre came to the point in March. He would not accept the displacement of Catholic Action by a Catholic political party, it would stand on its ground on all levels, continue to express its thoughts and present its policies while expecting adherence to them by 'all militant Catholics' when 'the religious and moral interests of the people' were involved. Nonetheless Catholic Action would not 'attempt to discipline, as it has never done in the past, deeds and activity that are merely political.'[23]

This was the classic enunciation of papal thought on the political activity of Catholics, as distinguished from their spiritual activity, that prevailed in Catholic social teaching, as enunciated by the popes, from the time of Leo XIII. The crux of it was the difficulty which arose in determining when a political act contained a religious element as, at least from the part of believing Catholics, there could be no question of regarding a religious act, especially if directed by the papacy, as purely or 'merely political'. The competence to decide whether acts which seemed to be 'merely political' contained in fact 'religious and moral interests' rested in the hands of the papacy and that problem Sturzo could solve in one way only. He could accept without question the papal dictate or foreswear his religious obedience as Romolo Murri had done. As an actor, indeed the chief actor, in the drama of the party which he founded, Sturzo was not, and never wished to be, fully autonomous. He accepted the claims of the papacy in regard to Catholic Action and, though he wanted the political activity of his party to be autonomous, he believed in the authority of the Church outside of which authority, as he himself said, 'there is no certainty'.[24] Nonetheless he hoped that such autonomy, with the progress of time and events, could be fostered and the very fact that his party was ever founded seemed to be an expression of the validity of that hope. Yet the slow development of that autonomy in the historical sense had been part of the whole relationship between Church and state in the diarchy between the two forces which had existed for many centuries in the Italian peninsula.[25] Sturzo was aware that so many contingent factors could foster or impede the progress of lay autonomy, chiefly perhaps the climate engendered by a change in the person holding the papal office and, although there was a lack of cordiality between Sturzo and Gasparri, whom he never met again after the audiences of late 1918, the tolerant attitude of Benedict XV made the first months of the party's activity relatively smooth.

Quick as it was to reflect changes in papal attitudes the *Osservatore Romano* was a good index of Vatican thinking on the new party. Short of any official sanction the paper made it clear that the PPI stood in a privileged relationship to Catholics by printing reports of its proceedings and those of its leader, Sturzo, in a way that was never done for other parties. Between January 1919 and the first Congress of the PPI at Bologna in June of that year, the development of the party and its proceedings were given space on 19 occasions and although much of the material was no more than a reproduction of the various communications sent to the paper by the party officials, their coverage indicated a high degree of interest, if not direct support.[26] Sturzo himself had retained his position as secretary of the special Catholic Action body, Pro Schola, an organization he himself had founded for the defence of private schools. As such he did not hesitate to proclaim 'freedom of teaching is a fundamental postulate for any political and moral action of Catholics' and *Osservatore Romano* acknowledged him as the 'tireless and valuable secretary general' of Pro Schola.[27] He was able to persuade Pro Schola, contrary to the view of Father Agostino Gemelli, that time was ripe for action on the education question and, although he was not present with the rest of the directorate when they had an audience with the pope on 4 March, he clearly kept himself occupied with the matter because on 7 March the parliamentary group of the PPI pledged itself to work for freedom of religious teaching in the school system.[28] In such ways it was evident that both with the pope and within powerful Vatican circles Sturzo as a priest and his party as a political group were not at odds on any fundamental issue and the mutual relations were harmonious, if not constant.

Catholic support for the new party was both widespread and valuable, especially when the Catholic papers of the so called 'trust' set up by Giovanni Grosoli some years previously gave their adherence to it. Those papers had been firmly linked to Catholic Action on the propaganda level and relied on the Bank of Rome and large financial concerns, especially those dealing in sugar, for support. The main journal was the Roman daily *Corriere d'Italia* which stated bluntly 'to the new political party … our paper cordially adheres', while others such as *Italia*, Milan; *Momento*, Turin; *Avvenire d'Italia*, Bologna and *Messaggero Toscano*, Pisa, also gave powerful support.[29] The *Perseveranza* of Milan in giving its support was delighted at the fine gesture of self-determination and maturity which revealed 'the decadence of all forms of tutelage'. On the other hand the important *L'Unità Cattolica* of Florence adopted a very cautious attitude on the grounds that the PPI was not a Catholic Action body, nor was it the representative or the exponent of Catholic Action or the pope. It thought nevertheless that, provided the party stuck to the Gospel and to the Church, it would do well.[30]

In like manner the local bodies of Catholic Action got behind the PPI to an extent which tended to cloud the issue of the autonomy and aconfessional character of the party. During the war, Catholic Action had suffered from the loss of much of its leadership which in large part had been later assumed by younger men who then tended to support the more positive and, at least in appearance, more valuable political action proffered by the Partito Popolare. It was generally acknowledged that the Popolari did not misuse their positions in Catholic Action, but the transference of papers and personnel from the apparatus of Catholic Action to the Partito Popolare certainly gave the appearance of the monopolization of the Catholic forces by the new political power.³¹ Stefano Jacini, the historian of the party in its early years, later admitted that within 24 hours of its founding the party 'counted on the adhesion of about twenty daily papers and about 50 weeklies the greater part of which stayed faithful until the end'.³²

This propaganda apparatus was directed from a press office which further confused the issue in that its chief was a priest, Guilio De Rossi, who was ably assisted by the capable polemicist Igino Giordani. Small wonder then that one side of the Tiber saw the new party as an extension of ecclesiastical political power in Italy, while the men in the Vatican began to wonder as they saw their control of the political activity of Catholics slipping from their grasp. In any case it was immediately apparent that the scope of the Electoral Union of Catholic Action had been pre-empted and compromised by the rise of the Partito Popolare. As a result it was dissolved and Catholic Action had no further apparent connections in the political field. As a final comment on this metamorphosis *Osservatore Romano* announced with regret the resignation of Sturzo from his general secretaryship of the Central Committee of Catholic Action and his assumption of the secretaryship of the Partito Popolare.³³

Nonetheless the Vatican was not prepared to let the field of Catholic Action be deserted without a struggle and to achieve this end it was decided to give every possible support to the mass movement called the Popular Union. As early as 24 January 1919 an appeal was made to all Catholics to join the Union which was seen as having a purely religious and social function and was thereby 'destined to reunite in full harmony of purpose and work all Italian Catholics' despite the political differences that may have existed amongst them.³⁴ By February the Union had formulated a new programme based on the education of the conscience of the people. It stressed the need to ensure the inviolability of the pope against 'sectarian irreverence' and in an Italy increasingly subject to civil unrest based on socialist inspired direct action 'to put before the people the principles of order and authority as the fundamental conditions of all strength and civil greatness'.[35] By March the claim was made that the Union had 950,000 members in 211 groups and although Dalla Torre admitted that, provided they held no office within it, members of the PPI could also be in the Union, he asserted vigorously that no political party could ever replace the Union itself.[36]

The prominence given to the new role of Catholic Action was illustrated by the fact that the *Osservatore Romano* began in April to run a full section under the headline 'Catholic Action' and reported at length on its various activities throughout the country.[37] Nonetheless it was clear that both Catholic Action and the PPI were being mutually affected by their inability to cooperate on other than the personal level and when Catholic Action celebrated the anniversary of Leo XIII's great encyclical *Rerum Novarum* in May 1919, the PPI, as a political party, was unable to participate.[38] Hence in its first few months of existence the seeds were sown of a conflict of loyalties between Catholic Action and the PPI which, although they were but dimly perceived at the time, were to bear later fruits.

On the parliamentary level the party was immediately joined by the nebulous block of 'Catholic deputies' who had kept themselves separate from other party alliances. Seventeen in number they were grouped together by Giovanni Bertini, Giovanni Longinotti and Guilio Rodinò and they were given the immediate, practical task of pressing for electoral reform based on the proportional system, a reform which the socialist party was also demanding. Within the year the aim of the party had been achieved and a new law accepting proportionalism was passed by the Nitti government.[39]

The composition of the party on the union level was based on adhesion to it by the Catholic 'white' unions which, while retaining their autonomy, nonetheless gave it their open support under the leadership of Achille Grandi and Guido Miglioli. These diverse elements that made it up gave the party more the nature of a movement than of a political structure with its own coherent unity. Its members ranged from old conservatives to young radicals, from large capitalists to small farmers, from directors of the Bank of Rome to small shareholders in credit societies. The party, according to Romolo Murri, was thus rendered dangerously frail in its structure and ideals. Murri wrote that it was even unable to 'take up a clear and firm position in the field of social justice because it was not a homogeneous and strong party but a gathering of men held together only by electoral interests and in it the participation of the clergy was by far the most important element ...'.[40] It was a harsh judgement to make of the Partito Popolare and it overlooked the effect that strong leadership can have even over diverse elements in times of grave import.

It was in an atmosphere of euphoria rising from the groundswell of support and the mushrooming of local branches right through the country that the party held its first Congress at Bologna in June 1919.[41] Inevitably, given its composition, there was immediate conflict on the question of the aconfessional nature of the party and opposition to it was led by the powerful figure of Father Agostino Gemelli who, together with Father Francesco Olgiati, had recently published a short work with the ominous title *The Platform of the Partito Popolare Italiano; as it is not and as it ought to be*.[42] Despite its brevity the book contained a serious argument which was well sustained by its authors. Its central thesis was that if the PPI was not a Catholic party with a Catholic platform and Catholic aims then it separated the religious principle from political activity and consequently differed little from other political parties. It deplored the lack of a 'courageous and dutiful affirmation of the necessity to solve the Roman Question' and it appealed for a continuation of the 'glorious guelph tradition' which had made Italy foremost amongst the nations of Europe.[43]

The tendency towards a confessional Catholic party had its roots in north Italy, especially at Milan and in the Veneto where the Church had remained firmly intransigent on the Roman Question and where Catholicism in Italy had its basic economic, cultural and political roots. Sturzo was well aware of these factors and as a result he was on the offensive from the very start with his nomination of Alcide De Gasperi as president of the Congress. As the representative of Trentino, united to Italy since the war, as the representative also of the economic and political struggle of the people of Trentino against the attempts of Austria to wean their allegiance away from Italy, De Gasperi seemed to fulfil the highest aspirations of the party to be truly national, to be an Italian party. In that context Sturzo affirmed the aconfessionalism of the party in a genuinely positive sense. While Gemelli and Olgiati had appealed in their work to the 'greatness of Italy' in whose name the party was asked to work for a solution to the Roman Question, Sturzo used the aconfessionalism of the party to affirm the greater work of resolving the question of Italy as a nation and, at that, a Christian nation. After stating that the party by its very existence had pre-empted the time worn monopoly of the liberals to represent the bourgeoisie, and the newer monopoly of the socialist to represent the proletariat, Sturzo turned to the question of aconfessionalism. He claimed that it was superfluous 'to explain why we didn't call ourselves a Catholic party: the two terms are antithetical; Catholicism is a religion, it is universal; a party is political, it is division.' Thus 'From the very beginning we have excluded religion as our political badge, and we want to stand clearly on the specific terrain of a party which has as its direct object the public life of the nation.'[44]

Sturzo's terminology, scholastic and precise in its clarity, could not veil his own deep conviction that the Roman Question was fundamentally a tactical matter to be decided in its own time by political bargaining. Thus it was neither sacred nor transcendental but temporal and expedient and any political party which espoused it as its primary or even as a fundamental objective was doomed to futility. He did not despise the past but praised the fruitful development of the Catholic movement from 1874 onwards which, as its final act, gave birth to the Partito Popolare. Now however it was time to unite on a common platform 'not of simple defence but of construction, not only negative but positive, not religious but social'. In affirming the positive nature of the party Sturzo was also prepared to renounce on its behalf the backing of the Church in all of its political acts and struggles which 'in our name alone we must and can fight, on the same grounds as the other parties that are opposed to us'. He took comfort in the fact that over 100,000 had already asked to join the party and that 850 branches were set up with more than 200 others awaiting approval and that 20 daily newspapers and 62 weeklies adhered to it. To him these were all signs the party could stand on its own feet.[45] The northern opposition to aconfessionalism quickly receded in the face of Sturzo's conviction and logic and, whatever else happened to it, the Partito Popolare never became a second face of Italian Catholic Action.[46]

The *Osservatore Romano* sent Francesco Zanetti to report the Congress and he gave a reasonably full report of its proceedings which was factual and without comment. At the end of the report the editor remarked that 'we intend to remain completely extraneous' to the proceedings of the party although the observation was made, with the customary rhetoric reserved for statements in regard to the papacy, that the demonstration in honour of Benedict, which lasted several minutes, was 'unanimous, spontaneous, sincere, imposing and moving'.[47] More provocative convictions on the origins of the PPI moved *Avanti* on behalf of the socialists to call the proceedings 'The Clerical Congress'; to say that private property and the capitalist system were the basis of the party and to reject its democratic and working-class claims as mere trickery because its basic aim was a theocracy. With some perception the paper also warned the PPI that if it tried to form a white as opposed to a red international its members might find themselves excommunicated because the Church itself was already the perfect embodiment of white internationalism.[48]

There was at least one aspect of 'white internationalism' which had been dear to the Vatican since 1870 and that was in regard to international Catholic solidarity on the Roman Question and the need for a solution to it. Thus it was one thing for Sturzo to set the Roman Question aside with seeming aplomb but it was another to allay Vatican fears that an apparent lack of unity amongst Catholics, especially Italian Catholics, would jeopardize the steps being taken towards its solution. The urgency of Vatican diplomatic activity towards a solution was not simply theoretical but practical in the political and economic sense.

In 1919 a book written by Nazzareno Casacca was published entitled *Il Papa e l'Italia* in which the claim of the Holy See for 'absolute independence from any earthly throne and the territory necessary to sustain that right' was proclaimed while Catholics who kept silent on the matter through 'human respect' were upbraided.[49] This was the kind of statement that the Vatican both understood and approved of while any concept that a true renewal of Italian national life, including the state, would automatically redound to the benefit of the Church was an ideal for some far distant parousia, even though proclaimed by Sturzo. In the Vatican school of diplomacy the Gospel was said to be the fundamental law, but everyone knew that its practitioners were men and its field the world. They were irreconcilables that only dreamers like Pascal II had attempted to wed when he had proposed as a solution to the Investiture Conflict in the twelfth century that the Church would give up her temporalities in return for freedom in the spiritual sphere.[50] Since then the realization was firmly fixed and acted upon by all the popes that without temporal means it was an unenviable task to preach the Gospel. In 1919 the Vatican was singularly devoid singularly of such means.

According to Gaetano Salvemini, Leo XIII had inherited a healthy financial situation from Pius IX but the Vatican had speculated in Roman building companies and lost in the 'construction crisis' of 1887.

Pius X had lived a precarious financial existence even selling gifts made to him in order to get by. During the war, the Vatican costs went up and the traditional voluntary means of support, Peter's Pence, had diminished, especially from its major source, France, where the anti-war politics of Benedict XV were unwelcome. The pope, furthermore, had aggravated the situation by spending large sums on civil and military prisoners of war. Moreover many religious congregations, French, Italian, Austrian and Hungarian, had been advised to deal with Austrian banking houses by those Vatican officials who believed in a German Axis victory. After the war the Vatican consequently felt obliged to contribute to the upkeep of those congregations which had been financially ruined. Finally the monetary crisis in Germany meant that German Catholics, who had previously contributed generously to Vatican finances, were unable to do so. North America in particular became the primary source for papal assistance after the war, but even so his circumstances were so straitened that Benedict often had to ask his rich visitors for a contribution.[51]

The financial and political situation demanded a quick solution to the Roman Question which would give both legal recognition to independence for a form of papal territorial sovereignty and some restitution for the losses suffered through the annexation of Rome and the Papal States. It so happened that while Sturzo was proclaiming his party's lack of enthusiasm for detailed proposals on the Roman Question at Bologna, Monsignor Bonaventura Cerretti, a high ranking Vatican official, was discussing a solution to it in Paris with Vittorio Emanuele Orlando, Prime Minister of Italy. The discussion eventually proved fruitless due partly to the opposition of the King who said that he would abdicate rather than accept a Concordat and that he held strongly to Giolitti's concept of the Church and state proceeding along two parallel lines. The little monarch, with an uncustomary degree of firmness, even promised to go out on the piazza with a rifle to uphold the *status quo*.[52] The fact that the Orlando government fell on 19 June

1919 also meant that the opportune moment was lost but it remained true that while a party based on so called Christian principles showed no inclination to cooperate with the Vatican, other, secular parties, were not so intransigent and perhaps offered greater scope for the future.

A concern for its position in the Italian peninsula was by no means the only problem preoccupying the minds of papal diplomats in 1918 and 1919. Already the 'spectre' that had hung over Europe for almost a century had begun to take on an awesome reality. Thus it was with more than passing interest that events in Russia were observed by the Vatican where as early as 4 July 1918 the conviction was widespread that the Russian Revolution would not simply disappear, especially in its 'inevitable consequences' which were seen as the 'ruin' and the 'irreparable end of a people'. Bolshevism was an 'infection' and the very term itself was 'the sacramental word of the overthrow of all order'. Woodrow Wilson visited the pope at the height of his Italian popularity in January 1919 and when a socialist deputy said that Italy had to make a choice between Wilson and Lenin, Wilson's principles were seen as reflecting 'that Christian civilization which sprang from the Gospel in the world', bolshevism was seen as 'inimical to all genuine civilization', and Father Giovanni Semeria, former general chaplain to the Italian army, proclaimed that it was the duty of all Italian Catholics to be Wilsonians given the Christian virtues of the American politician.[53]

To some extent the Russian situation was given constant point by the threat of a similar upheaval in Italy. The socialist party still retained the unity it had achieved in 1892 although its blending of left wingers, centralists and reformists was an unstable element that promised at any moment to split apart. *Avanti* still spoke for the party and it, like the *Osservatore Romano*, gave full treatment to the Russian Revolution while from his seat in parliament Claudio Treves asked the Italian government 'to support the permanence of the socialist republic in Russia'. To *Avanti* the Revolution was 'a gigantic work done by giants' and it was seen as the model for all revolutions. The Italian proletariat was invited to go beyond 'verbal manifestations' in displaying its solidarity towards 'Russia of the Soviets' and Catholics were assured that they need have no fear under socialism because Article 13 of the Soviet Constitution assured freedom of religion as well as irreligion.[54]

These assertions were met by the Vatican in *Osservatore Romano* with constant reminders of the intimate links between socialism and bolshevism. Socialism, it affirmed, 'tends towards the elimination of the individual to the advantage of the collectivity in a way that is ugly, thoughtless, tyrannical and often dishonest'. 'God, to the socialists does not exist' and in Russia and Hungary religious persecution had quickly followed the separation of Church and state.[55] In themselves such affirmations were little more than restatements of long held attitudes, but they were given point and even urgency by the events in Russia, Germany, Hungary and, to a lesser extent, in Italy where violence, especially in the north, was too frequently the password by which the extreme socialists proposed to usher in their own brand of earthly paradise. *Avanti* admitted what *Osservatore Romano* had already pointed out that the Russian revolution was not an isolated thing, but that it was an event which would spread eventually to embrace the world and the warning issued to all other political and religious groupings was explicit in the terminology and activity of the socialist movement in Italy during 1919.[56]

Under these circumstances it is scarcely to be wondered at that the proceedings of the PPI, especially in its deliberations on the social question, should be watched with some concern. Sturzo had never disguised his concern for the working class or his conviction of the necessity for a more even distribution of wealth. Nonetheless he rejected the concept of the intrinsic nature of the class struggle, and the tentative formulation given at the Congress by Guido Miglioli to proposals for a Christian party of the proletariat which would have a class basis were ignored.[57] As all the delegates knew, from the time of Leo XIII socialism had been condemned by the Church on the grounds of its materialism, its doctrine of the class struggle, its denials of private property and its use of violence. Such a simplification seemed to leave little room for manoeuvre in the enumeration of a social programme based on Christian principles, but, provided the use of terminology redolent of socialist principles in the above areas was avoided, then perhaps some progress could be made. Thus at Bologna it was possible for Remo Vigorelli, a delegate from Pavia with progressive tendencies, to add an amendment to the social programme of the party proposed by Achille Grandi. It read

> The Partito Popolare Italiano intends to champion the judicial norms and the provisions necessary to favour the gradual transition from and the ultimate removal of the present liberal capitalist economy which is based on the wage earner, to a more humane and Christian economy in which Capital, considered as productive insofar as it is subordinate to Labour, may be brought back to its natural function as a mere material agent of production. In this capacity it will be recompensed in well-defined limits, while to Labour on the other hand, whether intellectual or manual, the greatest fruit of the productive force will be assured.[58]

For his own part Sturzo himself drew on the fruits of his Sicilian experience as priest, mayor and Christian Democrat to propose policies on the land question that went well beyond the customary attitudes of previous administrations but, as such, proved acceptable to the Congress. The programme consequently contained a policy requesting that land be assigned to its cultivators by transfer or by contractual forms suitable to the prevailing local systems, and, in cases in which land had not been put to adequate use, it was suggested to expropriate it at public expense and share it amongst farmers' families.[59] Perhaps as a sop to those who would readily see the spectre of socialism behind such proposals, the policy also contained an invitation to the party to struggle against the attempted monopoly by the Socialist Party to represent the proletariat, and to demand equal treatment before the law for all organizations. The latter proposal was not to the liking of the General Confederation of Labour which was allied to the Socialist Party and wanted to be the unique voice of the union movement.[60]

During the Congress Father Gemelli had sounded his customary warning with 'There will also be a revolution in Italy: bolshevism is knocking at the doors'. To him the only answer was a return to Christ.[61] While one section of the Congress was firmly of the opinion that such a 'return' to Christ had to be spelt out in more specific terms, perhaps even terms which assailed the entrenched economic and social position of the wealthy, it was apparent that another section viewed with grave misgiving any tendency that seemed to smack even minimally of the long dreaded tenets of the socialist enemy. Thus Gemelli felt safe in replying to Miglioli's suggestion that the party should change its name to 'Party of the Christian Proletariat' with 'I have no feeling of solidarity with you because you talk like a socialist not like a Christian'.[62] It remained for Gemelli and Olgiati to take up this theme after the Congress and they were able to use *Unità Cattolica*, temporary replacement for *Osservatore Romano* during the strike of July–August 1919, as their vehicle.

In a long article the two priests gave their view of the reception given to their book and the ideas it contained by the Bologna Congress. To them there were too many 'sick' delegates who suffered from the disease of imitating and mimicking socialism. Miglioli was the worst afflicted and felt the need to prove with a concrete programme that he was in fact a Christian rather than a socialist. To the priests the right course of action was for 'Catholics themselves to bring about a revolution, that is to say substitute the Christian state in place of the liberal state, and oppose the reds and the bolshevists who wish to set up amongst us, as they have done in Russia or Hungary, a reign of terror and destruction'.[63] Those were heady words which confused the issues in emotive and personal terms without adding anything useful to the desire of the PPI to formulate its own programme and they serve to illustrate the wide rift that had opened between Sturzo and some other members of the clergy whose principles may indeed have been sound but whose grasp of the practical realities of Italian society on a political or economic level was weakened by the gulf between them and the complex nature of that society. *Vindex* in the next issue of *Unità Cattolica* came timidly to the defence of the PPI by stating that although it was not Catholic it was made up of Catholics who would never collaborate with the socialists, but the seeds of suspicion had been sown at Bologna and Sturzo's awareness of that suspicion made him determined to steer a centralist course in the party in order to ensure its survival.[64]

If one section of the party was concerned that it was too socialist another was troubled about its lack of the old element that had been the cohesive force in all Catholic groupings in the pre-war days — papalism. Old Battista Paganuzzi and 20 others formed a right-wing group and wrote to the directorate to complain about the presence of PPI men in the Nitti cabinet.[65] In their eyes Nitti's was a government which denied liberty and independence to the Holy See and to the pope, and no decent PPI man could acquiesce in that state of affairs. They promised that they themselves, as loyal papalists, would at least remain true to their ideals and struggle for the freedom of the papacy. The National Council of the party rejected this 'grave act of indiscipline' and threatened to expel its perpetrators if they persisted, thus moving the *Unità Cattolica* to remark that it was only because the PPI was not an official Catholic party that it had not yet provoked a rejection by the ecclesiastical authority, which seemed to contradict the assumption that according to accepted principles there could not exist any such thing as an official Catholic party![66] The directorate of the PPI must have welcomed the end of the strike which had caused the silence of the *Osservatore Romano* for in its more temperate columns the Roman paper had trod more gently when dealing with the PPI than had the determinedly papalist and rigid Florentine journal.

Despite the uneasiness of the alliances that made up the party one fact about the composition of the first Congress that did not escape the notice of observers was the presence of large numbers of clergy. Given his own position Sturzo was scarcely able to object to this manifestation of independent clerical, as distinct from ecclesiastical support, and it was futile for the *Civiltà Cattolica* to continue to represent the party as more dependent upon Rousseau than on Aquinas or Suarez for its doctrinal basis when such clerical solidarity, even from men not over disposed to theological speculation, was apparent.[67] Nonetheless, despite the fact that when Sturzo read Francesco Fanelli's disjointed analysis of his role as leader of the party some years later he took pains to illustrate his displeasure, rejection or simple, well merited derision of it by underlining sentences, putting in exclamation marks or even casting doubts on Fanelli's sanity, there was one accusation he did not deny. Fanelli singled out as a great weakness in Sturzo the fact that he had not rejected the hordes of inopportune priestly colleagues whose presence branded the party as clerical even in Gasparri's eyes, and who then deserted Sturzo in his hour of need. It was perhaps an accusation that Sturzo had often made to himself.[68]

In its first months of existence the party had given clear proof by its attitude to the Roman Question that it was no mere creature of the Vatican and in so doing it marked a stage in the development of one segment at least of the Catholic movement as well as illustrating that it had broken with the old conservative past. It was one thing to take that step which was a fruit of maturity as well as consistent with the aconfessional nature of the party itself. It was another to break with a past which had cemented in the minds of many Catholics the conviction that it was to their advantage politically, and that of the cause which they represented generally, to make alliances with other political figures or groupings for electoral advantages. Whether in regard to the early history of the Christian Democrat movement, the Gentiloni Pact or his own public activity in Sicily, Sturzo had always acted on the basic principle that alliances, promises, favours and anything that damaged the independence of his own group had to be avoided. At Bologna the question of political independence in electoral contests was fought out and, with the support of Sturzo, intransigence won the day.[69] It marked the party out as a political entity in its own right but it also meant that it had to prepare itself to oppose both men and measures within and without parliament even when opposition seemed perilous.

In the months from June 1919 to the end of the year the PPI devoted its total energy to preparing for its first electoral contest. This happened despite Sturzo's expressed wish not to look for immediate electoral success but to attend to the formation of a 'strong and mature political conscience' in the party.[70] But the formation of the party had engendered a great amount of enthusiasm while the increasing strength of Italian socialism and the atmosphere of urgency created by frequent strikes had given point to the crusading spirit in the party so the element of formation of consciences was quickly forgotten in the turmoil of electoral fervour. Stefano Jacini stressed that sense of urgency when he noted that at Bologna the very opening day of the Congress was clouded by the atmosphere of a general strike, while the streets were full of people carrying the red flag, and he saw all this as part of the accelerating 'revolutionary rhythm of Italian public life'.[71] It was in the context of this situation that the moderate support given to the party by the Vatican in the weeks prior to the election is explained. Everyone expected that the liberals would stay in power but 'against the very grave danger' of socialism it could do no harm to give a booster to 'Catholic popular action' — a clear reference to the PPI.[72]

While it was necessary to insist that ecclesiastical authority remained 'completely extraneous to all this jumbling of men and passions' it was equally necessary to insist on the moral obligation, accountable before God, not to vote for masons, bolshevists and their sympathisers.[73] Nitti's programme was given almost full approval by the paper, but it was left to Dalla Torre, in a letter sent to Italian Catholic Action on 11 November, to spell out a platform with which Catholics were in full agreement. He enunciated five main points on religious liberty, the family, education, labour and workers' unions, all of which were in full accord with the platform of the PPI.[74] That same day, after a ban of almost 50 years, the Vatican officially acknowledged the rights of Catholic citizens to take a role in the political life of the country. The *non expedit* was lifted in an official reply to a question put to the Sacred Penitentiary by Boncompagni and Santucci asking whether it was licit for Catholics to accept the office of deputy or senator in the Kingdom of Italy. The reply, in stately Latin, said yes, provided 'the candidates are sincerely disposed to conserve the laws of God and the Church'.[75]

To the extent that the Vatican had placed no obstacle in the path of the formation of the party, followed its first year of existence with interest and allowed it to be indirectly, but mildly, supported prior to the elections, it is reasonable to suppose that no widespread hostility to the party existed in high papal circles. Yet it is scarcely short of ingenuous to see in the changing nature of Italian society with its revolutionary overtones in the post war period a proof that the Vatican readily consented to the formation of the Partito Popolare, that it 'aimed at the realization by means of the PPI of an instrument of intervention in Italian political life', or that it had 'the approbation and support, even if tacit, of the Vatican'.[76] Short of examining Vatican archival material on this matter the case must rest with the public evidence which clearly indicates that the PPI was not a creature of the Vatican and that any judgement of it made by authoritative Vatican sources was largely negative. In short the Vatican acquiesced in the formation of the PPI because as a political party it could not prevent it. It may not be going too far to say that precisely because it was a political party it did not, indeed could not, give it its approval. To go further than that, one way or another, in assessing the role of the Vatican is to engage in mere speculation. The important thing is that the PPI went into its first election with private clerical support certainly, but without the direct support of the Vatican or of official Italian Catholic Action. The distinction may seem fine but when judged in the light of Sturzo's hopes for his party it is fundamental to the whole essence of his political economy. Without Vatican tolerance the PPI would have had to struggle for electoral support but with Vatican sanction in the official sense it would have ceased to be what Sturzo wanted it to be — an autonomous political party. To Sturzo it was better not to exist at all than to exist as a mere tool of the Vatican.

Although Sturzo had calculated that the party would hold about 60 seats in the new parliament the elections of 16 November 1919, conducted on the proportional system, resulted in its winning 100 seats.[77] It is probably little short of the truth to affirm with Arturo Jemolo that the party counted upon 'a second electoral office in all the presbyteries', because the lower clergy, more attuned to the real aspirations of their people than the Vatican, knew that the Catholic masses placed no hope in Nitti and a liberal government and had already begun to fear the excesses of socialism. Similarly Catholic Action gave some support to the PPI, if unofficial, and at a post-election meeting in Rome the newly elected PPI deputy, Egilberto Martire gave his grateful thanks to his friends of Young Catholic Action whom he called 'soldiers, today, of the political victory of the people of Italy'.[78]

The weakness of the clerical reed was not then apparent because what was so gratuitously and enthusiastically given could equally as readily be withdrawn, but it did help to consolidate the Catholic vote in the north, especially in the rural areas of Lombardy, Veneto and

Piedmont which won 38 seats between them and accounted for about one third of the votes, while in the Abruzzi and Molise it went down to seven per cent.[79] Salvemini analysed the voting figures and said that the 1,176,473 votes out of 5,682,000 cast for the Partito Popolare indicated the real strength of Italian Catholicism in the political arena in that it could count on about one fifth of the people for its support. The socialists recorded 1,835,000 votes; the so called constitutional parties 2,100,000; while half a million were divided up into minority parties.[80]

By any estimate the PPI had gained a resounding victory, both symbolic and factual. Frederick Chabod said with justice that the official return of Catholics to the life of the nation was 'the most notable event of twentieth century Italian history' and viewed in the light of the preceding half century such a statement was doubtless true.[81] At the same time one is entitled to wonder whether such a forceful entry into the public arena achieved much on the wider plane. The old liberal elements in Italian life were deeply displeased at this young, refractory party, the socialists were angered at the appeal it made to the Catholic working masses while in the Vatican there was concern and some degree of awe at the success of the organized Catholic laity.[82] As for Sturzo, all he could do was ponder on the thing he had helped create and perhaps ask himself whether, in the long run, such an easily gained victory would be pyrrhic, for it was clear to him that so far little indeed had been achieved in the formation of that solid, determined consciousness he so anxiously desired, For Sturzo conscience was 'the element which in the dynamic and dialectic of history gives life, value, stability and progress to society'.[83] It was an element which was singularly absent in large numbers of his party in 1919.

The only other major party with any degree of vitality was the socialist and they were delighted with their electoral success. They proclaimed a victory for the 'Symbol of the Soviets', promised that the revolution would be made by the Italian proletariat and likened their survival to that of Christ over death.[84] Neither they nor anyone else seemed very concerned about the fact that so many Italian citizens displayed either a lack of interest in the prevailing system or a distrust of the parties to the extent that only 50 per cent went to the polls. Clearly a large segment of the people was undecided as to their political allegiance and was awaiting some kind of an appeal that would strike a responsive chord in their breasts. A certain Benito Mussolini was on the top of the list run by the 'Fascio italiano di combattimento', but with only 5000 votes he was not elected. His platform contained a plank calling for the confiscation of all ecclesiastical goods and a month later he stated that he hated 'all forms of Christianity: from that of Jesus Christ to that of Marx'.[85] At least it can be said that he gave his game fair warning!

Notes

1. For the text of his speech see L. Sturzo, *Il Partito*, vol. 1 (Rome, 1955), pp. 32–58. The *Osservatore Romano* of 22 November ran an item that said Sturzo would give a talk in Rome on 26 November with the title 'Problemi del dopo guerra'. Clearly intended as a repeat of the Milan performance it did not take place. Curiously, Arturo Caroti, a socialist deputy, wrote an article in that same week on the need for a reform of Parliament. See *Avanti*, 28 November 1918.

2. The judgement of Palmiro Togliatti was harsh but relevant in that it expressed the conviction of many Italians. 'The Church, on account of its own organic structure, all the ideal stands that it defends and the ultimate scope to which all its activity tends, is the most "anti-democratic" power in the world.' P. Togliatti, *Momenti della storia d'Italia*, 2nd edn (Rome, 1973), pp. 26–7.

3. See G. Spataro, *I Democratici Cristiani dalla dittatura alla repubblica* (Verona, 1972), pp. 16–18.

4. For the correspondence between Cavazzoni and Sturzo see *Corriere d'Italia*, 20, 24 November 1918, pp. 8–9. The full text of Sturzo's letter is in P. Scoppola (ed.), *Dal neoguelfismo alla Democrazia Cristiana* (Rome, 1963), pp. 155–7.

5. *Corriere della Sera* of 21 January 1919 said that it would have been impossible to found a party had it not been known beforehand that the Vatican would place no veto in its path. It saw the foundation as a sign that the Catholics of Italy had come of age. For full reports on these press reactions see *Corriere d'Italia*, 21, 22, 23 January 1919.

6. See *Avanti*, 20, 22 January 1919.

7. See A. Cantano, *Il programma del Partito Popolare Italiano* (Turin, 1919). p. 6, and G. Rossini (ed.), 'Benedetto XV, i cattolici e la prima guerra mondiale' in *Atti del Convegno di Studio tenuto a Spoleto nei giorni 7–8–9 settembre 1962* (Rome, 1963), p. 201.

8. For this letter see G. De Rosa, 'Una lettera inedita del Card. Gasparri sul Partito Popolare' in *Analisi e Prospettive*, n. 1, January–February 1959, pp. 572–3.

9. See M. Missiroli, *Una battaglia perdita* (Milan, 1924), p. 83.

10. *O.R.*, 28 December 1918. The paper said 'our friends, even distant ones would not have given any weight to the proclaimed consent of the Holy See to the formation of a true and proper Catholic party in Italy'. Mussolini was also a keen observer of the rise of the PPI and wrote that it was the only party that could rival the socialists for the allegiance of the rural masses. See quote from his paper *Il Popolo d'Italia*, 24 January 1919, in B. Vigezzi (ed.), *1919–1925. Dopoguerra e fascismo. Politica e stampa in Italia* (Bari, 1965), p. 428.

11. See G. De Rossi, *Il primo anno di vita del Partito Popolare Italiano dalle origini al congresso di Napoli* (Rome, 1920), pp. 50 et seq.; G. Spataro, *I Democratici*, pp. 16–20; A.C. Gaudenti, *Luigi Sturzo*, pp. 33–6.

12. For the text of the appeal see L. Sturzo, *I discorsi politici* (Rome, 1951) pp. 3–5. The programme of the Party follows on pp. 6–7.

13. Ibid., p. 7. For further material on the political thought of Sturzo as crystallized in the PPI see G. De Rosa, *L'utopia politica di Luigi Sturzo* (Brescia, 1972) and G. Martinolli, *La concezione politica di Luigi Sturzo* (Trieste, 1971).

14. G. Salvemini, *Stato e Chiesa in Italia*, Elio Conti, (ed.) (Milan, 1969), p. 118. Lenin was widely revered in Italy in the post-war period when many workers called their children after him. There was also a Hymn to Lenin sung in 1919 to the tune of 'Cara piccina' which concluded 'Long live Lenin who is love itself / Who is a lighthouse of justice and freedom.' See G. Ruggero 'Le ripercussioni della rivoluzione russa in Italia' in, *Lo Stato Operaio*, no. 9–10 (Paris, November–December 1927), p. 993, and R. Vivarelli, *Il dopoguerra in Italia e l'avvento del fascismo* (1918–1922), vol. 1. (Naples, 1967), pp. 590–6.

15. See P. Scoppola (ed.), *Chiesa e Stato nella storia d'Italia* (Bari, 1967), p. 480.

16. For an account of the diplomatic moves see V.E. Orlando, *I miei rapporti di governo con la Santa Seda*, 2nd edn (Milan 1942), and C. Mollat, *La Question Romaine*, pp. 4ll–12.

17. The interview between Filippo Crispolti and Sturzo was also given in full in *Corriere d'Italia*, 24 January 1919.

18. *Civiltà Cattolica*, vol. 1, 15 February 1919, pp. 271–3. See also A. Arrò, *Il Partito*

Popolare Italiano e la Questione Romana (Turin, 1919).

19. R. Murri, *La Democrazia*, p. 77. Elena Aga Rossi, *Dal Partito Popolare alla Democrazia Cristiana* (Rocca San Casciano, 1969), in her excellent introduction simply repeated the thought of Murri when she said that 'the autonomy of the PPI did not represent a definitive conquest' (p. 17). She enlarged on it however by her comment that such autonomy 'had for the Church a value that was primarily instrumental; its limits were fixed by the measure in which it showed itself adaptable to the need to safeguard the existing social structure and to defend its conservative character' (ibid.).

20. Quoted from N. Valeri, *Da Giolitti a Mussolini Momenti dalla crisi del liberalismo*, (Florence, 1950), p. 120.

21. *O.R.* 20, 22 January 1919. For further on the PPI and Catholic Action see F. Crispolti, 'Il Partito Popolare Italiano' in *Nuova Antologia* (Rome, 1919), pp. 441–8.

22. M. Ferrara, *Luigi Sturzo* (Rome, 1925), pp. 35–6.

23. *O.R.*, 20 January and 28 March 1919. The audience took place on 14 January. *O.R.*, 15 January 1919.

24. See M. Ferrara, *Luigi Sturzo*, p. 19.

25. The Rome edition of *Il Messaggero* (30 April 1974), two weeks before the referendum on the divorce laws, in an editorial comment said 'The DC [lineal descendant of the Partito Popolare] has given great service to the country, but it has revealed the limits of its autonomy every time that it has been called to take up a position on questions concerning the relationship between State and Church'.

26. See *O.R.*, 20, 22, 31 January; 2, 6, 22, 28 February; 1, 3, 8, 14, 15, 28 March; 13, 15, 29 April; 11, 13, 18 May 1919.

27. Ibid., 4, 5 March 1919.

28. Ibid., 5, 8 March 1919.

29. *Corriere d'Italia*, 20 January 1919. See also F.L. Ferrari, *L'Azione Cattolica e il 'Regime'* (Florence, 1957), p. 4 and V. Castronovo, *La stampa italiana dall' Unità al fascismo* (Bari, 1973), p. 194 et seq.

30. For *Perseveranza* and *Unità Cattolica* of 22 January 1919 see (*Corriere d'Italia*, 23 January 1919).

31. See G. Castelli, *La chiesa e il fascismo* (Rome, 1951), p. 27. The Roman branch of Catholic Action went as far as discussing whether it would unite with the PPI. See *O.R.*, 22 February 1919.

32. S. Jacini, *Storia del Partito Popolare Italiano* (Milan, 1951), p. 28.

33. *O.R.*, 31 January 1919:

34. Ibid., 24 January, 1 February 1919.

35. Ibid., 11 February 1919. Filippo Meda said in October 1919 that the main reason

for the rapid development of the PPI was the evolution of socialism towards a revolutionary form. See F. Meda, *Scritti scelti*, G. Dore ed. (Rome, 1959), p. 295. See also S. Caretti, *La rivoluzione russa e il socialismo italiano* (Pisa, 1974), passim and G. Miglioli, *Con Roma e con Mosca. Quaranti anni di battaglie*, (Cremona, 1945) p. 21, where he says that Catholic fear of bolshevism reawakened conservatism and hence contributed to the growth of the PPI.

36. *O.R.*, 2, 28 March 1919.

37. Ibid., 17, 18, 19, 22, 21, 25 April 1919 and from then on constantly.

38. Ibid., May 1919, passim.

39. See G. De Rosa, *Il Partito Popolare Italiano* (Bari, 1972), pp. 16–17.

40. R. Murri, *La Democrazia*, p. 77. Murri's opinion of the widely divergent elements in the party was shared by S. Jacini, *Storia*, p. 283, and by G. Miglioli, *Con Roma*, p. 32.

41. For a complete and excellent account of the congresses of the PPI see F. Malgeri (ed.), *Gli atti dei congressi del Partito Popolare Italiano* (Brescia, 1969). On the congresses *Corriere d'Italia*, *Il Popolo Nuovo*, *Il Popolo* and *Osservatore Romano* also proved useful reading.

42. A. Gemelli and F. Olgiati, *Il programma del Partito Popolare Italiano. Come non è come dovrebbe essere* (Milan, 1919).

43. Ibid., pp. 10, 15, 59.

44. Ibid., p. 60. For Sturzo's speech see *I discorsi*, pp. 11–25.

45. Ibid., pp. 13, 14, 18.

46. Sturzo in interview with *Corriere d'Italia*, 18 June 1919. For Sturzo's conviction on the necessity of aconfessionalism see G. Caputo 'L'Enigma Popolare' in *Studi Cattolica*, No. 132, (Milan, February 1972), pp. 94–7.

47. *O.R.*, 15, 17, 18, 19 June 1919.

48. *Avanti*, 15, 16, 17 June 1919.

49. N. Casacca, *Il Papa e L'Italia* (Bologna, 1919), pp. 51–2. The book was given full coverage in *Unità Cattolica* on 29–30 July 1919. Due to a printers' strike in Rome *Osservatore Romano* was not published from 9 July to 10 September 1919 so the directors sent copies of *Unità Cattolica*, published in Florence, to subscribers in its stead. *Unità Cattolica* explained in its copy of 23–24 August that the *Osservatore* had been condemned to silence by 'a bolshevist strike'.

50. On being asked how the clergy would live under such a system the pope replied 'On alms'. It was an unacceptable solution. See K.F. Morrison, *The Investiture Controversy*, Chicago, 1971, pp. 68–9.

51. G. Salvemini, *Stato*, pp. 248–9.

52. See P. Scoppola (ed.), *Chiesa*, pp. 480–97; G. De Rosa, *Il Partito*, pp. 112–3.

53. *O.R.*, 4, 20 July, 23 October, 17 November 1918; 4, 13 January 1919 and *Corriere d'Italia*, 10 January 1919.

54. *Avanti*, 25 May, 7 July, 28 November 1918; 10 March, 11 April, 29 May 1919. On the development of the socialist movement in Italy see the excellent work of G. Arfè, *Storia del socialismo italiano* 1892–1926 (Turin, 1965).

55. *O.R.*, 4, 10 September 1918; 10 April 1919.

56. *Avanti*, 23 June 1919; *O.R.*, 28 March, 13 April 1919.

57. F. Malgeri (ed.), *Gli atti*, pp. 88–93. On the socialist thought of Miglioli see G. Marcucci Fanello, 'G Miglioli e il problema contadino' in *Storia e Politica* (Rome, 1968), pp. 669–82.

58. G. De Rosa, *Il Partito*, p. 24.

59. On Sturzo's ideas regarding the agrarian question see F. Rizzi, *Luigi Sturzo e la questione meridionale* (Rome, 1957) and M. Bandini, 'La questione agraria e il Partito Popolare', in *Saggi sul Partito Popolare Italiano* (Rome, 1969).

60. G. De Rosa, *Il Partito*, p. 25

61. *O.R.*, 17 June 1919.

62. See *Corriere d'Italia*, 15–19 June, for a full account of the Congress written by its editor Paolo Mattei Gentili who was also a foundation member of the party. It is fair to point out that both Miglioli and Gemelli followed the logic of their earlier views in that the former joined the Communist Party while the priest became an enthusiastic supporter of the fascist regime.

63. *Unità Cattolica*, 1–2, 2–3 August 1919. In October Gemelli and Olgiati were received by the pope in a private audience and Gemelli remained an intimate adviser to both Benedict and his successor. See *O.R.*, 27 October 1919.

64. *Unità Cattolica*, 4–5 August 1919.

65. A. Fiocchi, *P. Enrico Rosa S.J. Scrittore della Civiltà Cattolica (1870–1938)* (Rome, 1957), pp. 176–8, asserts that the Paganuzzi group was in constant contact with Rosa, editor of *Civiltà Cattolica*, and that its formation was approved of by Benedict XV.

66. *Unità Cattolica*, 19–20, 23–24, 26–27 August 1919. It is interesting that while the intransigent laymen of the PPI such as Paganuzzi would have no dealings with Nitti and his cabinet, Gasparri had no such misgivings. In October 1919 Gasparri gave Nitti full details of the precarious situation of Vatican finances and received the Prime Minister's assurance that the new laws on taxation to be introduced in November would not affect the Holy See. It is clear from their correspondence that Nitti and Gasparri were on close terms. See F.M. Broglio, *Italia e Santa Sede dalla Grande Guerra alla Conciliazione. Aspetti politici e giuridici* (Bari, 1966), pp. 60–65.

67. *Civiltà Cattolica*, vol. 1, 15 February 1919, p. 274.

68. Sturzo's well-marked copy of F. Fanelli, *Don Sturzo e il Partito Popolare Italiano* (Gubbio, 1923), is in the library of the Luigi Sturzo Institute, Rome. See pp. 171, 240–1, 247, 251. Salvemini is said to have calculated that more than 60,000 clerics belonged to the PPI between 1919–22. Even if half that number were accurate it was an alarmingly high proportion. See E. Rossi, *Il manganello e l'aspersorio*, 2nd edn (Bari, 1968), p. 37.

69. A.C. Gaudenti, *Sturzo*, p. 41 and F. Malgeri (ed.), *Gli atti*, p. 111.

70. See *Il Popolo Nuovo*, 8 June 1919. It was the official organ of the party and commenced as a weekly on 8 June 1919.

71. S. Jacini, *Storia*, p. 31. *Il Popolo Nuovo* ran a column called 'The chronicle of red violence' in which it documented the recurring atrocities perpetrated by the extreme socialists. See numbers of 16 and 26 October 1919. At the same time it had to defend the party against the liberal accusation that it too was 'red'. Ibid., 12 October, 2 November 1919.

72. *O.R.*, 21 October 1919.

73. Ibid., 8 November 1919.

74. Ibid., 10–11 November 1919.

75. *O.R.* 10–11 November 1919 and C.M. Buonaiuti, *Non expedit*, pp. 155–6.

76. E.A. Rossi, *Dal Partito*, pp. 15, 16. Rossi quotes from A. Gramsci and E. Pratt Howard rather than from Benedict XV, Sturzo or Gasparri to back up the assertions.

77. When the Nitti government introduced proportionalism in August 1919 it was proclaimed by the party as 'the most democratic law in the world' which would allow all parties to be represented in Parliament in an adequate manner. See *Il Popolo Nuovo*, 17 August 1919.

78. A.C. Jemolo, *Chiesa e Stato in Italia negli ultimi cento anni*, 2nd edn (Turin, 1963), p. 423; *Corriere d'Italia*, 22 November 1919. See also G. Salvemini, *Stato*, p. xx, where the assertion is made that the clergy organized the masses behind the PPI to win its seats.

79. There seems to be some argument about the precise figures of seats won with general agreement by modern historians that the party obtained 100 rather than the 99 mentioned, for example, by G. Spataro in *I Democratici*, p. 22.

80. G. Salvemini, *Stato*, p. 119.

81. F. Chabod, *L'Italia contemporanea (1919–1948)*, 4th edn (Turin, 1964), p. 43.

82. Salvemini thought that as well as taking many seats formerly held by the liberals, the PPI gained a vast number of votes that would have gone to the socialists had it not contested the elections. G. Salvemini, *Stato*, p. xx.

83. F. della Rocca (ed.), *Chiesa e Stato nel pensiero di L. Sturzo* (Rome, 1956), p. 61.

84. *Avanti*, 18, 23 November 1919. The *Osservatore Romano* saw a promising future for the socialists provided they stuck to a genuine pro worker platform and gave up their demagogic agitation, *O.R.*, 3 December 1919.

85. See quotes from Mussolini's paper *Popolo d'Italia*, 2 November – 12 December 1919 in G. Castelli, *La chiesa*, p. 27 and S. Jacini, *Storia*, p. 283.

3

DEMOCRACY WITHOUT DIRECTION

The new Italian parliament, with its fresh complement of enthusiastic but largely fledgling deputies from the Partito Popolare, faced formidable problems when it assembled in late 1919. The parliament contained a strong group of 156 socialist deputies who began by manifesting their contempt for the monarchy by the symbolic act of deserting the House when the King opened the session. They were described as resembling a group of 'madmen' as they entered the House 'singing the Red Flag, acclaiming Lenin and whistling at the King' after which they 'retired to the Aventine thus persevering in a negative criterion of sterile opposition'.[1] In many areas throughout the country there were violent conflicts between them and the marauding fascist bands and strikes crippled both industry and the public services constantly.[2]

To all but the blind it seemed clear that Benedict XV's summary of the war as a 'useless massacre' was justified when even the territorial claims of Italy to Fiume had proved fruitless, and the 'March on Fiume' led by Gabriele D'Annunzio became merely a prelude to a 'March' of another order three years later.[3] Meanwhile, the question of national unity of purpose had to be grappled with even though its attainment seemed impossible. The socialists had their vision of Italy's future according to the prophet Marx, and others, such as the Popolari, had theirs according to more ancient texts, but the government led by Nitti had none.[4] Italy was like a ship with several crews, commanded by a captain who did not know where it was going. So it was to remain until the 'strong man' came forward to grasp the helm, but in the interval its precious cargo of democracy, heritage of the Risorgimento, was squandered so that in that day little remained to be destroyed.

In the Vatican there were few signs of public rejoicing at the success of the Popolari although it was conceded that they had made an auspicious beginning. The *Osservatore Romano* went to some lengths to express its displeasure with the new electoral system that forced people to vote for a full list of candidates irrespective of their views on the suitability of some or many of them, and attributed the low overall vote to the new method and the lack of faith of the masses in the parliamentary system.[5] The more important aspect of proportionalism which would inevitably result in a mushrooming of parties of widely divergent views was overlooked. It carried in itself the seeds of disarray to the extent that, while the thirst for power would always result in enough men coming together to form a government, despite their divergent views on policy, it was more difficult to ensure the formation of a united opposition because without power men find it even more difficult to coalesce. To most observers the period 1919–22 seems to be marked in Italian parliamentary life by the lack of a strong, united government. No one seems to have been impressed by the equally evident lack of a strong, united opposition which could provide concrete criticism and ultimately an attractive alternative to the government.

In the House the old conservative journalist and leader of the Catholic economic forces, Filippo Crispolti, explained why it was impossible for the PPI to collaborate with the socialists. Apart from the time-worn expression of divergence from the socialists' materialistic concept of life and their insistence on the class struggle, an added incentive to keep clear from any alliance with them was their 'more recent and excessive tendencies subversive of any social order'.[6] It was all very well for the socialist deputies to reply that 'the discourse of the Crown ... is a dead letter' and that all they wanted was recognition of the socialist republic of the Soviets, but even *Avanti* had to admit that the party was no longer able to control the excesses of violence its members were engaging in, especially in the north where the party had its greatest strength.[7] The conflict between the socialists and the PPI was extended into the House when, on the first day in which the two parties met there, the PPI deputy, Angelo Mauri, accused both the socialists and fascists of violence against the PPI in the election campaign.[8]

Undeniably there were elements within the socialist party with whom some form of unity of purpose short of outright collaboration might have been possible. Filippo Turati was deeply convinced of the need for that unity in order to save the country from the economic and social crisis into which it was slipping. Equally he held views on violence by members of his own party which he called 'drunken bolshevism' and which to some extent coalesced with those held by the PPI. But he was under constant attack by the party which made it impossible for him to lead any move towards the formation of a united opposition in the parliament.[9] Giacomo Matteotti was another figure of moderation, but he explained to the House that no collaboration with the government was possible because it had no programme. As for the PPI he thought it also had no programme, nor would it ever have one because in its formulation on whatever level — international, economic or social — it would split between its conservative and its democratic elements. While Matteotti's criticism of the PPI had an element of truth about it, the socialists made no attempt to work with it even on issues such as the land question upon which both parties were clearly in basic agreement.[10] Thus there were constant verbal battles and even a physical one in the House mainly because the socialists deeply resented any attempt by the PPI to speak on behalf of the working masses or farmers although *Avanti* admitted that it had a large base amongst the latter.[11] What the Vatican thought of the possible similarities between the PPI and the socialists at this early stage is uncertain but Benito Mussolini did not hesitate to use them to stir the waters. He wrote,

> If one were to apply a little bolshevism in Italy the priests who, as everyone knows, have never worked since the time of Christ, would not eat. Then, in Rome itself, one could occupy the 11,000 rooms of the Vatican with their annexes and passages which would help solve the housing crisis. If that is what Miglioli wants it might be a good idea to ask what Cardinal Gasparri and the seraphic Professor Angeli of the *Osservatore Romano* think of it.[12]

Gripped with a bitter internal feud about the direction of their party, consumed by their impatient vision of the New Jerusalem that had sprung up in the Soviet East and determined to engage in obstructionist and intransigent tactics, it was no easy matter to find common ground with the socialists. With their contempt for parliament, their unruly and sometimes violent behaviour, their constant singing of 'the Red Flag' and their exultant rejection of anyone who did not share their views, the socialists, as a party, behaved exactly in the parliament of 1920 as the fascists were to behave in 1922. It was of little moment that the ultimate purpose of both parties differed because men who looked on could only see the stated immediate purpose, which was the destruction of the institution for which Italians had already suffered so much. If indeed it was so easy to destroy parliamentary democracy at the end of 1922 the reason partly was that the socialists, primarily, had helped so much to destroy it in 1920. In April 1920 a socialist deputy, Vincenzo Vacirca, suggested that when parliament was not in session a socialist parliament ought to sit to prepare for the day when power passed 'into the hands of the working classes'. The editor of *Avanti* approved of the idea because parliament 'is a dead man who speaks. Nor do we have any interest in giving him back life.'[13] Had it been mere rhetoric it would have been sufficiently damaging. Unfortunately, to many socialists it was an expression of reality which ignored the fact that in those crucial times the one thing Italy could least afford was a dead parliament.[14]

If it was a difficult task for the PPI to find common ground with the socialists it was scarcely less difficult to achieve unity of purpose with the government. It was clear to all that the election had resulted in a gain for the socialists and gave an impressive beginning to the PPI. It was equally clear that the party to suffer had been the liberals whose seats fell from 380 to 252.[15] Even in Turin, the revered birthplace of Italian liberalism, the liberals had come off badly in comparison with the socialists and the PPI. Certainly the war policies of the liberals had redounded against them by late 1919 in a country which, though allegedly victorious, was still reeling from the disasters to which it had been subjected. Over 4,000,000 Italian soldiers, of whom 670,000 died, had suffered in the war and the returning soldiers, so many of whom were unable to find work, were a constant reminder of the misery caused by war.[16] In the year since the Armistice the government had done little, but what was worse, it seemed to show so little promise of doing anything.

In the election campaign only Giolitti had anything cohesive to say with an important speech at Dronero in which he proposed the avoidance of future wars by ensuring that parliament, rather than the King and cabinet alone, would control international affairs and that large fortunes, especially those made during the war, should be taxed heavily. The socialists rejected him outright at the time but Togliatti later praised the speech as one of the few positive contributions to political thought in the period.[17] Thus it had been left to the socialists and the Popolari to get out on the piazzas and offer something to the people; in fact had it not been for the PPI the socialists would have had no opposition worth speaking of.[18] Nitti was a man little given to the practical formulation of a platform and his government was an inert one that had no programme except that of strengthening the force of the Carabinieri but the PPI had to consider cooperation with it in the certainty of sharing in its failure while perhaps gaining nothing from such a fruitless coalition.[19]

The PPI itself contained an array of new deputies in whom political convictions ranged from left to right to the extent that it bore closer resemblance to a movement of 'organized hope' rather than to a cohesive party.[20] Carlo Sforza, who was an under-secretary of state in the Nitti cabinet, watched the new PPI men as they assembled at their first session in the Parliament. To him there were ominous signs in the presence of old reactionaries like Crispolti mixed in with the young enthusiasts, but the main cause for concern was the number of deputies themselves rather than their quality. He thought that 50 would have been a more manageable number and he said that even Sturzo remarked to him that he personally was appalled to see so many successful candidates at their first attempt at an election.[21] Perhaps Sturzo also wondered at the background of his new deputies. They were heavily weighted towards the academic and professional world with 59 lawyers, seven university professors, six journalists, one secondary teacher, seven engineers, five bankers, five unionists, one worker, six farmers and three industrialists.[22]

Short of a common religious bond, a tenuous programme and a name, the main point of acknowledged unity in the party was Luigi Sturzo who, given his priesthood, held no seat in the parliament but directed the party from his position as general secretary. Sforza deplored the loss of Sturzo to the parliament because he was thus in no position to show publicly all the qualities of statesmanship that existed potentially in him, but at the time it seemed to Sturzo that he could satisfactorily lead from outside.[23] There is some slight evidence to suggest that Sturzo himself had hoped to stand for parliament because, in his letter to Santucci, Gasparri said that Sturzo was angered because the cardinal had refused him permission to do so.[24] Such a step was not without historical precedence and the then chancellor of Austria, Monsignor Ignaz Seipel, was a priest in good standing with the

Church. Apart however from Gasparri's assertion it seems unlikely that Sturzo sought parliamentary office and Gabriele De Rosa said that he had never come across any evidence to indicate that Sturzo had ever shown any inclination in that direction and that Sturzo himself had vigorously denied the truth of Gasparri's assertion when he, De Rosa, had brought it to Sturzo's attention.[25]

One thing the PPI did have on its platform and upon which there seemed to be party unity was the question of agrarian reform which it wanted the government to make a start on, especially in Sicily, and it posed action in that sector as part of its price of collaboration. Nitti did nothing and in the south many farmers, guided by the PPI, began to occupy idle land. But the cautious policy of selective collaboration of the PPI with the new government suffered a worse setback when Nitti chose to palliate the socialists through a series of deals with the red unions after strikes in the post offices and railways in January 1920. This left the white unions (who had refused to participate on the grounds that the strikes were purely political), and the PPI in a position in which they seemed to have no voice before a government with which they were attempting to collaborate, and in the corridors of Montecitorio the impression was widespread that Nitti was treating the PPI 'like a wife and the socialist party like a mistress'.[26] Furthermore, it left the white unionists at the mercy of the socialists who were only too anxious to exact reprisals for their refusal to engage in political strikes which were productive of nothing except increasing unrest on the part of the middle classes, misery and frustration on the part of the workers, a greater weakening of the country's economy and a hardening of resolve and organization of the incipient fascist movement.[27]

Nonetheless by March the PPI was able to put forward a nine point programme to the government on the basis of which it hoped for a form of collaboration which would benefit the country. The points covered the ground dear to Sturzo such as proportional representation in the coming communal and provincial administrative elections as well as a vote for women in all elections. The white unions were to be given proper representation on all national and local bodies in the same way as the red unions already enjoyed while the other points dealt with educational, agrarian and fiscal reform with, in the case of the latter, drastic measures in regard to war fortunes.[28] The crucial point was whether the government would be either willing or able to recognize the rights of the white unions to have their own separate organizational life and to speak on behalf of their members. Claudio Treves gave the socialist reaction to the PPI when in Parliament he called it simply another bourgeois party which, while having its roots in the soil of the proletariat, betrayed them by its fruits. To the socialists the nine points, and especially the one on the white unions, made up a rope offered by the PPI to Nitti and his government with which to hang themselves.[29] If Nitti agreed to the PPI request then his government would face serious industrial unrest; if he refused he ran the risk of losing the support of the PPI. Nitti refused, the PPI members of his cabinet gave up their positions and with some relief the party found itself free of its bonds with a government that showed no promise either for itself or for Italy.[30] Meanwhile, on the local level, the socialists wasted no time with verbal niceties and, culminating in a macabre celebration of May Day, 1920, there were brutal beatings resulting in injuries and loss of life to white unionists and PPI members.

In this atmosphere the PPI held its second Congress at Naples in early April 1920. Its growth had been impressive with 3,137 branches and 251,740 members so the delegates met with confidence in the party's future. At this meeting some further clarification was given to the party's platform on land and educational reform, and the debate on land reform became somewhat acrimonious when, speaking for the left wing, Arturo Osio of Milan claimed that the right to ownership resided in the man who worked the land to whom it ought to be given at his request. The right-wing reply to this was that 'private property is sacred and immutable: in the social field any form of collaboration by us with the socialists is impossible'. Sturzo easily maintained a balance between these extremes but he was pained to see the delegates from the south reveal their 'ancient and worn out fatalism' when one said 'We southerners are like the inhabitants of the Libyan desert. We have no roads and our plight is unknown to the rest of you.' On educational reform Sturzo took a radical view when he insisted that schools had to be built for the poor as well as the rich and that the system of public examinations had to be introduced into the private schools. However the main point agreed upon was the impossibility of taking a responsible role in any ministry which did not have a clear cut, progressive programme of economic reform. Furthermore it was decided to give no support to a government which refused to recognize the rights of the white unions and their auxiliary organizations. Sturzo insisted that the PPI was unique in that it alone fought against 'the centralist state, economic monopoly and communistic socialism'.

It was a widespread battlefield to engage a party on and it found its own echoes at Naples when the left, led by Miglioli, insisted upon more radical social reform and that the party free itself from 'any banking influence' meaning the Bank of Rome, while the right, led by Professor Vincenzo Del Giudice of the University of Perugia, still called for a deeper spiritual content and greater concern with Italian legislation affecting the Church. Miglioli was convinced that the party was 'confronted with a tremendous historical situation' by which he meant that the moment had come to decide whether the future lay with the right or the left. Meda, who knew where the choices lay, insisted that he personally had never excluded collaboration with the socialists but claimed that it was absurd to think about it 'when they continuously cry out to us that they don't want us', to which Miglioli replied 'Not true' and said it was up to the PPI to provoke them into collaboration.[31] For its own part *Osservatore Romano* thought too little attention was paid to the ideas of Del Giudice which were in perfect accord with Vatican thinking on the role of the Church in the Italian peninsula but were far removed from those of Sturzo and the progressive elements in the PPI. To Del Giudice the PPI was 'born in equivocation, lives and grows fat in equivocation' and only 'human respect' prevented it from facing the religious question in Italian life.[32]

Although *Avanti* was of the opinion that the Congress amounted to no more than the machinations of 'this little priest' in fact there were discordant notes struck against the dominance exercised by Sturzo over the party.[33] Sturzo was sufficiently to the left, despite his repeated anti socialism, to be able to contain that segment of the party that was in genuine contact with or represented the working class, and Miglioli, after many years of wandering from one ideological camp to another, never had a harsh word to say against Sturzo, while the left wing of the party stayed with him until the end.[34] On the other hand the right was never able to comprehend the mentality of Sturzo to whom aconfessionalism was so fundamental a premise for political activity that he appeared incapable of comprehending the consequences that could ensue from inflexible adhesion to it. It was almost as if Sturzo had decided that the centuries of involvement between Church and state in the Italian peninsula could be swept away by the simple expedient of granting autonomy to Catholics in political affairs. If that were so then his hope was ill founded for persons and events were already intertwining to make conflict inevitable despite, perhaps even because of, the inflexible adhesion of Sturzo to his belief in the aconfessionalism of the PPI.

Between the PPI, the Vatican, Catholic Action, the Catholic press and segments of the Italian banking world there were overlapping interests that made any decision of the party in Italian politics a matter of vital concern. It was perfectly clear already that no government in Italy which was made up of what remained of the old liberal parties could govern smoothly without the support of the PPI. This meant that were the PPI to collaborate with the socialists or even to assume a purely negative role in parliament then a stable government of the right was rendered impossible. Thus any proposals put forward by the PPI as the price of collaboration warranted careful consideration indeed. So far the party had exerted no pressure on the government in regard to a solution to the Roman Question, nor indeed did it seem that it would. In the economic field its proposals for 'land to the farmers' were unhappy music to the ears of the large landowners, many of them Catholics, to whom any genuine development in such an area could only bring social and financial change. Apart from heavier taxes for the wealthy the PPI seemed to have little else to offer as a solution to economic problems and in a tottering financial system that was of little use to the banking interests, or indeed to the wealthy.

As a result it was in an arena far removed from the actual meeting room of the party directorate that decisions were made that were to impinge heavily on its future. The president of the youth section of Catholic Action was Paolo Pericoli who was also an auditor of the Bank of Rome. The president of the Bank itself was Carlo Santucci who was a friend of Gasparri, known to the pope, a foundation member of the PPI and finally a party senator. Other men such as Martire, Cingolani, Grosoli and Colombo all moved to and fro between Catholic Action, the PPI, the Bank and the Catholic press almost as if it were one world as, indeed, on some levels it was.[35] In that world it came as a surprise that the PPI at Naples had decided it was going to be more than a simple bag of votes into which Nitti could dip at will for support. Nitti had decided to carry on the secret negotiations begun with Orlando towards a solution to the Roman Question and he hoped that the Holy See would guarantee the continued support of the PPI for his government even when he did not comply with the demands of the PPI.[36] There is no proof that the Vatican tried to bring pressure on the PPI in regard to the Roman Question or support for Nitti and in any case it would have been useless. Santucci, Martire, Grosoli and others all later proved they could be brought to see 'reason', but it was another thing to deal with Sturzo, Meda, Gronchi, Miglioli and De Gasperi.

Yet if the PPI was a difficult ally for the Holy See, Catholic Action still remained intact. Indeed Dalla Torre warned that 'if Catholic Action begins to falter, all political action may prove illusory'. There were clear signs that the Popular Union had come on evil days since the foundation of the PPI, but in the Vatican the conviction remained that Catholic Action was the unique means to form consciences and confront the problem of socialism.[37] In March 1920 Benedict wrote to Luigi Marolli, bishop of Bergamo, and warned in precise terms that the fulfilment of Christian duty, not social revolution, was the way ahead for the workers and when he spoke in late April it was clear that any initial honeymoon there may have been between the Vatican and the PPI was over. The pope was

> saddened to know that even amongst our best sons little is said of the Popular Union and it is an even more painful surprise to notice the silence that the Catholic press too often maintains in its regard... We do not want anyone to forget that the Popular Union is the principal agent of Catholic Action. If other activities have been able to arise, even recently, in different fields, they are nothing but little streams springing from the regal river. The streamlets of the Tiber and the Po can fade away while the Tiber and the Po will always continue their majestic course through the cities and villages ...[38]

Benedict's speech was clearly intended to reprove the PPI and the papers which supported it while, at the same time, emphasising the necessity for the continuation of Catholic Action. The PPI was unable to deny that the rise of the political party had seriously blunted the effectiveness of the Popular Union which, as well as losing personnel, had also lost part of its finality. It was a dilemma which no amount of mere good will could resolve because in any conflict of members and interests the PPI, by the sheer force of its vitality, had to prove the temporary winner but Catholic Action, though depleted, could survive because of its ties with the Church. Meanwhile, the PPI had to fight for its survival in the public, political arena and, at the same time, conduct a rear-guard action to ensure that Vatican tolerance did not turn to Vatican disapproval which would spell its doom. From the mid 1920s both areas of conflict became more and more evident for the PPI and it was only the muted sympathy of Benedict that toned down the urgency of the struggle during the remainder of his short pontificate.

In June 1920 one vital area of the Catholic press was brought even more firmly under the wing of the papacy and of Catholic Action when Giuseppe Dalla Torre became the editor of *Osservatore Romano*.[39] From then on even the communications that had issued so regularly to the paper from the 'little stream' called the PPI began to dry up and Catholic Action became more firmly the order of the day. When the PPI began to try to remedy its 'impressionable lack of Catholic thought', so grievous to the Vatican, by setting up circles of 'political and social culture' to help form the conscience of the people as well as its own members it was quickly pointed out that such a move was an invasion of the field of Catholic Action and beyond the scope of an 'a confessional political party'.[40] Ironically, given the true circumstances, *Avanti* ran a cartoon showing Capital and the Jesuits manipulating a puppet pope who in turn manipulated Sturzo and thence the PPI, ending with the government.[41]

Whatever he thought about the other links in the puppet mechanism remained unclear but Nitti soon came to realize that he could not count on the meek docility of the PPI or its unqualified support. In May his government fell, thus beginning that bewildering array of kaleidoscopic alliances that passed for governments in Italy until the end of 1922. The immediate cause of the fall was a contrary vote in the House on a matter of minor importance upon which the Popolari, the socialists and a few disinterested liberal groups had combined. In the long term the reason was basic discontent with Nitti's inactivity and on the part of the PPI a sense of resentment in that he refused consistently to accept their policies. Filippo Meda, the most widely respected of the PPI deputies, was invited to form a government, but, wearied as he had been with the burden of ministerial office, knowing that he would not get sufficient liberal support and having no personal ambition to lead the country, he refused.[42]

Though the socialists were delighted to see the government fall, as they continued to pin their hopes on the development of an anarchical situation, they blamed the PPI for deserting Nitti and were even more acrimonious when, in the absence of a viable alternative, Nitti again returned to power with the support of the PPI where the realization had dawned that at least for the present it was Nitti or no one.[43] It proved, in any case, an uneasy alliance despite the presence of two PPI ministers and four under-secretaries in the government and it came to an end when Nitti again fell from power on 10 June 1920 after a disagreement on the price of bread which had been pegged with the support of government subsidies. The PPI had agreed with Nitti's decision to raise the price, but wanted the government to take steps to see that the poorer classes would suffer the least. Nitti refused to comply with the PPI but he was afraid of the socialists causing unrest if he went ahead with his decision so he had no alternative but to resign. It is only just to note that Nitti probably had no option but to raise the price of bread as the government subsidy expended on it was causing a loss of 2 billion 400 million lire a year by 1919.[44]

Nitti had maintained a steady contact with Cardinal Gasparri for some time and in August 1920 he wrote to the Secretary of State with a full explanation of his attitude to the PPI. According to Nitti, Catholics, prior to the rise of the PPI, had voted for candidates with whom they felt some affinity. The PPI with its 'intransigence' had changed all that and hence the old guard of liberals and conservatives had to struggle against both the socialists and the Popolari. Was it any wonder to the cardinal that the PPI was hated and that in some circles there was a renewal of anti-clericalism with even talk of an attempt to introduce divorce laws? Added to that there was the increasing danger of pushing the lower bourgeois class into the arms of the socialists due to the stand taken up by the PPI in administrative elections. Nitti tolled another bell by pointing to the peril for the Church arising from the fact that as a priest was the leader of the PPI it made the Church in some way responsible for the party — a party always 'extraneous and contrary to all the parties of good order'. Finally in the statesman's opinion the very lowest aspects of Italian life were present in Sturzo who brought into politics 'the methods of Sicily and of Sicilian local life'. Sturzo and many of his followers were alleged to share the nationalist, political dream of Maurice Barrès himself and of 'the baleful behaviour of Barrès, Your Eminence and I share the same opinion.'[45]

Because no reply from Gasparri is available there is no way of knowing how Vatican circles reacted to the reflections of Nitti but Catholic Action immediately mounted a formidable campaign against any introduction of divorce laws; its directive body insisted that Catholics had to find unity with the forces of moderation against socialism on the grounds that *salus populi, suprema lex*, and a great deal of unease was expressed at the continued intransigence of the PPI.[46] For some months prior to the administrative elections in September there had been repeated instances of socialist violence especially in north Italy, violence frequently met with outbreaks of fascist outrages. Though *Avanti* denied or ignored any socialist complicity in the violence, *Corriere d'Italia* simply replied by giving chapter and verse of the incidents.[47]

Pope Benedict took it upon himself to address a letter in Latin to his brother bishops in the Veneto in which he asked the rich to be 'generous in giving, be inspired by equity and charity rather than by strict justice' and to the proletariat he said 'be on your guard for your Faith which you put in danger when your protests are excessive'. He made it clear that he did not defend the rich as such but only 'insofar as they are unjustly attacked' and he begged the workers to take their part in Catholic organizations.[48] A few days later Dalla Torre gave further point to this when he praised a certain Arrigo Pozzi who had strongly criticised the Popolari because they were worthless defenders, propagators or missionaries of the ideals of Christianity. The only real answer was the Popular Union if one were to remain Catholic.[49] When seven Catholics died as a result of socialist attacks at Sestri, Mantua and at Siena where a church was invaded, it was clear to the conservatives that Catholic forces had to be united or worse would follow.[50]

In this atmosphere the administrative elections took place and led by Sturzo the PPI decided to remain firm on its stand of intransigence, refuse to ally itself with other parties and present its own lists to the electors. This policy had been decided upon at the Naples Congress where intransigence in the administrative elections was seen as a 'necessity of life' for the PPI if it were to achieve its objective of cutting the bonds with the past.[51] However Sturzo was seen as the main architect of the policy especially when Meda refused to condone or defend intransigence in administrative elections and *Osservatore Romano* attacked the priest for the policy 'repeatedly recommended or, better, imposed' by him.[52] It was pointed out that all the PPI talk of the economic state of the south was fine, but what of its moral state if it failed to remain free from the 'cancer' of socialism that threatened it from the north? In Venice the Cardinal Patriarch begged for unity of the conservative forces 'to save Venice from the predatory and ferocious tyranny of Leninism' but there, as at Rome, where similar pleas were made, the PN refused to budge.[53] From Florence the *Unità Cattolica* thundered against the Popolari and especially took them to task for a party plank which they shared with the socialists — the vote for women. It was considered censurable on domestic and moral grounds and it threatened to bring confusion in its 'immature inopportunity'.[54]

At Milan when the dying archbishop, Cardinal Ferrari, distressed at the constant outbreaks of socialist violence, implored the PPI to think of the good of the Church, the pressure to comply and ally itself with the conservatives was immense, but the party refused to yield and the socialists won the election. *L'Italia* which was the local voice of Catholicism in the archdiocese and, as such, a powerful voice in the whole of north Italy was outraged at the lack of Catholic unity in the face of the socialist menace and from that event its disenchantment with, and eventual rejection of, the PPI stems.[55] Bergamo, stronghold of Catholic social activity for a century, saw a split in the party, but Sturzo still remained adamant. The local Catholic paper, *L'Eco di Bergamo*, deserted the party and a clerical moderate group stood in the elections. The seemingly impossible happened and the Popolari won. Overall the results in 8,327 communes gave 1,650 to the PPI and 2,166 to the socialists who gained impressive wins in Tuscany and Emilia, later to be centres of fascist violence.[56] To Sturzo no other course than intransigence was possible if the party were to remain true to its pledge of rejecting the tradition, stemming back to the days of the Gentiloni Pact, in which Catholics had been no more than a pool of easily caught votes for the old conservative parties.

The price however was high. Many Catholics were confused and divided, some Catholic papers that had previously supported the party such as *Venezia*, or that at the least had treated it with some degree of toleration such as *Unità Cattolica*, were now hostile while the Vatican regarded the PPI as having transgressed the bounds of morality and there were repeated denials by *Osservatore Romano* that the party was a Catholic one.[57] The opinion of the old conservative forces at Milan was summed up with the declaration that Sturzo was an idolator of intransigence and that his policy had meant the alienation of all decent people, even in parliament.[58] At Genoa the archbishop, Cardinal Tommaso Pio Boggiani, was one prelate who was not surprised at the behaviour of the PPI. In July he had warned his people in a pastoral letter of the danger the PPI posed to the Church by confusing Italian Catholics, breaking them away from ecclesiastical authority and not leading them along the 'true path to follow in public political life' —

the path mapped out by Pio IX in the Syllabus! Their intransigence in the administrative elections had only served to consolidate further the opinion of the cardinal and he forbad any Catholic who held a position in his Catholic Action groups to be associated on any official level with the PPI. It was all very well for the party to argue, in a well-reasoned article in *Il Popolo Nuovo*, that any course other than intransigence would have been fatal in that it would have weakened the PPI, which was the only real force opposed to bolshevism in the country, and that it was preferable to pay the price of losing a few hundred more communes to the socialists than that the PPI lose its integrity.[59] To the clerical mind the only way to stop bolshevism was the imposition of law and order and those concepts were enshrined in the old conservative forces of the right. It did not occur to them then that there might be another way of stifling socialism which would prove itself to be the negation of all the basic concepts of justice and morality.

On the parliamentary level the PPI revealed itself rather less intransigent when, after the two abortive attempts at collaboration with Nitti, it decided, against the better judgement of Sturzo to whom Giolitti was a spent and discredited force, to support the government formed by the old statesman.[60] Giolitti, apart from the attitude he had expressed in late 1919 with which the PPI was in large agreement, declared himself ready to act in the financial area to remedy the precarious economic situation of the country and to help him do this he asked Meda to become Treasury Minister. His government had as wide an array of talent as was available at the time but the absence of a left-wing element, which Giolitti wanted but the socialists refused, left him a prey to any extra parliamentary strategy the socialists could devise. The activity was not long in coming when in August, led by the metal workers, an occupation of factories took place, first at the Alfa Romeo plant in Milan followed by Turin and eventually throughout the peninsula.[61]

The event itself was rendered more significant by the revolutionary overtones it displayed rather than by any intrinsic value it had in itself. The socialists had called for a tightening of the cord around the neck of Italian democracy and when the occupation took place they saw it as 'an historical event of great magnitude ... a necessary moment of the revolutionary development and of the class war.' They called upon the workers and farmers to ready themselves to occupy 'the banks, the workshops, the land', asked the soldiers to join the workers and appealed to the proletariat of Italy to 'organize yourselves, discipline yourselves, arm yourselves'.[62] When the so called Parliament of the Proletariat met at Milan in early September it seemed to many that the Italy of tomorrow was to be bolshevist.[63]

Giolitti, from the start, decided to remain aloof but the hard-headedness of the industrialists was expressed in their refusal to negotiate on any terms except purely paternalistic ones. There was also the suspicion that they had tried to force the government's hand by leaving arms in the factories with the intended objective that the workers would worsen their cause by resorting to open violence. As a result the Prime Minister decided to act. He tried to force the industrialists to come to terms by threatening economic sanctions and he endeavoured to win the moderate socialist leaders, Treves, Turati and D'Aragona, away from the more determined elements. Over a month went by during which the government and the moderate socialists came to an agreement satisfactory to the less radical leaders in both the industrialist and workers' camps. The workers were given a greater share in the operation of the factories while overall control, to say nothing of ownership, rested in the hands of the industrialists. The workers had conducted themselves with restraint and in some instances impressive nobility and with hope in the future rather than resignation, they abandoned their occupation of the factories on 1 October 1920. It was to be the last united manifestation of working-class strength in Italy for a generation.

In its immediate consequences the results of the occupation of the factories were immense. The socialists could no longer contain their deep-rooted ideological divisions and, led by Amadeo Bordiga, the left began the formation of the Communist Party in October 1920.[64] The workers were isolated from the farmers, returned soldiers and middle classes who distrusted the soviet dream which the occupation seemed to embody, while the industrialists never forgave the slight done to them as owners.[65] Giolitti and his government had, correctly, taken a stand for both sides but it made his task in unifying the country almost impossible. The socialists who followed the moderate voices of Treves and Turati had seemed to betray the high, revolutionary promises they had so long held out, while the communists laid themselves open to the charge of being an alien force in society with their obsessive ideal of a soviet Italy. But the worst aspect of the whole thing was that the unionists were confused in that 'they felt they had been defeated but they could not see clearly how nor by whom' and as a result their leadership faltered and wavered leaving their followers bereft of purpose or finality.[66]

As for the PPI, with its young and weak links in the workers' world through the white unions, any choice heavily weighted to either side seemed precarious. To opt fully for the workers was to expose themselves to the charge of being sharers in the soviet dream, while not to do so was to align themselves with capitalism, conservatism and the miserable paternalism of the past. In the circumstances the party contented itself with vague affirmations of solidarity with the workers, discussed a learned discourse given by Sturzo, found itself, together with the white unions, repudiated by Giolitti and then assisted, albeit unwillingly, at the destruction of the workers' hopes when the projected law for worker control of the factories came to nothing.[67] In their inability to influence, much less direct, events the PPI did no more than share in the malaise that had gripped Italy whereby those who knew what direction the country ought to take possessed no means to lead it, while those who led it did not know what they were leading it to.

If any blame can be apportioned to Sturzo in this dilemma it stems from the fact that he never had the opportunity to understand the struggle of the industrialized working masses of north Italy. His experience in the south had equipped him with a deep understanding of, and a commitment to, the rural community and its work force but industrialization was foreign to him. Unlike Joseph Cardijn in Belgium, Sturzo failed to see that the alienated masses of the factories and workshops were the ultimate key to Italy's future and, as a result, he was incapable of taking up a cohesive position in their regard. Worse still, in the context of 1920, was Sturzo's inability to relate to or appreciate the role of the white unions. Giambattista Valente who claimed to be the founder of the white unions' Italian Confederation of Workers accused Sturzo of being a dictator, of wanting to use the Confederation for his own political purposes and of replacing him with Gronchi to further that aim.[68] Whatever the truth of such accusations the fact remains that Sturzo never realized the power inherent in the union movement which, when properly fostered and led, could have proved the bulwark of Italian democracy. In his favour it must be admitted that only a handful of Italian leaders saw the industrialized workers as anything but a discontented mass in the early 1920s and, as a result, they ignored the deep-seated yearning of the workers for justice and democracy.

In Italian life only two groups seemed to know where they were going. The communists had a creed, a model and a vision to work for and although the events of September–October 1920 seemed to indicate that Italy was not yet ready to pass through the revolutionary stage that would usher in the new era the communists could afford to wait and assist as best they could in the collapse of the capitalist system. On the other hand it was not easy for many people, especially in the middle classes, to await patiently their hour of deliverance. In their own way both the socialists and the Popolari, obsessed as both were with a doctrinal adherence to the dispossessed, had forgotten that class who were still the backbone of Italy. The small shopkeepers, the civil servants, the army, the returned soldiers who had been so despised by the socialists, the students who faced unemployment after seemingly fruitless years of study, the little people employed in vast numbers in service industries in which they eked out a miserable pittance all looked for a restoration in Italian life both economic and social. To them, strike after endless strike had brought irritation and frustration, violence with the loss of 2,500 lives in 1920 alone caused horror, government following government with a plethora of words and little action wrought havoc with any remaining faith they had in parliamentary democracy.[69]

Is it any wonder that on 15 October *Il Piccolo Giornale d'Italia* expressed the conviction of many when it wrote 'Italy needs A MAN of firm will who inscribes on his platform only one word: order.' It was idle for *Il Messaggero* on 16 October to observe that they couldn't find the 'MAN' amongst the wielders of power while at the same time recognizing the need for one to save Italy from the 'bolshevist pest'.[70] Equally the *Osservatore Romano* could do no more than express a Christian, personalist hope when Dalla Torre rejected the idea of one man and said that it was up to every man to save Italy because, if the bolshevists came to power, 'the whole country would be reduced to nothing more than one huge barracks'.[71]

Curiously enough the man was already on the scene awaiting his hour. His method was violence and his weapon the revolver. It was with contempt and derision that *Osservatore Romano* quoted an excerpt from Mussolini's *Il Fascio* but scarcely apt that it should have chosen Christmas Day to do so. 'The revolver is more beautiful than a woman. The woman talks too much, never arrives at a conclusion and betrays. The automatic speaks very little, but it makes itself understood immediately.'[72] The fascists were already giving constant proof that they believed in such loathsome banalities, while Mussolini himself was also beginning to believe in something else to which the *Osservatore Romano* could have usefully paid more attention. In October 1920 he said 'I think that Catholicism could be used as one of our strongest national forces for the expression of our Italian identity in the world.[73]

Notes

1. See *Corriere d'Italia*, 4 December 1920. The expression comes from Roman history when the people withdrew to the Aventine in protest against the abuse of power by the patricians. G. Ferrero, *Da Fiume a Roma. Storia di quattro anni (1919–1923)* (Milan, 1923), p. 37.

2. See E. Santarelli, *Il socialismo anarchico in Italia*, 2nd edn (Milan 1973).

3. R. Vivarelli, in his *Il dopoguerra*, p. 552, is of the opinion that the Fiume affair weakened the state at its very core because it helped the people think that 'any form of violence would be tolerated'. Ivanoe Bonomi saw the Paris Peace talks of 1919 as a severe blow to Italy in that the people thought they had been betrayed by their allies when Italy's claim to Fiume was rejected. See I. Bonomi, *La politica italiana dopo Vittorio Veneto* (Turin, 1953), pp. 41, 56.

4. The economic sector in the post-war period needed particular attention and Nitti seemed to have no concrete proposals to offer to solve its problems. Since 1914 the cost of living had risen by 390 per cent and the public debt in May 1919 was 78 billion lire. *Corriere della Sera*, 18 February, 12 May 1919, quoted in L. Einaudi, *Cronache economiche e politiche di un trentennio (1893–1925)*, vol. V (Turin, 1966), pp. 55–6, 142

5. *O.R.*, 17, 18 November 1919. *Civiltà Cattolica* was even more uneasy. To the Jesuits many PPI men had 'imitated to some extent the methods of the socialists', thus leading the people astray and leaving them an easier prey to socialism. *Civiltà Cattolica*, vol. 4, 6 December 1919, pp. 413–22.

6. *Avanti*, 10 December 1919. Crispolti was always uneasy about socialism and any tendency in the PPI to ally with it. He had no such fear of the right and abandoned the party for fascism in 1923. See F. Crispolti, *'I confessioni' di un clerico-fascista*, extracted from *Vita Sociale*, n. 123, September–December 1966, and E. Martire, *Filippo Crispolti, Note Biografiche* (Milan, 1943).

7. *Avanti*, 11 December 1919; *O.R.*, 12 December 1919.

8. *Corriere d'Italia*, 5 December 1920; Angelo Mauri was one of the old figures of the Catholic movement who stayed with the PPI until the end. He served as Minister for Agriculture under Bonomi, July 1921 – February 1922. See F. Magri, *Un pioniere*

dell'azione cattolica cristiana Angelo Mauri 1873–1936 (Milan, 1956).

9. *Avanti*, 31 July 1919; 5 March 1920.

10. Ibid., 30 March 1920. L. Gui, *Il Partito Popolare Italiano e i patti agrari* (Rome, 1956), p. 11, says that because the liberals were hostile and the socialists indifferent the PPI had scarcely any success with its land policies.

11. *Avanti*, 5, 11 February, 24 March 1920.

12. See *Il Popolo d'Italia*, 23 January 1920 in B. Vigezzi, (ed.) *1919–1925 Dopoguerra e fascismo. Politica e stampa in Italia*, p. 460

13. *Avanti*, 1 April 1920.

14. While Crispolti thought any claims that the PPI had stopped a socialist revolution in 1919 were exaggerated he was convinced, probably with some justification, that the PPI deputies prevented the socialist deputies from reducing the House in 1920 to a 'revolutionary constituency'. See F. Crispolti, *'I Confessioni'*, p. 438. The left never forgot the lesson of the early 1920s and the Italian Communist Party generally respected parliament and its proceedings.

15. *Corriere d'Italia*, 19 November 1919. Don Ernesto Buonaiuti pointed out that the PPI victory did nothing to harm the socialists but only the old parties of 'order'. Ibid., 21 November 1919. The term liberal is used to group the diverse elements of Italian political conservatism. In fact in the parliament of 1919 they were made up of Liberals 41 seats; Democrats 60; Liberals and Democratic Liberals 96; while the remaining 55 seats went to various minor parties. See E.P. Howard, *Il Partito Popolare Italiano* (Florence, 1957), p. 194. Edith Pratt Howard had the immense good fortune to work at Harvard with Gaetano Salvemini on her doctoral thesis on the PPI. It was published in Italian in 1957 with an introduction by Paolo Vittorelli, but regrettably no English version was ever published. Despite the fact that research in the last 20 years has added greatly to our knowledge of the PPI her work remains as 'an indispensable source for anyone who wants to understand the origins and causes of the fascist period and some decisive moments of the evolution of the catholic political movement in Italy'. See p. xxiv of Vittorelli's introduction.

16. *O.R.*, 25 February 1919. On the war and post-war economy see the excellent chapter in S.B. Clough, *The Economic History of Modern Italy* (New York, 1964), pp. 170–210.

17. *O.R.*, 25 February 1919; *Avanti*, 13 October 1919.

18. In 1920, 1,161,283 unionists were behind the PPI through the Catholic union movement. Of these 944,812 were farm workers so it was abundantly clear that in those circumstances the socialists could not expect to win the rural vote. See G. Salvemini, *Stato*, p. 241.

19. In 1947 when Nitti was again asked to form a government he said to Gronchi,

'There is no need to set out a platform', and he assured De Gaspari that if he did manage to set up a ministry it would never meet for longer than an hour! See G. Spataro, *I Democratici*, fn. 2, p. 23.

20. G. De Rosa, *Il Partito*, p. 33. In her thorough study of a region S. Colarizi, *Dopoguerra e fascismo in Puglia (1919–1926)* (Bari, 1971), maintains that the Catholic mass that voted for the PPI did so out of loyalty rather than conviction. The same phenomenon held true for many of the PPI deputies until their loyalty was put to the test.

21. G. Sforza, *L'Italia*, pp. 68–9.

22. V. Ambrosino 'Le Parti Populaire Italien', unpublished DIS thesis (Paris, 1965), p. 59.

23. C. Sforza, *L'Italia*, p. 71.

24. G. De Rosa, 'Una lettera', p. 573.

25. Interview with De Rosa, Rome, 13 December 1974. Senator Giuseppe Spataro in an interview in Rome, 15 December 1974, made the same assertion and told me that as Sturzo already held the party in his hand there was no need for him to enter parliament.

26. G. Andreotti, *De Gasperi e il suo tempo*, 2nd edn (Verona, 1964), p. 143, Montecitorio is the seat of the Italian Parliament.

27. It has been estimated that in 1919 there were 1,626 strikes with 1,078,869 participants and in 1920 there were 1,847 with 1,320,180 participants. In the latter year 55 million working days were lost with a loss of one billion lire in salaries. See F. Magri, *La Democrazia*, vol. 1, p. 86.

28. *Il Popolo Nuovo*, March 1920.

29. *Avanti*, 4 April, 13 March 1920.

30. L. Sturzo, *Italy and Fascismo*, trans. B. Carter (London, 1926), p. 99.

31. *Corriere d'Italia*, 13 April 1920. Again the paper gave a very full account of the Congress. See 8, 10, 13, 16 April 1920. See also F. Malgeri (ed.), *Gli atti*, pp. 113–218.

32. *O.R.* 10, 11 April 1920. See V. Del Giudice, *La Questione Romana ed i rapporti tra Stato e Chiesa fino alla Conciliazione* (Rome, 1947), and V. Del Giudice and A. Renier, *I massimi problemi del Partito Popolare innanzi al Congresso Nazionale di Napoli (8–10 Aprile 1920)* (Naples, 1920), pp. 1–4.

33. *Avanti*, 9 April 1920. *La Stampa*, 12 April 1920, said the PPI had one deputy, Sturzo, and 100 secretaries, not 100 deputies and one secretary. Quoted in E. Vercesi, *Il movimento cattolico in Italia, 1870–1922* (Florence, 1923), p. 189.

34. G. Miglioli, *Con Roma*, passim. The whole book contains not a single word of criticism of Sturzo while E. Vercesi, in *Il movimento*, is constantly critical of

the 'autocratic temperament' of Sturzo. See pp. 189–96. This book, written by a professional journalist, is profoundly anti Sturzo in tone but Filippo Meda wrote a preface to it in which he praised the work and did not defend Sturzo.

35. *O.R.*, 1, 7, 8 January, 23 April 1920, where there are details on both the Bank of Rome and Catholic Action. Martire, for example, was still vice president of Youth Catholic Action when elected a PPI deputy.

36. See G. Spataro, *I Democratici*, p. 27 and S. Jacini, *Storia*, p. 68. Sturzo said that Nitti told his friends that the PPI would have to continue to vote for him thanks to the intervention of the Vatican. L. Sturzo, *Popolarismo e fascismo* (Turin, 1925), p. 30.

37. *O.R.*, 18, 26 February; 26, 27, 30 April 1920. Early in 1920 Dalla Torre and Father Rosa, editor of *Civiltà Cattolica* had collaborated on an article 'Unione popolare e Partito popolare in Italia' which warned against the dangers to Catholic Action from involvement with the party. Dalla Torre then distributed 250 copies to the bishops See A. Fiocchi, *F. Enrico Rosa, S.J.*, p. 175 and *Civiltà Cattolica*, vol. 1, 21 February 1920, pp. 289–301.

38. Papal letter, 11 March 1920, in F. Magri, *L'Azione Cattolica in Italia*, vol. 1, 2 vols (Milan, 1952), p. 372; *O.R.*, 30 April 1920.

39. *O.R.*, 2 June 1920.

40. *O.R.*, 5, 6, 7–8, 16 June 1920.

41. *Avanti*, 9 May 1920.

42. G. Spataro, *I Democratici*, p. 27. See also *Corriere d'Italia*, 13, 20 May 1920. *O.R.*, 13 May 1920, was of the opinion that the PPI had taken an erroneous decision in opposing Nitti and thought it could give rise to 'unhappy consequences'.

43. *Avanti*, 8, 9, 14, 15, 20, 23 May 1920; *Il Popolo Nuovo*, 30 April 1920. Sturzo was opposed to the rebirth of the Nitti ministry, but he could not persuade the party directorate to accept his view. See F. Piva and F. Malgeri, *Vita*, p. 237.

44. L. Einaudi, *Cronache*, vol. v, p. 279.

45. The letter is found in F.M. Broglio, *Italia*, p. 386.

46. See *O.R.*, July, August, September 1920 passim on divorce, 12 September 1920 on unity and 10 September 1920 on PPI intransigence. Also *Corriere d'Italia* on divorce throughout August 1920. The PPI also joined in the anti-divorce campaign which was seen as a direct insult to them and their attempts at collaboration with the liberals. *Il Popolo Nuovo*, 18, 25 July 1920.

47. See *Corriere d'Italia*, 4, 5 May 1920; *Avanti*, 3, 4 May and for further instances 22, 24, 28, 29 June 1920.

48. *O.R.*, 21–22 June 1920 for text.

49. Ibid., 26 June 1920. Pozzi deplored the fact that many members of the Popular

Union had, wrongly, left it and joined the PPI. The experience of one year in Parliament and two Congresses proved to those Catholics, who held themselves to be such and who were determined to remain so, that the PPI was 'no longer enough and in fact was never enough'.

50. Ibid., 18 August 1920; *Corriere d'Italia*, 18 August 1920.

51. *Il Popolo Nuovo*, 25 April 1920.

52. *O.R*, 6, 7, 11 September 1920.

53. Ibid., quoting *Provincia di Padova*, 5 September 1920.

54. *Unità Cattolica*, 5 September 1920 in *O.R.*, 6 7 September 1920.

55. *L'Italia*, 30 October 1920 in B. Vigezzi, *L'Italia di fronte*, p. 561. The fact that Ferrari was much admired in PPI ranks made the decision to reject his plea a very difficult one.

56. For a succinct account of these elections see G. De Rosa, *Il Partito*, pp. 73–9.

57. *O.R.*, 6, 7, 15, 27, 8 September 1920.

58. *Corriere della Sera*, 3 October 1920.

59. See letter 'L'Azione Cattolica ed Il Partito Popolare Italiano' in *Civitas*, no. 18, 1 September 1920, reprinted in B. Malinverni (ed.), *Civitas: Antologia degli scritti più significativi apparsi dal 1919 al 1925* (Rome, 1963), pp. 71–7; *Il Popolo Nuovo*, 3 October 1920.

60. F. Piva and F. Malgeri, *Vita*, p. 237.

61. The justifiable unrest of the workers, their frustration at the refusal of the industrialists to meet their demands and their subsequent reaction can be studied in P. Spriano, *L'occupazione delle fabbriche* (Turin, 1964), and F. Catalano, *Potere economico e fascismo. La crisi del dopoguerra 1919–1921* (Milan, 1964), pp. 133, 164.

62. *Avanti*, 5 August, 2, 3, 7 September 1920.

63. The reactions of the various segments of Italian life can be seen in the prominence given to the event by such papers as *Il Messaggero, Corriere d'Italia, Osservatore Romano* and *Avanti* during August and September 1920.

64. See *Avanti*, October 1920, for proceedings of the Conference at Reggio Emilia which led to the official split. Writing in *Civitas*, Meda hoped for a Turati victory and that the socialist party would as a result take up its proper function as a reform movement once the communist dream had 'become no more than a sad memory in Italy'. See articles 'La Scissione Socialista' and 'Il Domani del Partito Socialista' in B. Malinverni (ed.), *Civitas*, pp. 89–3, 95–104. On the Italian Communist Party in its formative years see L. Cortesi, *Le origini del Partito Comunista Italiano. Il PSI dalla guerra di Libia alla scissione di Livorno* (Bari, 1972); J. Cammett, *Antonio Gramsci*

and the Origins of Italian Communism (Stanford, 1967); A. Tasca, *I primi dieci anni del PCI* (Bari, 1971).

65. G. Sabatucci, *I combattenti nel primo dopoguerra* (Bari, 1974), argues that the mass of the returned soldiers were not pro-fascist in 1919–20 but as 45 per cent of those mobilized were of farmer extraction they were not, in the main, pro socialist.

66. See P. Spriano, *L'occupazione*, pp. 151 and 162.

67. See G. De Rosa, *Il Partito*, pp. 54–73.

68. G. Valente (F. Malgeri, ed.), *Aspetti e momenti dell'azione sociale dei cattolici in Italia 1892–1926* (Rome, 1968), pp. 14, 207–9.

69. A look at the proceedings of parliament for 1920 reveals that scarcely any legislative act worth serious consideration was passed in that year. See *Atti Parlamentari, Camera, 1919–21*, vols 1–7 (Rome, 1919–21).

70. Both papers were quoted in *O.R.*, 21 October 1920.

71. Ibid., 21, 23 October 1920.

72. Ibid., 25 December 1920.

73. Quoted in F.M. Broglio, *Italia*, p. 75.

4

DEMOCRACY IN DECLINE

The year that saw Italy convulsed by violence, by strikes and by government inactivity also saw the coalescing of forces that shaped the destiny of the nation for another generation. The most important single factor that emerged in 1920 was a widespread feeling of reaction against those elements in society that wanted change, reconstruction or, as Sturzo saw it, the rehabilitation of the nation from its very core. People who had allowed themselves, albeit unwillingly, to be exploited economically, socially and in some senses spiritually for generations were reluctant to support the new forces that held promise of changing the situation. To an extent that defies analysis the socialists had wounded the sense of tradition and moderation that was so inherent in large segments of the Italian masses. Similarly the Popolari had alarmed the conservatism of the vocal elements of the upper classes who could express themselves eloquently through press and pulpit. And if those voices had been unequivocal in their condemnation of socialism they were soon to dispel any doubts they had entertained hitherto on the Partito Popolare.

Paolo Mattei-Gentili had been a journalist since his graduation in law at the University of Rome and in 1906 he joined the *Corriere d'Italia*, taking over its editorship within a few months. He was an intelligent, urbane Catholic conservative who threw in his lot with the PPI at its inception, helped in the formulation of its programme, became a member of its National Council in June 1919 and a deputy in the parliament in that same year. Until the end of 1920 he expressed no doubts about the value neither of the party nor of any of its actions and, indeed, in his paper he defended it constantly. In December 1920 he took the opportunity to sum up two years of the party's activity in a long editorial. Above all Mattei-Gentili was pleased that all the stupid talk of any form of collaboration with socialism was over. The PPI was a 'party of order' which did not share the violent spirit that animated socialism. While he did not think the party ought to agree with the ideas of fascism he wondered whether it was not time to conduct an examination of conscience within the party. He was especially concerned whether there was sufficient awareness in the party of the dangers of bolshevism and whether classes other than the proletariat were paid the attention they merited.[1]

There was a ready response to Mattei-Gentili's call for reappraisal, perhaps quickened by the fact that the socialists had engaged in a series of attacks on Catholics during December. One spectacular display of ill-bred virtuosity took place during the Midnight Mass of Christmas Eve in a little church outside Bologna. The priest was elderly and in poor health and the congregation defenceless. A band of enthusiasts singing the Red Flag invaded the church, emptied priest and people out into the winter's night and danced to the playing of the organ.[2] Against the charges that the party was not sufficiently aware of the danger of bolshevism Giulio De Rossi, director of the party's press office, replied with an extensive list of historical items to prove the contrary. The priest, however, weakened his case by refusing to indulge in any other critical estimate of bolshevism than the blunt assertion that it was kept alive by the 'social improvidence' of the legislative powers and the weakness of the bureaucratic apparatus which engaged in mere tendencies towards social amelioration rather than positive reform.[3]

This argument was followed by a long series of letters the central theme of which was the necessity for the party to be a strong centre party 'courageously at the head of the forces of legality'.[4] It was a correspondence rendered sterile and confusing by the silence of

Sturzo or any other genuinely progressive party leader and by the simple affirmation of moderate centralism by the other party members, including De Rossi. When Sturzo finally spoke up at Bergamo he was criticized because he had nothing to say about 'the moral content' of the party.[5] Such criticism only served to heighten the dilemma into which the PPI had allowed itself to be led. If it assumed a stand on moral grounds it was open to the accusation of overstepping the bounds set up by its aconfessionality, while if it remained neutral it was then open to the charge of being unchristian. It was rapidly developing into a situation in which only the fascists were seen as a salutary restraint against the socialists but in reality the socialist movement was weakening itself by engaging in its inexorable tendency to fissurize and fragment.

Those socialists who wanted their own movement to remain united were against any form of cooperation with the parties of the bourgeoisie. They included in their programme 'the eventual necessity of violence and admitted, at least in a provisional manner, the dictatorship of the proletariat'. As a result they stood firmly for 'Socialism and Revolution' hopeful that the workers would only listen to those who taught them to prepare for the final collision with the exploiting and oppressive bourgeoisie.[6] These extreme views were put forward by a determined group dedicated firstly to complete unity with and fidelity to the international movement based on Moscow and secondly to undertake and direct immediate action in the implementation of the revolutionary aims of socialism. The conflict reached a deadlock at the Party Congress held at Livorno in January 1921 at which the Moscow delegate, Kabaktchieff, propounded a hard line which required adhesion to the directives of Moscow, a change in name of the party to the Italian Communist Party and subservience of all its organs and auxiliary groupings to Moscow-based decisions.

Filippo Turati was unable to accept either the beliefs of Moscow or its directives. To him, 'The cult of violence ... is the cult of capitalism, not of socialism'. He thought that by engaging in violence the socialists helped to create 'both fascism and the PPI by intimidating the masses beyond measure'. With an intuitive look into the future he said 'As time passes you will perceive how, to some extent, Russian bolshevism is a form of oriental nationalism that now clings desperately to us in order to conserve its life and its power.' The majority at the Congress at least shared Turati's views on the international question and when the Moscow delegate spoke on the sixth day cries such as 'We are not slaves', 'We don't want papal legates' were heard. Finally when Turati was declared a heretic by Kabaktchieff, 'Long live the pope. Long live papachieff' greeted 'the Major excommunication' pronounced by the inept and probably confused foreigner who was unaccustomed to dissent. When the vote was taken, one third of the delegates declared themselves ready for the long Hegira to Moscow while the rest were more inclined to partake of the manna as they marched to their promised land. The party split was definite and the Communist Party in Italy was born.[7] It is not mere idle speculation to wonder whether the split would have taken place so promptly had both sectors not felt certain that because of the system of proportionalism, they were still assured of some of the crumbs of power with seats in the decadent parliament they so vigorously derided.

The split in the socialist party appeared as a bonus to the government and many parliamentarians thought with Filippo Meda that the Marxist dream was a 'bloody and useless oriental fantasy' and that it was a good thing the communists had taken their own path as now it might prove possible to work with the moderate element.[8] This hope Giolitti also shared to the extent that he thought the socialists would cooperate with him once the extreme elements were eliminated. It was another instance in which the liberal mind proved incapable of grasping the changed circumstances that had come about by the introduction into Italian life of political parties based on ideologies which limited their freedom of collaboration. Giolitti ultimately saw that the day of empirical opportunism was over and he was convinced that proportionalism was 'a veritable disaster'.[9] He failed to understand that his own day was done despite his 78 years and perhaps Ivanoe Bonomi, who knew and loved the old statesman, was one of the few who realized that even Giolitti had no strength left when he was smitten by the loss of his wife in May 1921.[10]

If it was one thing for Giolitti to try to understand the variations on the socialist theme it was another to assess fascism and here he seems to have been singularly incapable of arriving at any firm decision either as to its nature or purpose. The vigour with which he dealt with D'Annunzio in Fiume he was unable to apply in the face of fascism, and although a good deal of explanation and justification of Giolitti has been written by some Italian historians, the fact remains that he proved incapable of stemming, much less turning, the fascist tide.[11] Fascism had an ever increasing and seemingly respectable following amongst the middle classes, the army, returned soldiers and young people fired with a dream of false patriotism.[12] It was not a case of Giolitti either favouring or allowing the growth and development of the fascist phenomenon. It was rather that he imagined that it could be contained and even civilized within the framework of the old liberal state and, even more to the point, in a period when its violent excesses were daily more flagrant, he thought that the legal apparatus of that state could control it. That he was mistaken on both counts is manifestly a part of history. That he needs to be excused any more than the majority of his contemporaries, including large segments of the PPI who thought like him, is scarcely necessary.

In parliament itself Matteotti called fascism a bourgeois reactionary movement of violence, accused Giolitti of doing nothing to stop it and claimed that the socialists were not only defending themselves against the fascists but they were also fighting 'for the cause of our country and that of civilization itself'. From the PPI benches Miglioli condemned fascism for its violent repression of the struggle of the farmers and agricultural workers for justice and he poured scorn on the landlords who paid the fascists to put down the workers.[13] In retrospect it must be said that, on the parliamentary level, there were very few deputies who faced the fascist movement without equivocation and the events of Cremona in early 1922 reveal the weakness in those from whom genuine concerted resistance to fascism could have been expected. At Cremona, Miglioli had managed to arrange a kind of mutual defence pact between the peasants who belonged to the PPI and the socialist movement in order to give them the strength to resist the murderous assaults on them by fascist squads led by Roberto Farinacci. The pact came to nothing because both the PPI and the socialist leaders repudiated it — to the intense relief of the fascists who were fully aware that they could not face the concerted opposition of the Christian and socialist workers and farmers. Thus 'through the failure of a political strategy of alliances fascism forged ahead' and the work, sacrifice and idealism that had given birth to both socialism and Christian Democracy in Italy foundered on the prejudices of both sides.[14]

Despite the fact that he had not been forced to honour his promises to the PPI on agrarian, scholastic or even on electoral reform including a vote for women, Giolitti soon came to the conclusion that he was unable to continue in collaboration with the Popolari who had nonetheless given him loyal support.[15] His hopes of an alternative source of support were unrealistic so he decided to call an election in May 1921 still thinking he would be able to count on the support of the PPI who would be forced to opt for him as the alternative to the socialists.[16] What Giolitti did not seem to understand was that he was no longer dealing with the docile Catholic politicians of the past whose concept of responsible parliamentary activity rarely went beyond bolstering up liberal governments at the price of a mitigation of anti-clerical and masonic bigotry. The Popolari wanted to play a more positive role in Italian society and hence they refused to take part in the nondescript electoral block led by Giolitti which also comprised fascists. Giolitti was outraged at the conduct of the Popolari which he considered was as 'bestial' as that of the socialists, seemingly unaware that the main exponents of bestiality in the country were his own allies, the fascists, who gained a great deal of public respectability from the fact that they were allowed to stand on an electoral platform beside the 'statesman of Dronero'.[17]

During April and May 1921 the fascists' strength grew apace. Their 317 sections grew to 1001 and their membership from 80,476 to 187,098. Meanwhile the killing and wounding went on. There were 71 deaths, including those of 16 fascists and 31 socialists, and 216 people were seriously wounded between 16 and 31 May 1921. The *Osservatore Romano* ran a banner headline during these weeks which read 'The fascists versus the socialists'. It added the communists to the protagonists in late April and generally expressed horror at the incipient civil war. *Il Popolo Nuovo* had long since condemned fascism as a 'party of violence, of excess, outside the law and therefore a social danger and a constant cause of unrest, disquiet and malaise for our country'. It was judged as a 'blind, reactionary force' which might yet prove a greater danger than bolshevism and, indeed, in the opinion of the editor, had Giolitti been equal to his task of defending the state against bolshevist excesses the reaction of the fascists would have been blunted.[18]

The Popolari prepared for the election with confidence in their own and the country's future although they admitted the gravity of the situation, especially in the economic sector. Speaking for the party Giovanni Battista Bertone, who had been under-secretary of the Ministry of Finance in the Giolitti cabinet, pointed out that the situation was so grave as to demand the collaboration of the party with a government determined to restore its economic viability. The official deficit for 1920 was 14-billion lire and Bertone seemed to think that such a state of affairs was not unconnected with the prevalence of strikes in that year which had accounted for the loss of 28,898,227 days' work in industry and agriculture.[19] Sturzo himself had been unwearied hitherto in his emphasis on the economic situation as a prime cause of the nation's instability, yet by May 1921 he thought some improvement was evident.[20] Thus his main concern was whether the elections would result in a government prepared to uphold its authority, shake itself free from the parasitic state apparatus, give the people confidence and legislate for social amelioration without fear or favour. He also suggested that large parts of the state bureaucracy be abolished, that 'Three quarters at least of existing economic legislation be annulled' and that no new laws be made in that field for years to come. He admitted however that his criticism was harsh and he was prepared to recognize that 'in Italy the government, any government, is already prisoner of a bureaucracy which is tied ... to a new class of profiteers of the state' and its hope of freeing itself from that bureaucracy was remote without decisive action.[21]

Claiming that it was against revolution, reaction and violence and that it stood for economic, organic and spiritual freedom the PPI asked for the people's support while the communists asked the workers and farmers to vote for their party, for 'Russia and for the Revolution'.[22] The other parties had a less precise approach to the situation and the main point to emerge as a result of the recourse to the urns was the presence of 35 fascists and 15 communists in the new parliament. Because they increased their seats to 108, the Popolari announced 'behold, we have won' and even the socialists were not distressed although they had lost 23 seats.[23] One person in Italy had the experience to know, after a lifetime spent in political manoeuvring, that he had not won. Two weeks after the new parliament sat Giolitti resigned from his last ministry and in a symbolic sense the resignation of the man from Dronero spelt the end of Italian liberalism.

As had become customary there was the normal search for someone willing to accept the responsibility of forming a new ministry and after a refusal by Enrico De Nicola, president of the House, the former socialist, Ivanoe Bonomi, accepted the task and managed to put together a cabinet which included three Popolari.[24] Amongst them was Guilio Rodinò who became Minister of Justice which marked a departure from previous liberal governments in that no Catholic deputy had ever held the office. There was an outcry at the nomination which emanated from outraged liberal and masonic sources so the PPI issued an official warning that if the ministry fell on that account the party would not give its support to another ministry. For a party that was now fairly clearly the only remaining cohesive force in the centre of the spectrum of Italian political life it was a difficult position to sustain. On the extreme left the communists gave credit to the PPI as having at least the benefit of a democratic base but rejected it otherwise as an element for good in the country.[25] The socialists rejected the possibility of any form of 'hybrid union' between themselves and the PPI while on the right of the parliament the fascists were beginning to regard the PPI as an enemy at least as potentially dangerous as the socialists. Finally the Rodinò affair meant that the old struggle between liberal Italy and Catholic Italy was renewed in an atmosphere rendered well-nigh unsupportable by the widespread violence between fascists and socialists, violence which was beginning to involve the PPI and the white unions more and more as the situation worsened.[26]

In 1921 a group of leading Popolari which included Sturzo, Meda and Cavazzoni gave serious consideration to establishing a formal link between the various political bodies in Europe that had their base in the Catholic masses. Together with De Rossi, Cavazzoni had travelled widely in France, Holland, Belgium and Germany in 1920 making contacts, and in September 1921 Sturzo and De Gasperi visited Germany where they held extensive talks with the leaders of the Centre Party and met Adenauer who was then mayor of Cologne. De Gasperi and Sturzo came back convinced that collaboration with the socialists was, at least in principle, a good thing although they could not see it happening as yet in Italy where they thought the socialist movement had not matured to the extent that it had in Germany. Meanwhile De Gasperi felt that it was the task of the PPI, by moderation and understanding of the difficulties within the socialist movement, to help it towards maturity on the question of collaboration.[27]

Stefano Cavazzoni was regarded as one of the most influential leaders of Italian Catholicism, especially at Milan where he had long been an intimate of high ecclesiastics who placed much weight on his opinions. He also thought that, if it served to resolve the crisis in which the country manifestly found itself, collaboration between the Popolari and the socialists would be a useful thing.[28] The other Catholic leader, Filippo Meda, agreed with the idea but the socialists were less ready to depart from their long stated opinions and, at least officially, stuck to their policy of intransigence. To the hardline socialists there was only one programme, the class struggle, and one form of collaboration — with the proletariat. In order to convey the message to the less astute readers of *Avanti* its cartoonist depicted collaboration as a socialist lamb going to the aid of a bourgeois wolf which ostentatiously carried a rosary in its paw. In so doing volumes were spoken about the difference between socialism in Italy and socialism in other parts of Europe. In Italy the movement had inherited the anti-clericalism that was part and parcel of political society there and the basis of the socialist refusal to collaborate was the fear that in essence the PPI was a clerical party.[29]

In the Vatican itself no such convictions regarding the essence of the PPI were entertained. The attitude of Cardinal Gasparri was made public when Ernesto Buonaiuti had an article published in *Il Messaggero*, Rome, and *Il Secolo*, Milan, on 29 September 1921. Buonaiuti saw Gasparri regularly and in the discussion which formed the basis of the article, the cardinal expressed grave doubts on the activity of the PPI and was especially outraged at the attempts to form a 'white international'. Gasparri insisted that it was the responsibility of the Vatican alone to act in such a delicate field, that Sturzo's visit to Germany was 'an absolute calamity' and that his activity had no standing whatever. He concluded by affirming that Catholicism itself was 'the true white international' and that, if it continued its activity, all would be lost because of the PPI. One other thought that the Secretary of State confided to Buonaiuti was his certainty that no solution to the Roman Question would come through the activity of such politicians as Giolitti and Bonomi but that 'We still await our man'.[30]

Yet, if there was clarity in the Secretariat of State on some issues, the day-to-day behaviour of the political parties in Italy itself tended to make the task in the Vatican of remaining detached from day-to-day reality very difficult. Temporarily at least the possibility of any socialist–PPI collaboration seemed unlikely before the elections so Dalla Torre in *Osservatore Romano* restricted himself to despairing of all the parties in the field given their manifest inability to create the 'Discipline and authority, freedom and justice' the country needed. When the fascists showed some of their real attitudes to the Church by dropping leaflets on Poggibonsi which warned the people against the 'blacks' who 'use the great Christian idea only for their earthly ambitions' the Vatican organ told those Catholic papers with filo-fascist tendencies 'to meditate on their enthusiasms' and later, when the fascists in Udine started to proclaim 'To the gallows with the priests', the paper deemed it sufficient to report the curiosity without comment. By July the fascists had destroyed the Catholic newspaper offices at Udine, Treviso and Verona; the pope had composed a prayer for peace; the fascists and the socialists made a truce and the Vatican denied that it had handed over to 'any political party the defence and the care of its own interests'.[31] The peace between the fascists and socialists was taken seriously only by the latter while the former divided their energies between assaults on socialists, Catholic youth, Catholic associations and the PPI.[32]

In this situation the Vatican was unsparing in its criticism of fascism but the endemic violence to which the Italian people had been subjected so constantly since the war from the extremes of both right and left had engendered its own weariness so that a sort of hopelessness crept into the oft repeated appeals for internal peace. One last hope seemed to remain in the ancient form of Christian charity and the response to the Vatican's appeal for the starving Russians, eliciting 500,000,000 lire in the space of a few months, indicated a concern for human misery of which the Italian Communist Party showed meagre understanding when it warned the Russians that to accept any help from that direction would be paid for by the end of the revolution.[33]

It was in vain that the Bonomi cabinet tried to grapple with the mounting problem of fascist violence. It lacked the decisive parliamentary support that was required and the fascists took advantage of its weakness. Even in the economic sector, where the crisis became more evident with the collapse of the Banca Italiana di Sconto, the government was again helpless and the so-called democratic group, another variant fruit of the tree of proportionalism, passed over to the opposition benches.[34] Meanwhile the two political forces in the country with any remaining credibility were engaged in the seemingly endless pastime of holding congresses. The socialists held theirs at Milan while the Popolari met at Venice, both in October 1921. Giacomo Matteotti pleaded with the socialists to moderate their attitude to collaboration with anti-fascist forces even if it meant becoming a minor part of the government. This plea went unheeded by the majority who remained unimpressed when he pointed out that 'Whole regions live under terror' who cried out 'concern yourselves with this, say something to us'. Modigliani preferred to attack the 'army of Don Sturzo' which he thought was going from strength to strength while the socialists quarrelled amongst themselves but the Congress ended with no clarity as to how the agreed upon class struggle was to be fostered, nor indeed how the less popular policy of no collaboration was to be rendered an effective weapon in relieving the working masses, subject in increasing numbers to fascist violence, from their misery.[35]

The PPI met in Venice and the Vatican wished them well and hoped they would concern themselves with the real needs of the nation such as economic, agrarian and educational reform. It was also hoped that they would face one particular problem in the shape of the administration of the ecclesiastical patrimony. This matter had been a cause of grave concern to the Vatican since Giolitti had proposed a reform in the system of taxation after the war which would have required all ecclesiastical property to be held in name rather than under the title of an organization. Such a law would have meant a huge blow to the Church in taxation because the senior members of the religious orders would be those involved as property owners and given their age they would be subject to frequent replacement with consequent death duties in each case. It was a prospect that Gasparri viewed with considerable trepidation and it was an area in which the Vatican thought some help could be expected from the Popolari if they were to lay any claim to being loyal sons of the Church.[36] Whatever about their thoughts on ecclesiastical property the Popolari met with a crucifix on the table, many priests were present, there were cries of 'Long live Italy', 'Long live the Pope' and 'Long live the White International' while Sturzo spoke of their mission 'to elevate moral and social values in the field of political life'.[37]

The main problem the party discussed was that of collaboration with the socialists and the majority of those who spoke on the question were in favour of it in one way or another although Cavazzoni thought it unwise to think of narrow limits to collaboration, a reference to the ideas of Ferrari and Miglioli who insisted upon the exclusion of any form of collaboration with the fascists.[38] Cavazzoni warned the delegates that 'one cannot foretell history which is often stronger than our will' and Mattei-Gentili agreed that it would have been unwise to close doors at the Congress to any eventual collaboration with the right as no one could tell how matters would develop. The example he gave of an unknown element was fascism.[39] To the socialists and indeed to many delegates at the Congress the question of collaboration with the left must have seemed academic. The socialists had declared themselves against collaboration and there was no indication that they would deviate from that policy. Nonetheless *L'Osservatore Romano* appeared troubled and asked whether those who proposed a Christian renewal could collaborate with those who proposed a materialistic one, while *Avanti* rejoiced that the Popolari had begun to realize the hopelessness of any proposals aimed at collaboration.[40]

In this atmosphere of narrow loyalties in which the progressive forces of the country stood aloof from each other and refused to come together even on a tactical level, the forces of the right found no difficulties in their path. The fascists were more and more aided by the Carabinieri in their brutal suppression of the socialists and the movement had begun to attract the support of large financial and industrial interests who saw in fascism the only bulwark against a socialist state.[41] It was clear to very few that, by late 1921, there was no longer any real danger to Italian democracy from the left. It was equally clear that the fascist movement, with its overtones of barbarism and lunacy, was seen only by a handful of Italians as a threat to democracy.

Given the fragile state of the parliamentary system it is understandable that some people, concerned with the country's welfare, began to turn to other sources for the exercise of power. Outside of parliament, the traditional centre of authority and responsibility was the commune and from his early years in Sicily Sturzo had remained true to his conviction that no progress would ever be made in the development of Italian democracy unless it was based on the local regions. Sturzo took the opportunity at Venice to speak for over an hour on the theme of the decentralization of power to autonomous local bodies.[42] He saw the region as an integral part of the state but with its own unity of 'language, history, customs and relationships' and he outlined a programme in which the region could be granted the autonomy necessary to achieve its own unique vocation as the integral factor in society.[43] Small wonder that many thought such idealism was utopian given the prevailing political situation but to the priest politician it was basic to his understanding of the total revitalization of the Italian state. He had a concept of politics that transcended the power struggle in which the country was then immersed and he looked to a future in which men might come to realize that true power implied human and individual responsibility.

There was one priest at Venice who took a practical view of the needs of the times and who found it intolerable that the party would contemplate collaboration with anyone unless at the price of agrarian reform. To cries of 'Long live Miglioli', Father Rughi, delegate of the farmers of Cremona, said that while the left wing could not win at the present Congress it would do so in the future and its task meanwhile was to get on with giving 'land to the farmers'. The communist organ, *Ordine Nuovo*, took Rughi seriously enough to quote him, saw the PPI as a 'solid, united and disciplined organism' from which the old confessionalism had well-nigh vanished, judged the Congress as another step on the way to the assumption of power by the party and then spoilt its attempt at objective analysis by running a cartoon depicting Sturzo leading the masses to power, symbolized by the sun to which he was pointing and saying 'Behold there is our God'. Giolitti made no attempt at objectivity. To him Sturzo was 'an intransigent little priest without any superior qualities whatever who nonetheless dominates Italian political life'. This opinion was shared by Mussolini who thought that the spectacle of this 'mediocre little Sicilian priest' meddling in 'low politics' instead of caring for souls was 'truly mortifying'.[44]

It was fittingly symbolic that the last word at the Venice Congress should be spoken by old Marchese Giovanni Battista Paganuzzi. Venice was the last Congress of the PPI before the advent of the fascist state while Paganuzzi could look back almost 50 years to the Congress of Venice in 1874 at which the *Opera* were begun. In those years great changes had come over the Catholic movement in Italy but they had not changed Paganuzzi. As his *valedictum* he hoped that the pope would be given the necessary freedom to carry out his exalted office. Paganuzzi could not foretell the price the PPI would have to pay for the achievement of that objective nor did he have to ask himself the question whether the price was too high. Convinced papalist to the last, he died before the next Congress of the party.[45]

A month later, amidst violence in which seven people were killed and over 100 wounded, the fascists held their Congress in Rome and decided to transform their movement into a political party. They made no attempt to formulate a policy, deeming it sufficient to base any approach to the pragmatic business of running a country on the speeches their leader had given in the previous two years.[46] One particular point in those speeches had not gone unnoticed in Catholic circles. When parliament opened in June 1921 the newly elected deputy, Benito Mussolini, took occasion to spell out his conviction that the universality of Catholicism was the central glory of Rome and that Italy would benefit if it gave financial help to the Church to build schools, hospitals and churches.[47] It was a far cry from the anti-Catholic, irreligious Mussolini of a decade earlier but, if it said little on his inner convictions regarding religion, it said a good deal about the development of his political maturity.

Mussolini had used 'beautiful words' Ernesto Pucci wrote and 'There was already in that discourse a great omen for the future'. Even the *Popolo Nuovo* thought his new responsibilities may have changed Mussolini in that, at the very least, he now represented a new element of the right which was a far cry from the old liberal right that had so much detested the Church. The *Osservatore Romano* still hoped publicly for a solution to the Roman Question and expressed pleasure that it was being discussed in the press and in parliament 'with serenity and with respect towards pontifical authority'.[48] Thus when Mussolini told his followers at the Congress that a fascist regime would give 'full freedom to the Catholic Church in the exercise of its spiritual ministry' and promised an end to the discord between the state and the Holy See, his words quickened a response in the hearts of many who had been accustomed to hearing very different sentiments from Italy's parliamentary leaders since 1870. As a contrast, when Sturzo was interviewed in Germany in September 1921 he was cool in his replies to reporters who asked his attitude to the Roman Question, even to the extent of not seeming to regard it as a problem at all, which made even more remarkable the stated desire of Mussolini, who hitherto had shown little but contempt for the Church, to solve a problem so dear to the papacy.[49]

While the Vatican was inclined to discard the PPI as a source of support for its aims on a temporal level in Italy it was also irritated at the effect the party was having on Catholic Action. The Popular Union was not proving as successful as had been hoped and Gasparri expressed the unhappiness of the pope at the idea prevalent in some circles that the Union was finished, 'consumed and transmuted into a special form of political action'. The cardinal warned that such would prove a fatal error for Catholic activity in the lay sphere because, while political forms were changing and transitory, Catholic Action would remain intact.[50] Dalla Torre visited Bergamo, famed centre of Catholic activity, where he expressed Benedict's wish that there be further development of the Union in the diocese but by the end of the year it was officially acknowledged that in many parishes it was neither known of nor appreciated. Numbers were generally dropping, it was feared that they would get worse and the two main causes for such a state were seen as the setting up of the PH and the development of economic organizations under the direction of the white unions.[51] In Rome Benedict again deplored the situation in which Catholic papers still refused to give adequate space to Catholic Action while in their pages 'politics, even the least solid forms of it — hold the camp without rival'.[52] It was Benedict's last lament for on 22 January, after a short illness, he died, still praying for the peace which had eluded him from the beginning of his days as pope.

If the Church was bereft of a leader it at least had the time-honoured security of ultimately being able to provide one. The Italian state enjoyed no such security and during the very conclave which met to elect a successor to Benedict the Italian government was going through another of its now customary crises. The entry of 35 fascists into parliament had done nothing to render the movement of violence they represented more constitutional despite the fact that seven or eight of the new deputies had gone to fascism from the ranks of Catholic Action.[53] In Rome itself the clashes between the fascists and the workers during the fascist Congress had alarmed everyone and while it was one thing for the communists to applaud the 'Magnificent resistance of the Roman workers against the fascist invasion', to call for a general strike and to reply 'None' to the question 'What is the use of Parliament?', it was another thing for Ivanoe Bonomi to try to lead the country to stability.[54]

Bonomi was still imbued with many of the principles of his socialist past but he could evoke no positive response in those who had been his erstwhile comrades. The socialists deplored 'The new barbarian invasion' of Rome and Matteotti went into the House where, with his customary meticulous attention to detail, he gave chapter and verse on fascist violence. A fascist deputy, Piccinato, using the personal form, said 'You keep on saying the same old thing' to which Matteotti replied with words that, though nobly spoken, were unlikely to evoke any civilized response in their recipient. 'I beg you not to use the personal form of speech with me because I do not intend to have relationships of any kind whatever with you.'[55] Meanwhile Italy was steeped in violence and Bonomi's Minister of Justice, the PPI deputy Giulio Rodinò, was unable to do anything to restore it to a state of tranquillity.

Sturzo was deeply concerned at the gravity of the crisis through which the country was passing. He found time on 7 December to attend the opening of the new Catholic University of Milan which was Father Gemelli's brainchild, but to which the party had given its support. At its opening the only anxious note was the lack of recognition by the state and in this, as in so much else, the eventual blessing of a benevolent government was longed for. At the official ceremony Sturzo sat with and spoke on the same programme as Cardinal Achille Ratti, the newly appointed archbishop of Milan.[56] It was the last meeting between two men in whose hands so much of the future of both Church and state in Italy was to rest in the next few years, but there is no record that they discussed other than pleasantries. Sturzo was back in Rome a couple of weeks later where he met Bonomi to discuss the question of public order generally and that of unemployment in the south, but with the gradual dwindling of his support in the House there was little Bonomi could do except mark time until he judged it opportune to proffer his resignation.

To Giolitti and his followers it seemed that Bonomi was rendered ineffectual because he was forced to dance to the dictates of Sturzo, 'thereby submitting to the impositions of a party that has no ideals either for the Fatherland or for the Church but in practical terms looks only for electoral success'.[57] If there were doubts in lay circles about Sturzo's loyalty they were also being expressed in Vatican circles with Prince Michele Pignatelli writing to tell Gasparri that Sturzo had allegedly said 'as Political Secretary of the Party I never allow nor will I ever consent to a useless discussion in the heart of my party on the theme of the reconciliation between Church and State'.[58] It is not possible to do other than surmise at the effect such reports evoked in the Vatican but it is certain that Father De Rosa, still editor of *Civiltà Cattolica* and a priest whom the party still regarded as a friend, attributed the increasingly negative attitude of the Vatican to the PPI to the continued reluctance of Sturzo to make the Roman Question central to his party's initiative. In this atmosphere of uncertainty

Sturzo addressed himself to the problem of the 'Crisis and Renewal of the State' at a gathering at Florence on 18 January 1922 to mark the third anniversary of the founding of the party.[59] As the acknowledged head of the party even by those who resented his leadership, Sturzo's words were listened to with widespread attention as it was common knowledge that the government was on the verge of collapse.

Given also that 1922 was the year in which Italian democracy passed into the shadows for more than a generation, it is necessary to examine Sturzo's speech in detail in order to know whether, as leader of a party which then, and later, was regarded as at least partly responsible for the abject surrender of the forces of democracy, he had either a grasp of the reality of the situation or a plan to obviate disaster. In a sense Sturzo seemed to share the preoccupation of many of his countrymen at Italy's manifest lack of leadership, but his understanding of the situation was much more profound than that of the weak, the unsure, the frightened who sought only the 'man' rather than a political grouping that would lead Italy out of the chaos. Sturzo said,

> a man with a political ideal, an economic aim, an organic plan, like the men who unified Italy after 1848, is not found amongst us today; we ask in vain for a clear vision of our home affairs and of our relations with other nations. Democracy today suffers from the atrophy that struck the men of the French monarchy before the revolution of '89, and yet there has never been a more decisive moment in Italian history than the present one. There has never been a graver and more difficult period in which we ought to be able to ask those who are responsible for the destiny of the nation: Watchman, what of the night? To that question there must be a sure, masterly and resolute answer.

Sturzo did not blame the Italian people — who were hard working, sensible and capable of great sacrifices when given the material means necessary to overcome a crisis. To him it was idle to talk only of an economic solution because to do so implied the prior possession of a political idea. In his opinion only the socialists and the Popolari had a viable political idea while those in power were motivated only by expediency, and they had thus sold the economic interests of the nation into the hands of alien forces. As for the overall direction of the country it had been surrendered into the hands of the bureaucracy which had become 'the true and real holder of power and administration' but because of the limited interest and vision of each sector of the bureaucratic structure no good of a lasting nature could come from it. Parliament had devoted itself to interminable, generic debates and to 'political games' in which the mantle of power had been passed to and fro amongst men who did not share the general conscience of the people. Giolitti was especially singled out by Sturzo as a leader in whom one sought in vain for 'a constructive thought'; he was a 'liquidator more than an animator' and although some hoped that he would still be the man to bring equilibrium to the country it was a hope Sturzo clearly did not share. The PPI had collaborated with liberal governments in the past, 'regrettably not always with benefit to our party and to our ideals'. In the future the party would seek its autonomy because without freedom there was no way in which it could preserve its integrity. Sturzo thought that, with the decline of the old liberal democratic forces, three ideas alone seemed to hold any appeal to the masses: socialism, popularism and fascism. Socialism had lost its revolutionary drive the day it had taken a role in parliament and its one hope lay in collaboration.

Sturzo had concluded that fascism was too young to have any tradition, it lived 'on rhetoric alternated with violence' and it harmed democracy more than it harmed socialism because all that was not violence, anarchy and subversion in it was superficial and exterior to its real essence. Before it the bourgeois state had proved impotent and Giolitti revealed its impotence with particular clarity. With fascism Giolitti had used his old method of 'intoxicating it by holding it close and caressing it'. The result was that he had become its prisoner after having given part of the state organism into its hands. Fascism could only continue to profit by the increasing impotence of the state while it would pose as the new source of 'social reconstruction' which it would seek to achieve by 'physical violence'. Popularism, which 'denies revolution, admits the constitutionality of the state but wants its organic reform from the centre to the periphery, from the town council to the senate', had also contributed to the crisis of the state precisely because of its profound desire for reform and its idealism which had acted as a catalyst in Italian society. In that reform Sturzo included proportionalism, women's vote, a senate elected on a restrictive franchise, reconstruction of the bureaucratic structure, and finally the decentralization of administrative functions. This last goal Sturzo saw as the most important because it would result in that 'moral, economic and organic freedom which is denied in the name of the pantheistic, administrative and centralist state'.

While Sturzo did not indicate a detailed programme of immediately desirable action to be undertaken by the state he did embark on a pungent, critical analysis of the economic situation in which he stressed the need for financial and political policies which eschewed any form of state socialism. Nonetheless it must be admitted that in the realm of practical policy his speech was an appeal and an emphasis on principle rather than an enunciation of practical steps to which, as a priest, he was forced to restrict his observations. In the morass into which Italy was falling perhaps little else could be expected than a sure signpost which would lead to firm ground. With his demand for the absolute refusal of any connivance with violence or subversion, his rejection of political alliances that time had proven useless, his emphasis on genuine economic reform and his appeal for a conscientious drive towards state reform, Sturzo had given a signpost. To what extent he would or even could be listened to was another matter.

When Bonomi resigned in early February 1922 the Popolari were dismayed and disgusted.[60] Rightly they saw the hand of Giolitti and his followers in the collapse of the government and, as a consequence, the determination of Sturzo and De Gasperi to refuse any further collaboration with them was strengthened. As they saw it Giolitti had been 'the exponent of the degeneration of political democracy in Italy', where he had used his power for the sole purpose of maintaining the strength of 'that vast clientele of persons and interests which until recently had propped up parliamentary life to the detriment of the wellbeing and real needs of the country'.[61] Giolitti endeavoured to have the Vatican intervene on his behalf and persuade Sturzo to lift his veto against him, but it was a vain attempt and one which the Vatican denied had ever taken place.[62] Ever since the imposition of the so called veto against Giolitti historians have expended much energy in examining the rights and wrongs of the matter. Nino Valeri, biographer of Giolitti, saw the veto as successful in 'blocking the attempt by the sole politician capable (perhaps) at that moment of making fascism return to legality'.[63] The force of that statement is the 'perhaps'. Giolitti had not been capable of achieving that objective in 1921 and there is nothing to indicate that he would have been more capable in 1922. But the point at issue is fundamental to an understanding of Sturzo and his ideal vision of the role of his party. To him Giolitti was a reactionary bourgeois opportunist whose day was done.[64] In his speech at Florence a fortnight before Sturzo had made it perfectly clear that Giolitti would not return to power with his approval and he had spelt out his reasons. When he acted on that decision one criticism only can be made of Sturzo which is more a judgement of Italian parliamentary life than it is of Sturzo. It was one thing to reject Giolitti but where in that parliament was there a viable alternative as leader of the country?[65]

In England the political joust at Rome was watched with interest and while the *Observer* thought the PPI was the crux of the parliamentary system *The Times* said that Sturzo, called 'Little Lenin' in Italy, was 'the strongest force in Italian politics' and the *Daily Mail* reported that 'after the Pope and the King Don Sturzo is the best known and most powerful man in Italy' and 'the invisible dictator of the House'.[66] It was an unenviable position for a man to be in with his country verging on collapse. The fact that he was a priest, subject still to ecclesiastical authority and unable to take an official parliamentary role in the crisis did not make either Sturzo's or the PPI's task any easier. His priesthood possibly made it easier for Sturzo to lead the PPI with its origins in Christian Democracy, but it made it impossible for him to lead Italy and what Italy so anxiously sought in early 1922 was a leader.

The search for a leader, in the parliamentary sense at least, was tortuous indeed. After De Nicola and Orlando failed to form a government Bonomi tried again unsuccessfully and Giolitti himself was thwarted at another attempt when Orlando and De Nicola refused to work with him. The King, 'judging him the most authoritative parliamentarian of the popolari group' asked Meda to try to form a government but Meda, without asking the opinion of the leaders of the party, refused to undertake the task perhaps because 'he was personally not against Giolitti'.[67] The refusal of Meda at such a critical moment rightly earned Sturzo's displeasure. The King did not ask Meda simply as a private member of the House although the Italian constitution gave no official recognition to political parties. He was asked because his candidature would have had, if actualized, the backing of a powerful group in the parliament and in the country at large. It was not simply a question of Meda's personal inclinations but also that of the country and of the party of which he was a member, a party he did not bother to consult regarding his decision and from which he ought to have had the decency to resign had he differed seriously from it on the veto to Giolitti. In the event of his proving unable to form a government his candidature would have clarified the air by showing exactly where the other parties, and in particular the nebulous groupings that coalesced around Giolitti, stood in relation to the PPI. As a result the PPI would have been relieved of much of the opprobrium cast upon it for its alleged refusal to collaborate with the liberal democratic forces in an attempt to ensure stability of government in 1922.

Most of the participants were wearied by the length if not the fatigues of the tournament by the end of February so that eventually a rag-bag government composed of liberals, followers of Giolitti, Salandra, Nitti, reformists and Popolari, was formed. It was led by Luigi Facta who was a friend of Giolitti and one of his foreign ministers. This was seen by Sturzo as the worst possible solution and he was personally unfavourable to the participation of the Popolari in the minority.[68] Later he regretted that a decision against Facta had not been made at the time as it could have resulted in a conflict between the party directorate and the parliamentary group, a conflict which was bound to arise eventually given the composition of the two groups. He also recognized, too late to draw any useful fruit from his knowledge that, during and to an extent because of the crisis of early 1922, the 'democrats' in parliament had moved to the right and the right was already fascist.[69]

From Milan a steady stream of correspondence flowed from the pen of Anna Kuliscioff to her beloved Filippo Turati at Rome. To her the Popolari were 'much better, a hundred times better' than the old liberal groupings under Giolitti. She was fed up with the reluctance of the socialists to collaborate and pleaded with Turati to get on and do it. The only party they could collaborate with was the PPI but far better for Italy to have that coalition in power than one between Giolitti and the fascists. In either case there would be civil war but Kuliscioff thought it would be less 'homicidal' to the mass of Italians if the socialists and the PPI were in office. Dismayed to hear that Facta had been given office she warned Turati that the fascists were preparing for a civil war, but her words were lost in that vortex of swelling ambitions, vain rivalries and ideological posturings that now passed for parliament.[70]

Notes

1. *Corriere d'Italia*, 20 December 1920.

2. Ibid., 1 January 1921. For other violence see *O.R.*, 4, 5 December 1921. Another event that had attracted attention was the killing of Father Angelico Galassi, who was murdered by the reds as he came out of a church door in the company of his elderly mother. See L. Bedeschi, *L 'Emilia amazza i preti* (Bologna, 1951), p. 7.

3. *Il Popolo Nuovo*, 2 January 1921.

4. *Corriere d'Italia*, 5, 25 January 1921. The quote comes from the letter of Livio Tovini, 18 January 1921. Tovini was an old guard conservative who supported Mussolini after 1922.

5. *O.R.*, 14, 15 January 1921.

6. *Avanti*, 1, 13 January 1921.

7. Ibid., 17, 20 January 1921. See also G. De Rosa, *I partiti politici in Italia* (Bergamo, 1972), pp. 117–3, for documentation on the Livorno Congress.

8. See F. Meda 'La Scissione socialista', in B. Malinverni (ed.), *Civitas*, pp. 89–93.

9. G. De Rosa, *Giolitti e il fascismo. In alcune sue lettere inedite* (Rome, 1957). Letter of 5 April 1923 to Camillo Corradini, p. 19.

10. I. Bonomi, *La politica italiana dopo Vittorio Veneto* (Turin, 1953), p. 161.

11. See N. Valeri, *Giovanni Giolitti*, pp. 307–19; G. De Rosa, *Il Partito*, pp. 80–97; I. Bonomi, *La politica*, p. 159. A. Lyttelton, *The Seizure of Power* (London, 1973), is a masterly analysis by an English scholar of the rise and consolidation of fascism in Italy. On the early period see chap. 3 in particular.

12. Although the occupation of Fiume between September 1919 and February 1921 ended satisfactorily for the Italian state, the example of unbalanced rhetoric, poetic nonsense and ritual verbalism such as 'Eia, eia, alala' and 'A noi' used by D'Annunzio attracted much attention, swayed the minds of impressionable young people and set a pattern for fascist ritualism. On this, see R. De Felice (ed.), *La penultima ventura* (Milan, 1974), passim.

13. *Avanti*, 1 and 5 February 1921; P. Alatri, *L 'antifascismo italiano*, 2 vols (Rome, 1961), vol. 1, pp. 85–98.

14. G. Marcucci-Fannelo, 'G. Miglioli e Il problema contadino', in *Storia e Politica*, 7th vol., part IV, pp. 672–3; R.A. Webster, *Christian Democracy in Italy 1860–1960* (London, 1961), pp. 70–71; A. Ossicini, 'Ricordo di Guido Miglioli. Un cristiano e il socialismo' in *Paese Sera*, 16 November 1974.

15. *Il Popolo Nuovo*, 4 January, 15 August 1920; 20 February, 6, 27 March, 10 April, 1 May 1921.

16. G. De Rosa, *Il Partito*, p. 96.

17. Giolitti referred to the 'bestial conduct' of the socialists and the PPI in a letter to C. Chiaravoglio republished in *Studi Cattolici*, February 1972, p. 123–4.

18. *O.R.*, February–May 1921, passim; *Il Popolo Nuovo*, 19 December 1920, 20 January, 6 February, 15, 22 May 1921.

19. See Bertone's policy speech in *Il Popolo Nuovo*, 1 May 1921. Bertone was probably favourably inclined towards a return of the Giolitti government. He had acted as a go between from Giolitti to Sturzo in 1920. See F. Malgeri, *Gli atti*, p. 670.

20. Apart from a fall in the number of days lost by strikes in 1921 it is difficult to see where Sturzo based his optimism. See S.B. Clough, *The Economic History*, pp. 202–10, for the more pessimistic view of an economic historian.

21. Sturzo's speech is found in *I discorsi*, pp. 75–106. It was given at the Augusteo, Rome, 2 May 1921, and repeated later at Turin and Milan.

22. *Il Popolo Nuovo*, 15 May 1921; *Ordine Nuovo*, 15 May 1921.

23. *Il Popolo Nuovo*, 22 May 1921; *Avanti*, 19 May 1921.

24. The communists called Bonomi, 'the traitor'. Bonomi had been expelled from the socialist party in 1912 at which time he was editor of *Avanti*. See *Ordine Nuovo*, 5 July 1921.

25. Ibid., 9 June 1921.

26. *Avanti*, 27 May 1921; A.C. Gaudenti, *Sturzo*, p. 47.

27. See A. Gammaldi 'Il Pensiero Politico di Alcide De Gasperi' unpublished doctoral thesis (Rome, 1972–3), pp. 26–7; *Corriere d'Italia*, 30 September 1921; M. Rumor, *Omaggio a Luigi Sturzo* (Rome, 1964), pp. 26–7.

28. L. Cavazzoni (ed.), *Stefano Cavazzoni* (Milan, 1955), p. 54.

29. *Corriere d'Italia*, 29 June 1921; *Avanti*, 27 May, 1 June, 3 September, 11 November 1921.

30. E. Buonaiuti, *Pellegrino di Roma* (Rome, 1945), pp. 199–204.

31. *O.R.*, 16, 27 February, 9 March, 22 April, 27 May, 15, 17, 22 July, 4, 5 August 1921.

32. Writing in Rome in June 1921 Mario Missiroli saw some hope in a socialist–fascist truce. He dreamt of a new democracy arising on the ashes of the old with fascism as its 'conscience' but he warned that, as fascism lacked a programme, it would have to reconcile itself with socialism or it would fail. M. Missiroli, *Il fascismo e la crisi italiana* (Bologna, 1921), p. 60.

33. *O.R.*, 20 November 1921; *Ordine Nuovo*, 10 August 1921.

34. The Banca Italiana di Sconto was formed in 1914 and grew enormously during the war. Its failure was an ominous blow to the economic sector. See S.B. Clough, *The Economic History*, pp. 205–6.

35. *Avanti*, 13, 15 October 1921; *Ordine Nuovo*, 13 October 1921, *Corriere d'Italia*, 13, 14, 15 October 1921. For fascist violence in Ferrara led by the local *ras* Italo Balbo, see the careful study by A. Roveri, *Le origini del fascismo a Ferrara: 1918–1921* (Milan, 1974). Roveri holds that it was its agrarian fascism that gave the movement its initial importance, not the personal leadership of Mussolini who simply went along with it (pp. 75–6).

36. E. Buonaiuti, *Pellegrino*, pp. 201 and 211.

37. *O.R.*, 21, 22 October 1921.

38. See *Il Popolo Nuovo*, 16 October 13 November 1921, for full reports of the Congress. Also G. De Rosa, *Il Partito*, pp. 114–20, and F. Malgeri (ed.), *Gli atti*, pp. 219–385.

39. *Corriere d'Italia*, 26 October 1921.

40. *O.R.*, 27 October 1921; *Avanti*, 20 25 October 1921; G. Petrocchi in *Collaborazionismo e ricostruzione Popolare* (Rome, 1923), pp. 111–31, deals at length with the Venice Congress and the question of collaboration with the socialists.

41. See P. Melograni, *Gli Industriali e Mussolini. Rapporti tra Confindustria e fascismo dal 1919 al 1929* (Milan, 1972), and G. Grilli, *Grande capitale, destra cattolica. Trent'anni di vita politica italiana* (Florence, 1959). Grilli gives a version of a song sung by the Carabinieri in which they asserted that they were fascists as well as Carabinieri and that it was their desire to arrest 'only the socialists', p. 466.

42. See L. Sturzo, *I discorsi*, pp. 143–79.

43. Ibid., p. 155.

44. *Ordine Nuovo*, 21, 24, 26 October 1921; F. Malgeri (ed.), *Gli atti*, pp. 267–78. Mussolini quoted in F. Meda, 'Luigi Sturzo' in B. Malinverni, *Civitas*, p. 461. Mussolini also warned that unless Sturzo stopped his activity Italy could witness an outburst of anti-clericalism compared to which the anti-clericalism of the past would appear to be 'a harmless game among children'. Ibid., p. 462.

45. Ibid., pp. 359, 367. In his own inimitable fashion Salvemini makes fun of this incident in his *Stato*, p. 237. I would prefer to believe that the young cynic who told Salvemini how the Popolari kept applauding Paganuzzi until he stopped speaking was not representative of the majority of delegates. Salvemini himself is constantly crude in his attack on the Roman Question — a crudity perhaps equalled only by the vigour with which some of its proponents upheld it.

46. See F.L. Ferrari, *Le Regime Fasciste Italien* (Paris, 1928), p. 49.

47. *Atti parlamentari. Camera, Discussioni 21 June 1921*, pp. 89–98 and E. Pucci, *La pace del Laterano* (Florence, 1929), pp. 67–8.

48. Ibid., *Il Popolo Nuovo*, 26 June 1921; *O.R.*, 2 September 1921.

49. See report of Sturzo's interview in *Corriere d'Italia*, 23 September 1921.

50. Gasparri to Bartolomeo Pietromarchi, 19 May 1921, in *O.R.*, 23 24 May, 1921.
51. See *Il movimento cattolico Bergamasco — 1913–1921* (Bergamo, 1921), p. 1–7.
52. *O.R.*, 1 January 1921.
53. Sturzo lamented this fact in July 1921. See F. Piva and F. Malgeri, *Vita*, p. 253.
54. *Ordine Nuovo*, 12 November–12 December 1921.
55. *Avanti*, 3 December and *Corriere d'Italia*, 4 December 1921.
56. See F. Magri, *L'Azione*, vol. 1, p. 556.
57. Rolando Ricci to Giolitti, 28 August 1921 in N. Valeri, *Giovanni Giolitti*, pp. 324. S. Ricci was the Italian ambassador to Washington.
58. Pignatelli to Gasparri, 11 January 1922, in F.M. Broglio, *Italia*, p. 99.
59. L. Sturzo, *I discorsi*, pp. 181–214.
60. *Il Popolo Nuovo*, 5 February 1922.
61. Ibid., 26 February, 5 March 1922.
62. See F.M. Broglio, *Italia*, pp. 84–5 and *O.R.*, 24, 27 8 February 1922.
63. N. Valeri, *Giovanni Giolitti*, p. 326. Mario Missiroli reprinted in *Una battaglia* two articles he wrote on 25, 28 February 1922 in which he defended Sturzo and the PPI vigorously. To him Sturzo had stood up for democracy in rejecting Giolitti and in any case the PPI had done no more than exercise its prerogative as a political party. See pp. 221–34.
64. See P. Alatri, *Le origini del fascismo*, 2nd edn (Novara, 1963), p. 1–17.
65. In the Sturzo Institute there is a copy of S. Jacini, *Il regime fascista* (Milan, 1947), which, by the notes on its pages was clearly read by Sturzo and in parts disagreed with. On p. 30 Jacini said that the main fault with the veto against Giolitti was that there was no alternative. Sturzo made no mark of disagreement with that.
66. *Observer*, 12 February, *The Times*, 3 March, *Daily Mail*, n.d. but early March 1922, quoted in *Il Popolo Nuovo*, 26 March 1922.
67. See G. Spataro, *I Democratici*, p. 41, and G. De Rosa, *Il Partito*, pp. 1–10.
68. Sturzo's solution to the crisis was one that was truly parliamentary but under the circumstances scarcely practical. He thought that the new leader ought to be chosen by the House itself and that once elected he would have the right to select his ministers. In both cases the King would be called upon to do no more than express his formal approval. See F.L. Ferrari, *Le Regime*, p. 41.
69. See L. Sturzo, *Popolarismo e fascismo*, pp. 50, 51.
70. F. Turati and A. Kuliscioff, *Carteggio*, A. Schiavi (ed.), vol. 5, *Dopoguerra e fascismo* (Turin, 1952), letters of 19 January, 23, 24 February, 7, 13 March 1922, pp. 534–70.

5

THE SEARCH FOR A LEADER

Benedict XV was elected in 1914 and died in 1922 at the age of 67. With judgements such as 'Cold, mediocre, obstinate' and 'Tomorrow history will have already forgotten him' the left-wing press in Italy dismissed his memory.[1] Together with Sturzo he was regarded as the 'creator of the Partito Popolare' and it was confidently asserted that Sturzo would 'attempt to be one of the great electors of the new pope by means of a cardinal friend'.[2] It was also claimed that the new pope would make or break the PPI, although the communists, on the grounds that 'the sons have become stronger than the mother' were convinced that the PPI now had an independent life of its own and thus a changed papacy would not affect it.[3] No one can tell what effect any of this had on the cardinals as they entered the Conclave. One thing however is certain. They knew that matters had reached a critical stage in Italian affairs for that very day, 3 February 1922, the Bonomi government fell.

The dominant personality at the Conclave was 'the great weaver' of Vatican politics, Pietro Gasparri.[4] The Secretary of State knew that the position of the Church in Italy was fraught with difficulty given the appalling instability of the country and the state of economic chaos to which Vatican finances had been reduced. The least that could be done was to ensure the election of a strong pope with some experience of Italian and international affairs and Gasparri knew the very man, Achille Ratti, a priest of humble origins. For seven years prior to 1918 Ratti had been Vatican librarian and, during those years, Gasparri had learnt that behind that unassuming visage there was a quick mind and a determined will. With Gasparri to back him, Ratti had become an ecclesiastical diplomat in 1918 with a difficult posting in Warsaw as his task. Within three years he went from librarian to cardinal archbishop of Milan, the chief see in Italy, apart from Rome.

Gasparri put in some earnest work during the Conclave so that on the fourth day Ratti, who had only gained two votes in the first ballot, was elected with 42 votes.[5] It was 6 February 1922 and the *Osservatore Romano* ran the banner headline *Habemus Papam*. As pope he took the name Pius, the eleventh of the line. He blessed the crowds from the Loggia and he confirmed Gasparri as secretary of state, which was an unusual departure from normal practice.[6] One of those who had followed the election with interest and had stood with the crowds awaiting the white smoke from the Sistine was Benito Mussolini who wondered aloud to his companions Giacomo Acerbo and Caleazzo Ciano how anyone could fail to be impressed by the power of the Church and the grandeur of it all.[7]

Pius became pope at the age of 65 and since the day in 1867 when, aged 10, he had entered the seminary, his whole life had centred on the Church.[8] After completing his studies in Rome he returned to Milan in 1882 and spent a few months as a parish priest. These months were his first and last contact with the people in a direct pastoral ministry because, for the next 30 years, books were his life, first in the seminary at Milan where he taught and later when he became prefect of the great Ambrosian library there and published articles in the field of medieval history.[9] Although he experienced something of the new spirit of Christian Democracy through contact with Filippo Meda and Stefano Jacini at Milan the events that most directly influenced his papacy took place when he was sent as papal representative to Poland in 1918.

He arrived in Warsaw when Poland was being invaded by Soviet troops and he was present there in August 1920 when they attacked the city and were repulsed. If that was a day he always rejoiced in, the armistice between Russia and Poland of 18 March 1921 was one he grieved over because it left 3,500,000 Latin Catholics in Soviet hands. As papal nuncio in Poland his post included large parts of Eastern Europe which gave him a specialized knowledge of the USSR. He is said to have come to the conclusion that atheism was at the basis of the Soviet system, the scope of which was not simply economic reform but 'the transformation of men on the atheistic model'. This system Moscow 'hoped to impose on the whole world' and that conviction Pius always tried to share with others as pope.[10] When he returned to Milan as archbishop on 8 September 1921 Ratti began to share his other great conviction with his hearers. To him Rome was 'truly the capital of the world' because it was the pope's city and if Italians did not yet realize that fact it would dawn on them. It was necessary only for an Italian to go out of Italy to discover that Catholics elsewhere were convinced of it.[11] According to Mussolini, who expressed delight at his election, the five months spent by Ratti as archbishop were long enough for the Milanese fascists to establish cordial relations with him. On the occasion of a ceremony in honour of the Unknown Soldier he had allowed them to come into the Duomo brandishing their fascist pennants.[12]

The new pope was welcomed by the PPI; pleasure was expressed at the confirmation of Gasparri and the party directorate turned its mind to the problem of collaboration with the socialists.[13] Although Filippo Turati spoke without authority he had expressed himself in favour of 'a programmatic and tactical pact' between the socialists and the Popolari. He recognized that their differing attitude to the teaching of religion in the primary schools was an obstacle, but he thought it could be resolved by the Popolari acknowledging that the more important aspect of the educational problem was the lack of schools as such.[14] To this the Popolari replied that Italy was bound to commence its reconstruction from the school with the 'spiritual renewal of the Nation' as its first task. Writing in *Corriere d'Italia* Paolo Mattei-

Gentili tried to urge prudence in the matter. To him collaboration with the socialists was too important to be rushed into simply because of the pressure of fascist violence, but to others the question was not quite so academic. A socialist deputy, Lino Ziocchi, said in the House on 16 March that the masses who voted for the socialists were looking to an alliance with the Popolari because such was their last resort given the impotence of the government to restrain the fascists.[15]

The past violence of rabid socialists in north Italy, so often directed against Catholics and Catholic associations, was hard to forget, but it is equally clear that there was no threat from that quarter to Catholics in March 1922. Furthermore it is even clearer that the prime source of violence, repeated *ad nauseum* daily and directed mainly against the workers and their associations, emanated from the fascist squads. In fact Sturzo himself had been the target for a fascist assault at Venice in March 1922 and it was only by good fortune that he escaped while Giuseppe Spataro had been beaten up in September 1921 and there were constant assaults against Catholic groups in early 1922.[16] In that context it is almost impossible to understand the attitude of the two leaders of Milanese Catholicism, Meda and Cavazzoni, who refused to vote for a motion in the House which condemned fascist violence. Meda said the PPI was against all violence and would accordingly vote only for a less specific motion while Cavazzoni insisted that the 'red violence of the past be remembered'. There were cries of 'Jesuits', 'Hypocrites' and 'Go with the fascists' and when the vote was taken in a depleted House of 254 members the PPI deputies abstained and, out of 154 votes, there were 82 for and 72 against. Giolitti voted against the motion and Matteotti said 'for the first time in your life you are sincere'.[17] To those who watched the proceedings in the House on those fateful days when the parliament itself was still free to condemn fascism, the responses of the PPI spoke volumes. The socialist deputy Modigliani, said that the abstention of the Popolari removed one further 'equivocation' while the communists thought it unmasked the apparent anti-fascism of the parliamentary heads of the PPI and gave further strength to their own conviction that the only course was that of the 'direct action of the masses'.[18]

By the middle of 1922 it was apparent to those who were concerned about Italy's future that the state was in crisis and even many Catholic bishops who visited Rome in that period warned Pius XI that, in their opinion, the country was on the verge of a civil war.[19] By July, 8,000,000 were out of work, fascism was 'causing the streets of the Fatherland to run with blood' and Mussolini's judgement that the only hope for Italy was a military dictatorship was shared by so many that Bonomi wrote with justice that it was all very well to criticize the parliament of 1922 'in a country that looked with sympathy at the armed men who were preparing to abolish it'[20] Turati still hoped to be able to collaborate with 'the better part of capitalism' in order to build a socialist future; Gramsci was theorizing on the necessary role of the Popolari in 'the development of the Italian proletariat towards communism'; the new daily paper of the unitarian socialists, *La Giustizia*, was sure the Vatican would not block 'an agreement between the socialists and the popolari' but the leader of the left wing of the socialist party, called the maximalists, Giacinto Serrati, still insisted 'Always alone against everyone else' and collaboration foundered in a welter of words and heart searchings amongst men of principle, while the armed bands thrived in the air of general malaise that spread down from the highest levels of the government.[21] It was perhaps inevitable, but nonetheless tragic, that at that moment the Facta government fell.

It was difficult for the Popolari to disassociate themselves from the prevailing air of dissatisfaction with the government, even though they knew that, as in February it had been fruitless to accept Facta, now it was equally fruitless to reject him in July. Sturzo knew that there was no viable alternative to Facta while the socialists remained committed to intransigence, but he was unable to have his view prevail as indeed he had been unable to prevent Facta's initial rise to power in

February.[22] On the other side Turati watched while the unitarians and maximalists continued their bitter feud as to the path to choose and with the tones of a biblical prophet the old socialist told the parliament

> It is not simply a matter of the fall of a Government, nor even that of a regime, but of an entire civilization. That is why this is a decisive hour. At this moment it is a question of deciding whether Italy will continue to be a civilized nation or whether it will return to barbarism.[23]

With the fall of Facta the stage was set for a fascist takeover and it is necessary to ask why it was possible for it to be so rapid and complete in its bid for power. Some contemporary Italians insisted that only something that was specifically apposite to the Italian situation could have produced fascism as its result. Francesco Luigi Ferrari probably expressed this view most bluntly when he wrote in 1929 that there was no genuine democracy in Italy before the advent of fascism because neither the monarchy nor the parliament fitted any known pattern of an operative democracy, nor was there any democratic spirit in the people who had never been involved in the work of Italian unification. As a result the fascists dared and attempted to do in 1922 what the left could probably have done in 1919 and 1920 at one stroke. All they had to do was to overthrow the cardboard institutions of a democracy which really never existed.[24] While it is the prerogative of Italians to judge harshly their own house it is sometimes possible for the stranger to throw another light on a situation in which emotionally he is not so involved. It is perhaps in the person of Luigi Facta that some explanation can be discerned for the rapid success of fascism in Italy.

Emilio Lussu was a member of the parliamentary commission that reported to Facta on the extent of fascist violence in the summer of 1922. Lussu painted the picture of Facta as a semi-imbecilic figure who reacted as if he was being told of births rather than of deaths. Smiling, Facta said, 'I cherish the hope that things will get better soon ...' As a result, Facta's nickname became 'I cherish the hope'.[25] In a sense Facta seems to have embodied some characteristics of the Italian people that can only be considered weaknesses when taken in isolation and exaggerated beyond their importance. Long centuries of economic dependence, with the ever present hope that, either through the beneficent action of an overlord or the fruitful product of a rich harvest, things would get better had bred a sense of hopeful expectance in the Italian peasantry. This confidence the Church had reinforced with the constantly recurring theme of hope as expressed in her liturgy and feasts. How many Italians really believed in August 1922 that Mussolini was a dangerous, brutal megalomaniac who would end in destroying his country and its pride in itself'? Who believed that the marauding bands of fascists largely made up of thugs, adventurers and otherwise idle youth would prove to be such an alien element in a placid, decent and industrious society? Who believed that once in power it would be impossible to absorb the fascist phenomenon into the body politic and render it another, different but docile element of the democratic spectrum? Finally, who believed that the summer of 1922 would not be just another of those moments of temporary depression after which nerves frayed by heat would relax again in a mild and pleasant autumn in which all things, including even the economy, would take a turn for the better?

Turati perhaps knew the truth but he was rendered impotent by the high minded socialist theoreticians who surrounded him. If the communists knew it they accepted it as a stage in the emancipation of the proletariat and hence did nothing to prevent it. Sturzo and the Popolari clearly believed that only through the due processes of the democratic state would it be possible to work out a solution. The liberals and the so-called democrats were incapable of sensing the urgency of the moment while the King thought only of the retention of his throne. It was not that Italy lacked democracy — a force and a spirit that is always in the making. It was simply that the Italians failed to judge the moment, the man and his movement in that intricate complex of converging factors that brought fascism to power. If Facta lived in the hope of a better tomorrow, so also did the vast majority of Italians to whom another government crisis was of little consequence. The important things were to get in the harvest, save something if possible for a few days rest in mid August and generally get by until things changed for the better.

The crisis of July 1922 was the closest to which the PPI came to forming a government, but it was an attempt that failed when perhaps a strongly knit party under the leadership of a man of standing and firmness of character could have led Italy along the path of democracy. The unique and acknowledged leader of the party was undoubtedly Sturzo, but Sturzo either by his own choice or by his compliance with an order from the Vatican was unable to step forward. The alternative was Filippo Meda who was called by the King when it became apparent that neither Orlando nor Bonomi were able to form a government. Sturzo sent him a telegram at Milan asking him to 'sacrifice himself and form a government'.[26] Meda came to Rome and met the King on the morning of 27 July at the Quirinale. He went straight to the meeting without consulting either Sturzo or any of the members of the party directorate as if he was uneasy about being subjected to persuasion in his decision. The Milanese lawyer gave the King one reason only for his 'great refusal'. He declared that to become prime minister was to accept an office that was 'incompatible with the exercise of his profession'. Later he admitted that the threats of the fascists who were demanding a role in government made him, and others, little disposed to undertake a task requiring 'initiative and sacrifice'. Meda repaired to his hotel, removed his 'stiffelius' and took the train to Milan.

Sturzo, aware of the meeting with the King, despatched Spataro to the Minerva, Meda's hotel, to tell him that if he had refused the offer he was to return to the Quirinale and inform the King that the PPI was prepared to assume government with another leader. It was too late given that Meda had already left the city.[27] Although the King was able to express his understanding and appreciation of Meda's refusal, even to the extent of thinking his motive did him honour, Meda's friends in the PPI were never able to comprehend him and they later saw his refusal as the last occasion Italian democracy was offered to avoid the coming of fascism.[28] Perhaps in the Vatican Meda was better understood for the only comment was that his refusal was 'generally expected' and in the atmosphere engendered by Mussolini with his now open policy of warnings and blandishments to the Church it was perhaps a relief that Meda had not offered to lead an anti-fascist government.[29] To Mussolini the PPI was neither a Catholic nor a Christian party but one 'dangerous to the interests of religion and faithless to those of the fatherland'. Sturzo was worse again in the judgement of Mussolini who warned,

> There are two popes in Italy: the first, don Sturzo, has the care of the flesh, the second, Pius XI has the care of souls. Isn't it possible that don Sturzo is the antipope and an instrument of Satan?... Grave tempests will arise on the horizon of the Church if the PPI continues ... its materialistic, tyrannical and antichristian politics.[30]

As early as January 1922 a veritable campaign had been mounted in the Catholic press against the PPI on the grounds that it was no substitute for Catholic Action.[31] In June, a kind of counter party to the PPI was founded by Marquis Cornaggia Medici who was a Catholic conservative from Milan and a friend of long standing of Pius XI. He called it the Italian Constitutional Union and he claimed that the pope knew and approved of his ideas and initiative. The Union failed, however, to attract a following and quickly withered away but it is significant that *Osservatore Romano*, in contrast to its repeated disclaimer of any Vatican connection with the PPI, made no such statement in regard to Cornaggia Medici's Union.[32] Even to the uninitiated it was apparent that there was a hardening of resolve in the Vatican since the election of Pius XI and although it was still only obliquely directed against the PPI with such things as the republication of Cardinal Boggiani's attack of July 1920 it was beginning to seem that there were grounds for unity between the Vatican and Mussolini in regard to Sturzo's party.[33] In August Mussolini wrote 'we are now confronted with a party that is infected with socialism and is therefore both anti-Catholic and anti-Christian'.[34] Pius XI, Gasparri and Dalla Torre would not have gone that far as yet but the continued talk of the possibility of collaboration between the PPI and the socialists was anathema to a pope who regarded socialism with horror.

Meanwhile the task of forming Italy's 65th cabinet since 1848 was exacerbated by the attitude of Giolitti whose power was still immense given the following he held intact in parliament. Giolitti had not forgiven Sturzo for his veto in January, even though he probably looked to the Vatican as its source, and he viewed with contempt any move to set up a coalition between the Popolari and the socialists which he referred to as a 'Don Sturzo–Treves–Turati marriage'. As far as he was concerned the Popolari were responsible for the situation that had arisen and he was determined to remain aloof from any attempt to form a government himself, fearful perhaps that he would meet another Sturzo veto. Giolitti was convinced that any government which had as its main purpose the containment of fascism would plunge the country into civil war and from that situation he thanked God that he was removed personally.[35] Given Giolitti's 'veto' against any government that would deal decisively with the fascists any further attempt to form a centre-left coalition was out of the question. All that remained was extra-parliamentary action and the socialists chose that moment to call a General Strike.

Filippo Turati had done his best to bring some semblance of sanity into the political situation. He had met with Sturzo, he had visited the King, he had considered the possibility of taking a portfolio in a coalition, anti-fascist cabinet and it had all come to nothing except to prompt derision of his actions by Giolitti and by the communists and maximalists.[36] He can hardly be blamed if he concurred when the time worn weapon of the strike was put forward, even though he knew that the communists and maximalists would see it as a revolutionary rather than a constitutional and legal act.[37] It proved an utterly futile weapon in that the workers' movement was disorganized, the people were weary of disorder and the fascists were strong. It was all over in two days and Turati and later, Nenni, admitted a complete and total defeat.[38] The fascists had judged the strike as an attempt to ensure a left government and, while asking his own railway, port and telegraph men to work, Mussolini had threatened 'to take the place of the State' if the strike were not over in 48 hours.[39] In the Vatican the situation was judged with a detachment and clarity scarcely possible to the men involved in the rough and tumble of political action. A commentator in *Osservatore Romano* lamented that with one stroke the fascists had been enabled to make up all the ground they had lost in popular esteem on account of their violence and, as a result of the strike, they were now in a position to claim that they were the true defenders of the people and the nation.[40] One other observer of the scene seems to have remained impassive. The King, having shuffled and played the gamut of Italy's political leaders, laid down the final ace in that last game over which he would have any control for the remainder of his reign. The card in question was called Facta and, full of confidence as always, poor Luigi came back to power after two weeks of rest. He had not had much time to ponder on any useful changes in his cabinet so the old hands were all there ranging from Popolari to fascist sympathizers with a core of liberals, democrats and mere functionaries in the centre. The second Facta government showed as little likelihood of being able to deal with the situation as the first. Above all the government was incapable of restraining the surge to power of Mussolini.

The abundant historical texts that deal with the final few weeks of Italian democracy starkly reveal the apparently hopeless nature of the situation. Yet it is just to point out that all the factors were still present that could have given rise to a democratic solution. The Parliament was weak but it still retained the freedom to act, the army in the main was loyal, while the same could be said of the police. The apparatus of the state remained in the greater part under the control of government, the judiciary was intact at all its important levels and the economy was by no means bankrupt. No external forces were bringing pressure to bear to cause a collapse and no serious commentators prophesied a quick end to Italian democracy.[41] One thing seemed to be lacking in the nation and it was the very thing that had plagued Italy since her constitutional unification. There was a lack of unity of purpose resulting in an individual pursuit of conflicting aims which rendered sterile any attempt to weld the nation into its expression as a political body that could resist the attack of an aggressor.

It was Italy's desperate fate to be in such a position at the moment when she numbered amongst her citizens one who proclaimed himself capable of giving her unity of purpose, pride of nationhood and direction for the future. That his purpose and direction were less than clear, that his concept of nationhood was primitive and violent seemed to matter little. No one could then clearly foresee the agony into which he would ultimately plunge Italy.[42] No one could dream of the chords his example would strike in the diseased mind of a teutonic monster. No one could look down the dark tunnel that would lead to a maelstrom of horror for Europe and the world, a tunnel into which Western Europe stepped when one of its ancient nations, Italy, bowed to the dictator in October 1922. The only thing that seemed to matter at that moment was that the strong man promised a better future. So few asked to see his credentials because in their hearts they perhaps knew he had none.[43]

If it is necessary to introduce Benito Mussolini in this narrative it is because his period as dictator and his fall from power have clouded his formative years. The 'Duce' transcended the man who was already 39 years old in 1922 and the myth that has given place to the man since his death has obscured the factors that made him. It is a curious fact that in Italian journalism and political commentary before 1922 there is surprisingly little material that gives any insight into Mussolini, and once he came to power it was as if his past had never been. He became the man of the moment. Here and there his name crops up prior to 1920 as, for example, the bitter, derisive account of him by 'Ariel' in *Il Popolo Nuovo* where he was said to have a frightening face and a voice which, rather than speaking, exploded like a pistol shot. The question was asked 'What terrible physiological catastrophe has contaminated this soul?', and the prophecy was made that tomorrow, if he could, he would be a 'cruel tyrant', a 'pocket edition of Nero'.[44] But such descriptions are far from giving any real insight and it has been left to modern historians to grapple with the problem of Mussolini the man.[45] In his bid for absolute power Mussolini more than once called Sturzo his number one enemy, which indicates that whatever else, he neither underestimated Sturzo nor ignored him. In his public writings Sturzo chose to reject any serious analysis of Mussolini which perhaps indicated that, like the vast majority of Italians, he disregarded the man as an unimportant and transitory phenomenon.

Benito Mussolini was born on 29 July 1883 at Predappio, a small town in the Romagna between Bologna and the Adriatic Sea. His socialist father named him after Benito Jaurez, executioner of Emperor Maximilian of Mexico. His mother was a teacher who had to work hard to keep the family in the frugalities of life as his father, a blacksmith, was often without work. In the family atmosphere Benito picked up from his father the first elements of revolutionary socialism tinged with bitter anti-clericalism, while his mother did her best to make him a Catholic Christian. At school he learnt rapidly and easily, at play he was violent and provocative, personally he loved animals and music. After two years in Switzerland, 1902–4, acting as a socialist agitator and manual worker he was expelled, returned and was expelled again, so he decided to do his military service. At this time he proclaimed himself a 'true heretic' and there is no evidence to suggest that he had any other interest in religion apart from his constant propensity to attack and, when it suited his purposes, manipulate it.

After his military service in 1905–6 he turned to the life of political agitator earning three-months solitary confinement in 1908 which he managed to avoid serving. In the following year he went to Trento as editor of *L'Avvenire*, engaged in violent polemics with Alcide De Gasperi and after six months was expelled again. He came back to Forli and lived with Rachele Guidi by whom he had a daughter, Edda, in 1910. In 1915, a month after the birth of his son to Ida Dalser whom he had known from his days in Trento, he married Rachele in a civil ceremony. Meanwhile he became the acknowledged leader of the socialist party in and about Forli, edited its paper, proclaimed himself a revolutionary, anti-masonic and anti-parliament and served a five-and-a-half months' prison sentence in late 1911–early 1912, for his political activities. In the party he was both 'loved and esteemed' as a 'man of character and incorruptibility' and was looked upon by all as its local inspirational figure.

He came to national prominence at Reggio Emilia in 1912 when, at the socialist conference in July, he moved the motion leading to the expulsion of Bissolati and Bonomi as 'reformists' and Lenin praised the conference for choosing the 'correct path'. His clear-sighted grasp of the exigencies of revolutionary socialism led to his appointment as editor of *Avanti*, the socialist national daily based in Milan. To the paper he gave a startlingly violent and intransigent form but meanwhile he built the circulation rapidly from 35,000 to 60,000 in less than two years. As the war clouds gathered he stuck to the party line of absolute neutralism but by October 1914 he had become an equally convinced interventionist. He left *Avanti* and with French government and local industrialist funds, founded *Popolo d'Italia* on 15 November 1914 which, together with his warmongering, earned him his expulsion from the socialist party that nonetheless mourned the passing of such a capable leader.

From December 1915 to February 1917 Mussolini served with courage and initiative in the Italian army, rose to the rank of corporal and was severely wounded. The defeat of Italian Arms at Caporetto at the end of 1917 grieved him deeply, so deeply that Renzo De Felice, his biographer, traces to it his loss of belief in socialism and the seeds of his fascist ideas. He now believed parliament was an utterly useless facade, democracy a failure and the road to the future lay under the direction of a dictatorship. These ideas he propagated in *Popolo d'Italia* and on 23 March 1919 he founded, at Milan, the *Fasci di Combattimento*. Of the 50 or so who joined Mussolini on that Sunday most were former shock troops of the Italian army, but the new movement was of the right, anti-democratic and initially elitist. It looked to the farming, commercial and industrial bourgeoisie for support and quickly found it, especially in the north.

Mussolini wrote in his paper on 18 March 1919 'We want the material and spiritual elevation of Italian citizens ... and the greatness of our people in the world'. These were the very sentiments that had captured so many Italians in the crazed beauty of D'Annunzian rhetoric but with Mussolini the aberrant idea clothed itself in the movement and with him also there was the sense of destiny. Mussolini seemed to say that, with him, something would happen to Italy and her people. Even in his personal qualities he seemed to encapsulate ideals held precious by many but possessed by so few. An acute contemporary observer, Giovanni Gasti, Inspector General of the Security Service, gave a summary of the fascist leader.[46] Mussolini was very strong physically, working from noon to 3 a.m. daily and was abstemious in food and drink. He was sensual, emotive, impulsive, sentimental, prodigal, intelligent, courageous and audacious. He had the ability to make friends and enemies with equal facility, and those in the latter category had cause to know it. However, his main characteristic was ambition. He always wanted to lead and dominate and especially when he found himself at the head of what he considered a new force in

Italy. Gasti added that he believed in Mussolini's patriotism although he admitted he was very prone to rapid changes.

From the start the fascist movement was anti-bolshevist and quickly assumed the role of implacable adversary of the socialists with its own reprisals of sackings, burnings, assaults and murder in response to those of the socialists. Mussolini was not fascism, despite Churchill's assertion that he was, but to it he gave the qualities of violent and dedicated leadership that it needed. He was the embodiment of its alleged nationalism in a situation in which many Italians were longing to see the country recognized as an important European power. He threw off his garb of anti-clericalism and taught his followers that the Church was a major factor in Italian life. He even proclaimed his loyalty to the formerly despised monarchy, he made contacts with the big financial and political forces of old liberal Italy and he stood for and won a seat in the parliament he had once regarded with contempt. His movement grew apace with 20,000 members in 1919, 250,000 in 1921 and 300,000 in 1922. Arrayed behind its 'Duce' it aimed to take control of the Italian state. In its path stood a weakling king, an optimistic prime minister, a divided parliament, and 'a government that doesn't know how to live and doesn't want to die'.[47]

By early August 1922 Mussolini was prompted to remark that the 'march on Rome has started' with the claim that the fascists controlled the Adriatic, the Tyrrhenian coasts and the valley of the Tiber.[48] It was no idle boast although the already well-established tactic of confusing the public by threats was as much behind his rhetoric as any firm decision to proceed with the march at that time. But unrest was widespread with constant murders and wounding of innocents as well as the destruction of buildings. Pius XI was sufficiently concerned with the situation to compose a letter to the bishops of Italy in which he deplored the 'war of fratricide' in the nation, indicated that a return to God was the only solution and requested the bishops to continue their 'work of pacification'.[49] On 11 August the Parliament rose to take its summer recess and while the editor of *Corriere d'Italia* had an unshakeable faith in a rosy future, the editor of *Civiltà Cattolica* was not so sure. It was to be many years before the prestigious Jesuit publication again took a firm stand on fascism but it then said that it 'has the violent spirit of socialism, not only imitating it but even surpassing it with its bullying, killings and barbarities'. The conclusion was that Catholics could not approve of or help fascism any more than they could help socialism 'since one and the other are opposed to the most elemental principles of christianity'.[50] It was a singularly unfortunate position into which Catholics were thus forced by the logic of the Jesuits because to refuse to work with the socialists was to ensure a fascist victory.

Despite the fact that no concrete steps had been taken towards collaboration between the Socialists and the Popolari, Catholic fears on the question were raised in a letter which Count Santucci drew up and which seven other PPI senators signed and addressed to Sturzo. The letter bore the date 18 September 1922 and its publication caused a good deal of comment.[51] The PPI in its official paper *Il Popolo Nuovo* played the incident down, but the left-wing press saw it as the desperate cry of the right-wing, financially strong elements in the PPI, for a hardening of the anti-socialist line and a shift to the right. The letter clearly rejected any possibility of an alliance with forces that denied God, the nation and the family which, in the emotive language of the period, summed up socialism. Essentially the purpose of its backers was to obstruct any action of the party that may have resulted in the creation of an effective antifascist force and, although *La Giustizia* and *Ordine Nuovo* saw the power of the Banco di Roma behind it with its president, Santucci, its vice president, Grosoli, and Nava, the president of the Banco Ambrosiano, an affiliate of the Banco di Roma, as three of its motivators, the issue was a wider one.[52] The conservative elements of the PPI were unchanged in their adhesion to the old form of the liberal, capitalist state despite their well-intentioned but, for the PPI, fatal adhesion to the party. To them, change in the social order was acceptable provided it meant no threat was aimed at good order, stability and the rights of big business. Above all they were concerned to see the rectification of those issues over which the liberal state and the Church had differed, such as religious education in the primary schools and the all-important Roman Question. That the Banco di Roma was a leading issue to the Catholic conservatives given its threatened stability is undoubted. Nonetheless the question went deeper. Socialism, despite its fissurization, remained the declared enemy while Mussolini and his fascists had indicated their willingness not only to shore up the old bourgeois class, but also to look with favour on the Church in Italy, and it is not surprising that *Corriere d'Italia*, increasingly the voice of conservatism in the PPI, agreed wholeheartedly with the letter of the right-wing senators.[53]

In the Vatican itself even Pius XI had begun to think of Mussolini with feelings of hope and shared the view now widely held in high clerical circles that nothing could be expected from the government of Italy as it then stood.[54] The youth wing of Catholic Action met for a Congress at Rome in early September 1922 and in their elections the democratic, pro PPI elements which were explicitly called 'anti-fascist' won against the conservative forces led by Egilberto Martire. When the delegates were received in audience by Pius at the end of the Congress he glumly told them that no hope for the future lay in politics or economic activity, but only in 'the Christian formation of individual persons'.[55] Provided it meant that the Vatican remained aloof from direct intervention into the political arena, that theme was a worthy one and it preoccupied Pius for the rest of his pontificate. Meanwhile, as if to favour the progress of national disintegration, the socialists met for their XIX Congress at Rome in early October 1922 and the moderate, pro-collaboration elements led by Turati, Treves and Matteotti were expelled and went off to form a new party of unitarian socialists. Turati knew that the split had taken place too late to be of any benefit and in its own way it showed how far socialism had degenerated into a form of 'squalor without precedent' in Italy.[56] The power of a united left was gravely weakened because in place of the old socialist party, in less than two years, three separate entities had been formed none of which had the strength to confront fascism alone. Only the fascists stood to gain by the dissolution of socialism as, given the fact that the white unions supported the PPI, the working masses of Italy were split four ways and not even the imminent threat to their political freedom proved sufficient to give them unity of purpose.[57]

By October it was clear that the only alternative to fascism was a composite government led by Giolitti in which the PPI would take some cabinet posts.[58] As in February, so too in October, Sturzo was accused of refusing to collaborate with Giolitti and thus having paved the way for fascism. Sforza said that he personally had informed Giolitti that Sturzo did not oppose his return to power in October and similar assurances were given him by others.[59] Yet, if it is clear that Sturzo posed no veto to a Giolitti cabinet in October, it is equally clear that he would have nothing to do with a prime minister who asked the PPI to have its ministers in a cabinet alongside fascist ministers. Sturzo himself later affirmed that he had informed Giolitti's intermediary, Camillo Corradini, that he would not consent to a Giolitti cabinet unless it was anti-fascist so that any veto by Sturzo in October was not directed individually against Giolitti but against the fascists.[60] Thus it was not Luigi Sturzo who failed Italy in October 1922 although he has often been blamed for his attitude to Giolitti's attempt to form a government.[61] Nor can it be said that Giolitti failed Italy for the simple reason that as a man and as a politician he was long since past taking the decisive action necessary to avoid the collapse of democracy. Equally it is not just to lay the blame, as Sforza does, at Facta's feet calling him a 'traitor' on account of his 'cowardice and stupidity'.[62] By October 1922 the Italian nation was in such disarray that it contained not a shred of that consensus of informed opinion that lies at the very heart of democracy. Put simply, democracy had not proved a workable alternative to that chaos which since the war had engulfed Italy. The war itself, with its own logic of brutal force, had held the nation together during the years of conflict and now, once again, the only alternative to chaos was force.

According to the PPI historian, Stefano Jacini, 'the party directorate was vigilant and serene in that turbulent autumn of 1922' but it had taken pains to warn Facta of the gravity of the situation 'without shaking his olympic calm'.[63] By October the conviction had grown that an impasse was being reached so the party launched a final appeal to the people in which it stated bluntly that the very institutions of the Italian State were in danger and that the government was so weakened that it was forced 'to tolerate every seditious act and every violent reprisal by factions'.[64] The appeal was a futile gesture because the party itself was already rent asunder on the parliamentary level where many members were beginning to look to their positions in an uncertain electoral future. Its mass following was as yet unshaken despite the vacillating manoeuvres of the leadership but the people could only stand by helpless as the situation deteriorated. The only other voice in the nation capable of awakening a response in the Catholic masses was that in the Vatican. But Pius remained silent while doing all he could to have the bishops dissuade their clergy from any further involvement with the PPI. It was all very well for Sturzo to fear for the future of the country and to 'eat his heart out over the stupidity and unworthy conduct of these clericals' who were undermining his party, but the Vatican had taken the part of the so called 'clericals' and against the Vatican Sturzo was powerless.[65]

On 2 October 1922 Gasparri sent a strongly worded papal reminder to the bishops in which it was laid down that the Holy See was 'totally extraneous' to the PPI and that the clergy were to have nothing to do with it. It was in a less than convincing tone that *Corriere d'Italia*, still tentatively upholding the PPI, asserted that the document did not reject the party outright while the socialists for their part hit hard at 'Papa Ratti' and the Catholic liberalism of his friends, the Lombardy moderates, who were allegedly selling it out.[66] Sturzo and the democratic forces of the PPI could not come out against the Vatican on such an issue if for no other reason than their adhesion to the principle of aconfessionality, which on the one hand led them to accept the presence of large numbers of the clergy in the party, and on the other to acknowledge the right of the Vatican to discipline those same clergy in matters political. Thus when Dalla Torre, in the *Osservatore Romano*, asserted with wearied repetitiveness on 25 October that the PPI had no connection with the Vatican, that Catholic Action was its only concern in the field of lay activity and that the existence of the PPI did not mean that the Vatican had abdicated its rights in the civil order, the PPI could make no reply.[67] It was clear to all that the PPI could not look to the Vatican for protection or favour even though it had never claimed either in the past. What was even clearer was that the Vatican had decided that the PPI was an irritating and embarrassing element in Italian life and that all steps possible would be taken to dispel any equivocation as to alleged links between it and the Church.

It was unlikely that any resolute leader bent on power would overlook his opportunity at a moment when the nation was in such disarray so the National Council of the fascist party met at Naples on 24–26 October to plan the march on Rome and Mussolini stayed long enough to engage in his customary bombast and decide that his hour had come.[68] He left Naples on 26 October for Milan but, between changing trains in Rome, he found time to meet Paul Palermi, Grand Master of one branch of Italian masonry, and be assured of masonic support. Being already assured of the support of the other branch he set out for Milan where he awaited his call with an eye to the Italian border that promised safety in the event of a mishap. Back at Naples the blackshirted leaders began the mobilization of their forces and summoned by an anxious prime minister the 'little King' arrived in Rome on 27 October and told Facta at the station that the city must be defended at all costs.

There can be no doubt that Rome could have been defended from any armed assault. Giovanni Amendola, writing in *Il Mondo* on 27 October 1922 said 'Let us stay calm because the state still has the force and the capacity to defend itself'.[69] General Pietro Badoglio, army chief of staff, regarded the fascists as a 'rabble' and said 'Give me full power for a week and no trace will remain of fascism'.[70] But Mussolini had taken pains to proclaim his own and his followers' loyalty to the monarchy and at the Naples Congress the King's name had been cheered to the echo. Moreover the King knew that his cousin, the Duke of Aosta, was close to the fascist leaders and that he would move with them against the monarchy if they were thwarted. Finally, in his favour, it must be admitted that the King feared one thing above all, a civil war. To avoid that horror Vittorio Emanuele was prepared to accept any solution that had the shadow of constitutionality and Mussolini had played on that weakness.[71]

Facta, who was beginning to lose his cherished confidence, wasn't sure what course to follow except that he personally was expendable so he decided on the resignation of his ministry which he communicated to the King and went home to bed. His sleep was cut short by those who thought that dignity, if not Italy, ought to be preserved by some attempt at resistance so, having drawn up an order proclaiming a state of siege, he took it to the King who, afraid for his throne, refused to sign it.[72] Facta then resigned for the last time while Mussolini, commissioned by the King to form a government, took a sleeper from Milan and arrived to take office on 30 October 1922.[73] The fascist march on Rome was in itself a symbolic farce but it is recorded that Sturzo stood at a window of Villa Ruffo Scaletta and watched as the blackshirts entered the city carrying banners with their ghastly symbols of death. He turned his face to the wall and wept. Sturzo wept for Italy, but he wept too for the priesthood because he had seen the priests who walked behind the blackshirts.[74]

Notes

1. *Avanti*, 24 January 1922; *Ordine Nuovo*, 23 January 1922. As an example of an historical slant of another kind, a life of Benedict XV published in Rome when relations between the Church and the fascist state were at their height makes no mention of the PPI, the lifting of the *non expedit* or of Sturzo see F. Vistalli, *Benedetto XV* (Rome, 1928).

2. *Giornale d'Italia*, 23 January 1922; *Il Popolo Nuovo*, 29 January 1922; *Corriere d'Italia*, 26 January 1922.

3. *Ordine Nuovo*, 25 January 1922.

4. See *Il Cardinale Pietro Gasparri* with introduction by Pietro Piolanti (Rome, 1960), pp. 98–100; also the pungent chapter on 'The politics of Pius XI' in G. Salvemini, *Stato*, pp. 257–65.

5. *Il Cardinale*, pp. 53 and 180 and F.M. Taliani, *Vita del card. Gasparri, segretario di stato e povero prete* (Milan, 1939), pp. 165–7. Gasparri obtained 24 votes which he quickly transferred to Ratti in a block thus ensuring his election.

6. After Gasparri's death in 1934 Pius told Archbishop Bernadini, nephew of Gasparri, how the cardinal had visited him the evening before his election suggesting the papal name and the gesture to Italy by blessing from the Loggia which was a practice that had been discontinued after Pius IX See *Il Cardinale*, p. 180.

7. See F. Pucci, *La pace*, pp. 89–91. The *Manchester Guardian*, 7 February 1922, acclaimed the election on the grounds that Pius was 'the only pope to have walked the streets of Manchester' which he visited in 1900. See A. Berselli, *L'Opinione pubblica inglise e l'avvento del fascismo 1919–1925* (Milan, 1971), p. 57.

8. For an excellent study of Pius and his pontificate see 'Pio XI nel trentesimo della morte (1939–1969)' in Raccolta di studi e di memorie (Milan, 1969).

9. N. Malvezzi, *Pio XI nei suoi scritti* (Milan, 1923), *passim*.

10. W. Meysztowicz, 'La Nunziatura di Achille Ratti in Polonia' in *Pio XI nel trentesimo*, pp. 177–206.

11. See F. Cattaneo, 'Achille Ratti prete e arcivescovo di Milano' in ibid., pp. 107–62.

12. See E. Pucci, *La pace*, p. 91. It is worth noting that though relations between the new archbishop and the fascists became cordial they were not so from the beginning for, on the day of his entry into the city, the fascists tried to break up ceremonies in his honour while the socialist mayor refused to attend the ceremonies. *O.R.*, 10 September 1921.

13. *Il Popolo Nuovo*, 29 January, 12 February 1922. At the death of Benedict, Sturzo sent a telegram of condolence to Gasparri on behalf of the party and requested all PPI members to join with Catholic associations in ceremonies in his memory. *O.R.*, 23 January 1922.

14. *Ordine Nuovo*, 4 March 1922.

15. *Il Popolo Nuovo*, 12 March 1922; *Corriere d'Italia*, 5 March 1922; *Ordine Nuovo*, 17 March 1922.

16. See A. Kuliscioff to F. Turanti, 1 April 1922, in *Carteggio*, vol. 5, pp. 578–9, and G. Marcucci Fanello, *Storia della F.U.C.I.* (Rome, 1971), p. 88.

17. *Ordine Nuovo*, 19 March 1922; G. Andreotti, *De Gasperi*, p. 146, states that Cavazzoni was a friend of Mussolini and had been so since their years in Milan.

18. *Ordine Nuovo*, 20 March 1922.

19. See A. Martini, 'Pio XI e l'Italia' in *Pio XI nel trentesimo*, p. 536. By 31 May 1922, *Ordine Nuovo* thought Italy was already in a state of civil war.

20. I. Bonomi, *Dal socialismo*, p. 122.

21. See *O.R.*, 7 July 1922; *La Giustizia*, 1–2 July 1922; *Avanti*, 16 June 1922. For the quote from Gramsci see *Studi Cattolici*, no. 132 (Milan, February 1972), p. 120.

22. L. Sturzo, *Popolarismo*, p. 44.

23. *Avanti*, 20 July 1922.

24. See S. Mastellone, *Uno scritto poco conosciuto di Francesco Luigi Ferrari* (Florence, 1969), pp. 257–61. Even after World War II Salvemini was still asking whether pre-fascist Italy was a democracy. See P. Scoppola, 'Per una valutazione del Popolarismo' in *Quaderni di Cultura e Storia Sociale*, Anno 11, no. 5 (Livorno, May 1953), p. 186. For an analysis of fascism see A. Hamilton, *The Appeal of Fascism* (New York, 1973), and A. Lyttelton, *Italian Fascisms from Pareto to Gentile* (London, 1973).

25. See E. Lussu, *Marcia su Roma e dintorni* (Rome, 1945), p. 32.

26. See G. De Rosa, *Il Partito*, p. 153.

27. For an account of these events see G. Spataro, *I Democratici*, pp. 45 S. Senator Giuseppe Spataro told me that the two men whom the directorate had in mind as alternatives to Meda were Angelo Mauri and Giulio Rodinò, both ex ministers. Interview 15 December 1974.

28. Interview 15 December 1974.

29. *O.R.*, 31 July 1922. Both Gabriele De Rosa and Senator Spataro's secretary, Mrs Marcucci Fanello, reacted vigorously to my suggestion that ecclesiastical pressure was brought to bear on Meda to have him refuse the appointment. Interview 15 December 1974.

30. *Popolo d'Italia*, 25, 27 July 1922, in B. Vigezzi, *1919–1925*, p. 447.

31. G. Salvemini, *Stato*, p. 225, quotes from *O R.*; *Cittadino di Brescia*; *Avvenire d'Italia* and *Unità Cattolica* to illustrate the point.

32. E.P. Howard, *Il Partito*, p. 364. The pope sent a telegram to Cornaggia to encourage the new body. Ibid.

33. See *O.R.*, 30 July 1922, where Boggiani's pastoral letters were held up as most useful to Catholic readers.

34. Mussolini in *Popolo d'Italia*, 19 August 1922, quoted in D. Allegra, *Come ha operato il Vaticano nel corso del regime fascista a sostengo della reazione* (Rome, 1954), p. 43.

35. See G. De Rosa, *Giolitti*, p. 17. Missiroli thought Giolitti's attitude to the PPI was little short of 'satanic'. M. Missiroli, *Una battaglia*, pp. 277–83.

36. *Ordine Nuovo*, 30 July 1922. In June and July Sturzo, Turati, Treves, Modiglioni and Matteotti met frequently in Rome to discuss collaborating to form a government. They were interrupted by the fall of the Facta cabinet. See G. De Rosa, *Il Partito*, p. 143.

37. L. Sturzo in *Popolarismo*, p. 64.

38. See I. Bonomi, *Dal socialismo*, pp. 44–5. Nenni said the strike, which was an act of 'despair', 'put the seal on the socialist rout'. P. Nenni, *Storia di quattro anni, (1919–1922)*, 2nd ed. (Turin, 1946), pp. 211–14.

39. *Popolo d'Italia*, 1 August 1922, in B. Vigezzi, *1919 1925*, p. 482.

40. *O.R.*, 2 August 1922.

41. F. Guarneri, *Battaglie economiche tra le due grandi guerre* (Milan, 1953), vol. 1, pp. 79–80 with improvements in agriculture, industry and in the balance of payments. See also R. Romeo, *Breve storia della grande industria in Italia*, 3rd edn (Florence, 1967).

42. I. Bonomi, *Dal socialismo*, pp. 92–3, states that in his opinion the Italian people were so nauseated in 1922 with their parliament that they didn't care a whit what Mussolini did to it.

43. In September 1922 Filippo Meda likened the fascist movement to a 'volcano in full eruption' but admitted that even a vulcanologist would be hard put to predict its course. To him it was so violent that no Catholic could support it. As became clearer day by day, such observations in a violent era were of little effect. See 'Il fascismo e i cattolici' in B. Malinverni (ed.), *Civitas*, pp. 163–72.

44. *Il Popolo Nuovo*, 16, 19 October 1919.

45. In particular see R. De Felice, *Mussolini il rivoluzionario, 1883–1920* (Turin, 1965), and *Mussolini il facista, 1921–1925* (Turin, 1966); 1. Kirkpatrick, *Mussolini:*

A Study in Power (New York, 1964); chap. 3 of A.J. Gregor, *The Ideology of Fascism: The Rationale of Totalitarianism* (New York, 1969) is a serious study of the formation of the young Mussolini.

46. See 'Rapporto dell' ispettore generale di PS. G. Gasti su Mussolini e I Fasci di combattimento (Giugno 1919)' in R. De Felice, *Mussolini il rivoluzionario*, pp. 725–37.

47. *La Giustizia*, 13 October 1922.

48. *Ordine Nuovo*, 13 August 1922.

49. *O.R.*, 9 August 1922. For an account of the violence in August–September 1922 see F.L. Ferrari, *Le Regime*, p. 43.

50. *Corriere d'Italia*, 12 August 1922; *Civiltà Cattolica*, vol. 3, 19 August 1922, p. 363. For a good overview of the attitude of the Jesuit magazine to fascism see the two articles by B. Talluri, 'La *Civiltà Cattolica* e Il Fascismo 1922–1924' in *Studi Senesi*, (Siena, 1966), pp. 285–330, and 'La *Civiltà Cattolica* e Il Fascismo 1925–1929' in ibid., vol. LXXVIII (III Serie, XV), Fasc. 2, pp. 257–98.

51. See *O.R.*, 21 September; *Corriere d'Italia*, 20, 21 September and *La Giustizia*, 22 September 1922. See also P. Scoppola, *Dal neoguelfismo*, pp. 176–80. For the text of the letter see *Corriere d'Italia*, 20 September 1922.

52. See *Ordine Nuovo*, 20 September 1922; *La Giustizia*, 22 September 1922. The letter itself is a good example of some of the lack of clarity which surrounds certain episodes in the history of the PPI. G. De Rosa, *Il Partito*, p. 164, gives the names of eight PPI senators who signed it. G. Spataro, *I Democratici*   p. 50, says six senators signed it with Soderini voting against it. G. Salvemini, *Stato*, p. 264, has eight signatures including Soderini. The list of names given by De Rosa tallies with that in *Corriere d'Italia*, 20 September 1922, as I personally verified it, yet Salvemini cites that paper as his source. In fact Soderini did not become a senator until 1923. E.P. Howard, *Il Partito*, p. 382, wisely avoided any details as to the signatories.

53. *Corriere d'Italia*, 21 September 1922.

54. See G. Pucci, *La pace*, p. 86.

55. *Civiltà Cattolica*, vol. 4, 7 October 1922, p. 55.

56. See G. Arfe, *Storia*, pp. 311–12.

57. On the disintegration of the forces of the left see A. Davidson, 'The Italian Communist Party 1921–1924; An Inner Party Dispute' in *ANU Historical Journal*, vol. no. 1, Canberra, October 1964, pp. 84–97.

58. G. De Rosa, *Il Partito*, pp. 166–182, deals admirably with this confusing episode.

59. C. Sforza, *L'Italia*, p. 71.

60. L. Sturzo, *Italy and Fascismo*, p. 116. It must be conceded that Sturzo, like

Gramsci, regarded Giolitti with grave suspicion. To them he was a reactionary who had betrayed the south and their deep preoccupation with the south was basic to their mental outlook. See F Rizzo, *Luigi Sturzo e la questione meridionale* (Rome, 1957), p. 30, and P. Alatri, *Le origini*, p. 117.

61. See M. Viana, *La monarchia e il fascismo* (Rome, 1951), p. 184.

62. C. Sforza, *L'Italia*, p. 120.

63. S. Jacini, *I popolari*, p. 97.

64. *Il Popolo Nuovo*, 22 October 1922.

65. For Sturzo's frame of mind in early October, see G. Donati's letter to his wife, 7 October 1922, in G. Rossini (ed.), *Il delitto Matteotti tra il Viminale e l'Aventino* (Bologna, 1966), p. 18. F. Fanelli, *Don Sturzo*, p. 49, claimed that the PPI was by definition anti-clerical and thus it was hated by the clericals who considered it rebellious and heretical. In the context clerical does not mean clergy but laymen who allowed themselves to be directed in political matters by the Vatican. It ought to be said that there was at least one cleric in the Vatican in 1922 who had decidedly anti-fascist and pro Partito Popolare views. His name was Angelo Roncalli, now better known as Pope John XXIII. See L. Bedeschi (ed.), *La terza pagina de Il Popolo 1923–1925* (Rome, 1973), p. 30.

66. See *Corriere d'Italia*, 20 October 1922 and *La Giustizia*, 21 October 1922. The text of the letter was made public on 20 October in *Giornale d'Italia*. See also F.L. Ferrari, *L'Azione*, pp. 19–20.

67. *O.R.*, 25 October 1922.

68. Donati wrote to his wife on 27 October saying that the fascists knew the time had come for them to act and that if they did not do so 'it will never come to pass for them again'. See G. Rossini (ed.), *Il delitto*, p. 19.

69. G. Amendola. *La democrazia italiana contro il fascismo 1922–1924* (Naples; 1960), pp. 60–1.

70. E. Lussu, *Marcia*, p. 33.

71. M. Viana, *La monarchia*, p. 696, defends Vittorio Emanuele whom he calls a 'scapegoat for the errors and failures of his accusers'.

72. F.L. Ferrari, *Le Regime*, pp. 53–4, admits that the decision of the King not to repulse fascism with force was shared by the majority of Italians.

73. For the events of late October 1922 see R. De Felice, *Mussolini il fascista*; A. Lyttelton, *The Seizure of Power*; A. Repaci, *La Marcia* and E. Lussu, *Marcia*.

74. See G. De Rosa, *Rufo Ruffo Della Scaletta e Luigi Sturzo* (Rome 1961), pp. 7–8.

6

THE STICK AND THE CARROT

Since 1920 the fascist movement had threatened the stability of Italian democracy by violence and yet when it came to power in late October 1922 it was able to do so by peaceful means. No resistance was met as the blackshirts came into Rome. No protest was offered when Mussolini formed a cabinet. No cry of rage or despair was raised by king, parliament or people and the murmur of anguish from the left was muted in the atmosphere of general euphoria. Throughout the country things quietly settled down to normalcy and the fact that parliament, the highest expression of the nation's will, remained unfettered, albeit temporarily, passed almost unnoticed. By his alternate threats and blandishments, by his violence to some and his protection of others, by his assurance to the monarchy and the Church, above all by his promise of order, authority and progress, Mussolini had revealed his keen sense of the appropriate. He had lulled most of his compatriots into a torpor so deep that they were unaware of the violence that had been done to their liberties. That chapter in Italian history known as the Risorgimento was closed and some children born in 1922 were to grow to adulthood before another would open. Many others would die as Italy lived through the years of its courtesanship and in the end, due in part to their resistance, struggled to freedom again.

Some voices were quickly stifled under the new regime. *Avanti* was immediately subject to aggression with its head office sacked, but it managed to come out again on 14 November when Pietro Nenni declared the death of 'bourgeois democracy', the culpability of the King and the judgement that the new government had been put there by the industrial and agricultural corporations.[1] *Ordine Nuovo* was subject to military occupation but from 4 November until the end of the year it managed to survive as a single sheet done on a hand press to eventually disappear into that clandestine underground from which the Italian Communist Party, both within and without Italy, carried on its anti-fascist campaign while the regime endured. Its last word to Sturzo warned that Mussolini was trying to get an audience with Pius in order to destroy the PPI's influence in the Vatican. 'It remains to be seen whether he will gain his objective' it said but thought that the projected audience would be considered 'inopportune.'[2] *La Giustizia* was suppressed for 10 days after which it appeared again on 8 November and was able to survive until the end of 1924.[3] The other papers varied initially in their assessment of the new regime, but eventually only those that were prepared to adopt an attitude of complete subservience were able to survive beyond 1925. After that date the freedom of the press went the way of the other freedoms normally associated with a democracy.

On the very day that the existence of the Italian state in its democratic form was in the balance Pius XI made an appeal to the Italian people with a letter to the bishops. In 'this land so blessed by God' he uttered 'a word of charity and peace' asking all to be inspired by 'christian principles of order' which they could manifest by 'limiting, and if necessary, sacrificing their own wishes for the public good'.[4] It was a document inspired by its historical circumstances to the extent that it reflected the general desire amongst Italians for a return to a normal state of affairs. That some segments of society would have to accept the sacrifice of their legitimate interests in order to achieve civil equilibrium was apparent, but it could only be a matter of conjecture whether Pius had any specific element in mind. Any appeal on his part was scarcely likely to evoke a positive response in political circles except from the members of the PPI and Dalla Torre was quick to remind those men who were 'solicitous above all for the welfare of the people' of their duty to collaborate with Mussolini.[5]

It is somewhat surprising that at such a delicate moment Gasparri and Pius permitted *Osservatore Romano* to use its columns for what amounted to a posthumous repudiation of the PPI by the pope who, allegedly, had helped to found it. The paper ran a letter from an obscure gentleman who, signing himself as 'The Honourable Monti-Guarnieri', claimed to have been a friend of Benedict XV and he now intended to dispel any notion that the late pope had ever considered recognizing the PPI as a Catholic party. On one occasion while walking in the Vatican gardens Benedict reportedly said to his honourable companion, 'the Pope has nothing to do with the Partito Popolare. I have not recognized it as a Party and I do not wish to recognize it now in order to be free to disown it when it suits me!' The pope asked his confidant to communicate this message to others and apparently Monti-Guarnieri decided that the time was now ripe to do so. His conviction on the matter was seemingly shared by Dalla Torre for lest, in the excitement of the moment, the letter may have been overlooked by readers it was run again in full in the next edition of *Osservatore Romano* alongside the news that Mussolini had arrived in Rome.[6] As an interested student of Vatican affairs both in relation to its attitude to himself as well as to the PPI, it is a reasonable assumption that the contents, the timing, the repetition and even the position of the letter were not lost on Mussolini.

Within the PPI there was some initial hesitation when it was known that Mussolini wanted the party to participate in his ministry and to support his government. It was apparent that without the support of the PPI members the new prime minister would not have a majority in the parliament and in that case it would have been necessary to dissolve the House and call for new elections, a situation which would have unleashed another fascist wave of terror throughout the country.[7]

In such circumstances it is understandable that even the more detached members of the party directorate, to whom the decision was left given its urgency, were inclined to take a less intransigent stand, while the members of the right wing were already committed to collaboration. Cavazzoni had been in regular contact with Mussolini in Milan and there was no uncertainty as to his attitude; Grosoli and Mattei-Gentili gave him firm support while the latter knew that Mussolini had promised him a cabinet post.

Unsurprisingly Sturzo was firmly opposed to collaboration and Giuseppe Donati, an old Murri follower whom Sturzo had invited to Rome to set up a party paper, was adamant that the PPI ought to refuse any form of association with the regime. Donati pointed out to the party leaders that 'certain kinds of unfaithfulness to moral principles are invariably paid for in the long run', and he strengthened Sturzo's opposition to collaboration but it was in vain. Sturzo was unable to prevail over those members of the party directorate who opposed him and, in his absence, the decision was taken to collaborate with the fascist government. A few months later Stefano Jacini who was present at that fateful meeting and acquiesced, unwillingly, in the ultimate decision wrote 'If we were mistaken, which God forbid, it would spell ruin for Italy'.[8]

As a result of the directorate decision Cavazzoni and De Gasperi went to tell Mussolini that the party was prepared to collaborate provided he gave an assurance to introduce state examinations in all schools, not to vary the electoral laws and to guarantee the freedom of the workers' associations. The Duce promised all this and asserted that he personally would take the Ministry of the Interior in order to ensure the authority of the state against his fascist bands. With these assurances the party accepted the nomination of Cavazzoni as Minister of Labour, Vincenzo Tangorra as Minister of the Treasury and four others as under-secretaries, including Giovanni Gronchi, general secretary of the white unions, as under-secretary of Industry Commerce. In the

Vatican there was an almost audible sigh of relief, down in the city the offices of *Corriere d'Italia* echoed the sentiments of the cautious while Meda, clearer now than he had been in the past, told Sturzo that while he deplored the step taken by the party, he recognized that there was little option given the attitude of the Vatican. As for the future he was unwilling to speak except to say that he very much feared that 'facts themselves will speak with too much eloquence'.[9]

Spataro, who was a witness to these events, made the enigmatic statement that the party could still have gone back on the decision to collaborate but that Sturzo, clearly the only one who could lead the dissent, made it clear for the first time 'that his priestly status impeded him from acting in full liberty.'[10] Spataro did not then spell out what precise agency so transcribed the freedom of the priest, but he later made it clear that Sturzo was fully aware of the hope placed in the new regime in the Vatican, and to have dashed those hopes at that time by refusing to allow his party to collaborate was well-nigh impossible for Sturzo to whom the highest loyalty remained the Church.[11] His only other course was to have resigned his position as secretary of the party but, again, to have taken a stand on conscience when around him so many, including the pope, saw no question of conscience involved, was to assume a role that required clarity of vision and intensity of purpose which even Sturzo at that moment was unable to muster. To his credit it must be said that Sturzo neither fostered nor approved of collaboration. That he acquiesced in it perhaps says no more than that he had been mistaken four years before when he allowed so many to join the party who did not then, nor ever would or could, share his own ideals and convictions.

Another persuasive factor that helped some of the leading members of the party to follow the road of collaboration was the precarious financial situation into which the Banco di Roma had fallen.[12] Some facts about the Bank are obscure but it is clear that it was the repository of large segments of Vatican finance, that its president and vice-president, Santucci and Grosoli, were both PPI senators, Vatican intimates and committed to a form of clerical conservatism, and that its relationship with the PPI and its financial domination of many segments of the smaller banking and cooperative ventures of the white unions was deplored by Sturzo and some other members of the party. Furthermore, there was a link with the Bank and the papers of the trust set up by Grosoli some years before and those papers which had hitherto given their support to the PPI, especially the *Corriere d'Italia* in Rome, were organs which it was in the interest of the new regime either to win over or to neutralize.[13] Within two weeks of taking power Mussolini signed an order telling Vincenzo Tangorra, Minister of the Treasury, to take steps to save the Banco di Roma and at the same time he expressed the desire that the bank would prove itself worthy to be saved.[14] According to Alberto De Stefani, Mussolini saw the saving of the Banco di Roma as a means of inducing the political forces of the Church to support the regimen and eventually of facilitating the conciliation of Church and state in Italy. Although it must be admitted that De Stefani was a leading member of the fascist regime, there is no proof that in this matter he departed from the truth.[15]

Eight years later Francesco Luigi Ferrari wrote to Father Rosa from his exile in Paris. Ferrari had read an article in *Osservatore Romano* of 20 December 1930 which rejected an accusation of Mussolini that the Catholic banks had failed the people by replying that it wasn't the Church but the PPI that was responsible. Ferrari asked Rosa whether the Vatican organ had already forgotten 'the direct and indirect pressure brought to bear on the Partito Popolare to get it to give the fascist government the backing it asked for in compensation for the saving of the Banco di Roma, the immunity of its administrators and the payment of its creditors?' Ferrari did not deny that such pressure had proved successful because he was present at a meeting at which Grosoli, Mattei-Gentili and Cavazzoni had pleaded with Sturzo and the party directorate to collaborate with Mussolini.'[16]

If saving the bank was part of the hidden price of collaboration Mussolini was quick to make other public gestures that were equally conciliatory to the Church. He made it clear that nothing further would be done to enact laws interfering with taxation or ecclesiastical property as envisaged by Giolitti, laws which, if put into effect, would have done grave harm to the religious orders. He extended state examinations to all schools thus removing the disability under which students in Catholic schools had laboured under the liberal regimes of the past, and he restored the crucifix to the schools, thereby removing a long standing source of discontent amongst Catholics.[17] Meanwhile he continued to make extravagant statements that must have given pause to those who remembered his flamboyant atheism and anti-clericalism of the past. On 21 November he declared before a group of journalists 'My spirit is profoundly religious; religion is a fundamental force that must be respected and defended ... Catholicism is a great spiritual and moral power and I trust that the relations between the Italian State and the Vatican from now on will be very friendly.'[18] All of this specious activity naturally threw the masons into disarray. They had given very extensive financial support to the fascist bid for power and had been rewarded with five cabinet posts, but they had not bargained for such a reversal of liberal Italy's attitude to the Church. To those amongst them who were internationalists it was full of foreboding for the future as it seemed to imply that Italy was in the process of again becoming the centre of international Catholicism in fact as well as name.[19]

It would be fatuous to assume that these gestures were seen in the Vatican in any other light than conciliatory moves in an attempt to soften Catholic apprehension. Nonetheless the pope himself was inclined to the view that much could be achieved in an Italian state with Mussolini at its head and his secretary of state, Cardinal Gasparri, held to a like view. A few days after Mussolini came to power Pius is alleged to have said to Count Ambrogio Caccia Dominioni, president of the diocesan branch of Catholic Action at Milan, 'I believe that with Mussolini it will be possible to get a lot done'.[20] The hope that had been held out initially in some Vatican circles that, with a powerful Catholic party in the country, the situation of the Church in Italy would have undergone considerable improvement, had long since waned. Sturzo had made it clear that his party was dedicated to a total renewal of Italian society without favour to any element within it, even to the Vatican, and hitherto the PPI had shown little inclination to weaken its stand because of ecclesiastical pressure. Yet in the new circumstance it was imperative to ensure that the Catholic political force either gave wholehearted support to the fascist regime or, at the worst, abstained from active opposition to it. Even the *New Witness* in London expressed the opinion that if the fascists and the PPI could work together 'Italy is saved' and if such a view was tenable in London, it was even more firmly held in the Vatican.[21]

The PPI thus found itself in the invidious position of being a leading partner in a government about whose head and on whose principles and policies large segments of the party held grave misgivings. The mere act of coming to power could not erase the past and the fascist past was clouded with violence, duplicity and intrigue. A good deal of that violence had been directed against the Popolari as well as against the socialists and those who had suffered under it were unable to forget it even though they may have tried to forgive it. Miglioli, Francesco Luigi Ferrari, Donati and Sturzo himself were neither blind nor weak, but they were unable to outweigh the apparently positive elements in the new situation. First, they could not deny that Italy had all but lacked a government in any real sense since the initial Facta cabinet in February. Secondly, Mussolini was a constitutionally elected member of parliament who had been invited to form a cabinet by the King himself and the accusation that the King had acted under duress was thin, given that the same monarch had refused to lift a finger to bring the forces of the state to bear against the fascist menace. Thirdly, Mussolini had gone out of his way to ensure that the PPI was represented in his cabinet and had given two important posts to PPI members. Finally, the greater part of national and even international opinion was in favour of the new regime. Thousands of telegrams of congratulations had poured in to Mussolini, many of them from foreign heads of state with promises by England, France and America of cordial cooperation.[22]

Thus Mussolini knew where he stood when in his first speech in the House he insulted and blandished in turn the very parliament itself, promised to contain fascist violence, declared his respect for all religions, but especially Catholicism, and prayed 'May God assist me to bring my work to a victorious end'. To this admixture of bombast and blasphemy it was noble of Turati to reply by accusing Mussolini of treating the House with contempt and stating that 'This Italian parliament has ceased to exist' but his was an enunciation of 'absolute, irreducible and proud opposition' and he was in a minority.[23] To most Italians it was clear that parliament had not ceased to exist and the question as to whether it any longer represented the democratic will of the people had to be left for time and events to clarify. As for the PPI, with only two votes against and five abstentions, it voted full financial and administrative powers to the new government and hoped for the best.[24] To Sturzo it was shameful to see the members of his party sit silent and acquiescent in parliament and be mocked by a man for whom Sturzo felt only profound contempt. He understood that many of them feared for 'their own persons' and that foreboding was real because he had begun to fear the loss of something more precious to him than life itself. To his friends he confided that he feared the fate of Murri — excommunication by the Church.[25] Donati wrote to his wife on 10 December 1922, 'Sturzo is now the target of a dogged and jesuitical attack by the clerical fascists and I believe I am one of the few who remain faithful to him.'[26]

Between the end of October and the middle of December the pressure on Sturzo to conform; to accept the advice of the prudent and to hope that things would become normal was enormous. His old companion Meda had decided to adopt a wait and see attitude, to hope that the new government would bring 'order, discipline and internal peace to Italy' and to refrain from pronouncing a final verdict on the régime.[27] Yet Sturzo already knew that the only internal peace that would come to those who opposed Mussolini and his regime was that induced by unconsciousness, death, exile or by the indignity of the ingestion of castor oil. Even Pius XI knew it for he had warned Father Rosa not to write anything critical of the regime in *Civiltà Cattolica* because to do so was to invite violent reprisals against his person.[28] But Sturzo and Pius XI had differing concepts of what was at stake and what was prudent for a pope may not have applied to a priest even though a political one.

On 17 December Mussolini's promised containment of fascist violence proved ineffective when, as a reprisal for the death of two fascists, 22 anti-fascist workers were killed at Turin and their bodies thrown into the Po. Three days later Sturzo arrived in the city to address a public gathering and throughout Italy his words were awaited by some in hope, by others in fear and by the majority, content now with the illusion of peace, with discontent. It was his first such opportunity since the coming to power of Mussolini and he had long pondered on what he would say, but he spoke, as always, without flights of oratory, humour or sarcasm.[29] As in January 1922 at Rome, so now at Turin, he embarked on 'a careful analysis' of the present situation. Accepting the existence of the Mussolini government as a constitutional fact he spoke as the leader of a minority party in coalition with that government. At no stage did he give the faintest hint that he approved either of the way Mussolini had come to power or of his party's collaboration with the fascist government. At the same time he gave little indication of foreseeing the darker side of Italy's future under fascism and he clearly still hoped that time and events would work together to normalize and constitutionalize the fascist movement. In that context he was prepared to give his support provided some things were clear. Firstly, he would not brook any interference with the proportional system; secondly, he would uphold always the autonomy and right to existence of his party and thirdly, he rejected either the tendency on the part of the fascist state to use or absorb the Church or the tendency of the Church to meddle in the political arena for its own ends.

All of this Sturzo said in lengthy and thoughtful cadences without rancour or bombast. To those who could read as they ran it was plain what he meant. To Mussolini, to Pius XI, to Gasparri, to Santucci, to Grosoli and to the fascist leadership the little Sicilian priest gave fair warning of where he stood. He could only hope that his party would stand with him and that his message would be understood, but it produced only irritation and incomprehension. The fascists and their followers were annoyed that he had not done what they could never expect. Sturzo would not give them outright support. The socialists and the anti-fascists were upset that he had not condemned fascism and collaboration in ringing terms. To *Avanti* the speech was 'unclear' and not genuinely anti-fascist while *La Giustizia* thought it an 'abstract and general analysis' and Amendola in *Il Mondo* wrote, 'We, and with us the whole country — wanted to know what the PPI intended to do. We found ourselves being served up involved dissertations or simple enunciations of premises without practical application to today's reality.'[30] These criticisms would have been fair comment had they been applied to those who had refused to collaborate in any form. As it was they missed their mark in Sturzo because he had permitted collaboration, albeit unwillingly, and to him it was a question of making the most of it and trying to keep his party intact for the battle that he knew lay ahead.

It is only just to note that in one keen observer some chord was struck for, to his credit, one Vatican commentator wrote with restrained and dignified prose of the speech.[31] But Dalla Torre's voice, if indeed it was his, was only one voice in the Vatican and the other from there was not slow to speak. Pius XI had been on Peter's Chair for almost a year and the time had come for his first encyclical. Its title was *Ubi arcano Dei*, and its official date was 23 December 1922. Pius spoke from Rome which he regarded as the divinely designated capital of the whole world because 'it is the seat of a divine sovereignty that, passing beyond the confines of nations and states, embraces all men and all peoples'. Rising above all questions of party politics, the pope made it clear that henceforth the aim of the papacy was to be Catholic Action, 'to us most dear'. To those who might wonder whether such an aim may prove disruptive of the civil order, Pius promised that Catholic Action would remain within its own sphere of the spiritual and moral formation of the faithful. Finally the prelate who had spoken so clearly on the Roman Question at Milan returned to it now from the Vatican as pope. He assured all Italians that 'Italy has nothing and will have nothing to fear from the Holy See' and that he was prepared to await the hour of God for a solution to the problem which had bedevilled relations between Church and state since 1870. To him that hour would be 'amongst the most solemn and fruitful both for the restoration of the Reign of Christ as well as for the pacification of Italy and the world'.[32]

Apart from the fact that the encyclical contained no hint that Italy's new regime was viewed with other than strict neutrality, it contained little to dismay the fascists or to console the Popolari. Yet Pius had made two things abundantly clear. First, the role of the Church in the Italian peninsula was henceforth to express itself in the civic order through a centralized form of Catholic Action which Pius himself intended to control.[33] Secondly, his words let everyone understand that the time was fast approaching for a reconciliation of Church and state in Italy. Pius did not give any sign that he doubted the good will, ability or cooperation of the then ruling regime in the country. Nor did the pope indicate that any help would be needed from foreign powers or from other local political forces. *Ubi arcano Dei* was a document which Mussolini assuredly read with relief and one which Sturzo equally assuredly read with apprehension. For his part Mussolini gave his personal token of appreciation to Pius with the gift of the library of the Ghigi family. It seems that Pius, in his days as Vatican librarian, had tried to buy the library but the price was too high. When Mussolini had the matter brought to his attention he arranged for its acquisition and presentation to the Vatican.[34] He followed this with the much more decisive gesture of decreeing that henceforth the Catholic catechism was obligatory in the state schools and was to be taught to all children except those whose parents requested an explicit abstention. This was a step which delighted the hearts of all in the Vatican as it overthrew the old law of 1908. That law, which had left the option on religious teaching to the municipalities, had caused a constant state of tension in the numerous places where opinion was divided on the matter.[35] *La Giustizia* summed it up neatly when it said 'Mussolini has done more for clericalism in three months than the Partito Popolare in ten years' while Mario Bendiscioli, professor of the History of Christianity at the University of Milan, was even more to the point when he later wrote, 'The Holy See ... fully appreciated the direct and spontaneous guarantees that this [fascist] policy offered to Italian ecclesiastical life and therefore it had no difficulty in abandoning the Partito Popolare to its destiny.'[36]

Sturzo was powerless to combat the forces that were beginning to coalesce against his party. He was disgusted at the way the PPI deputies had placed expediency before principle; he knew that Italian democracy was in jeopardy and he feared Mussolini's attempt to lull Catholics as he realized that in such a way any will in the party to resist the new regime would be undermined. Large sections of the PPI at its top level had remained fundamentally conservative, tied to the past forms of state and Church and dependent upon a stable, capitalist economy for their existence. Sturzo could not hope to awaken any response in such people although some, such as Mattei-Gentili, still supported the party while insisting that 'a new historical period' had opened in Italy in the face of which men and parties may have to decline given the power of its revolutionary force.

But other voices were carrying their message in clearer terms and Father Giovanni Semeria, a nationally known and widely respected military chaplain, summed them up when he warned of the grave consequences that would ensue if Mussolini fell from power. 'Today it is not a question — let us be deeply convinced — of saving a party, ours or others: it is a question of saving the country', wrote Semeria and, while many agreed with him, Sturzo was not prepared to accept meekly the sacrifice of a party he believed could still offer to the nation a genuine force of social, political and even spiritual renewal instead of the spurious one offered by the fascists.[37] But, as Donati noted, Sturzo had lost any chance he ever had of leading the party from inside parliament where he would have been able to stand up to Mussolini, and outside he could only try to rally around him men who would help in the battle.[38] Fortunately, in the persons of Ferrari, Donati, De Gasperi, Spataro and others of the younger group, they were not lacking. They firmly rejected the idea that, as *L'Italia* of Milan put it, collaboration, 'absolute, loyal and fervently active' was the only road open to those Catholics to whom the preservation of the interests of the Church were the main motive for political action.[39]

Two of the most potent weapons that Sturzo used in those early days of resistance to fascism were *Il Domani d'Italia* of Milan and *Il Popolo* of Rome. The Milan paper had Alberto Canaletti-Gaudenti, Guido Migliolo and Luigi and Gerolamo Meda behind it, but Francesco Luigi Ferrari was its driving spirit. *Il Domani* was named after a weekly that had been directed by Romolo Murri in 1901 and took as its motto 'Let us hold up high the little flame of this night until the dawn of tomorrow' — a resolve to which it held fast until the end.[40] Beginning on 24 December 1922 the paper immediately took a left, intransigent and anti-collaborationist line. This prompted the *Corriere d'Italia* to lament from Rome the presence of such a disruptive force in a party which Mattei-Gentili, Grosoli, Santucci and even Filippo Meda now hoped would quietly submit to giving loyal support to Mussolini and his regime.[41] *Il Popolo* came out for the first time in Rome on 5 April 1923. It was founded by Giuseppe Donati and it immediately became the most potent weapon of the democratic element in the party in the struggle against fascism even though Mussolini, never expecting the way the paper would develop, had given his approval for its foundation.[42] In Rome, in particular, where the *Corriere d'Italia* was rapidly moving towards a pro-fascist stance, *Il Popolo* became the voice of the party. At Milan and in the north where *L'Italia* had adopted a favourable stance towards the regime *Il Domani* was able to keep alive the spirit of the party even though, lacking the financial support of the big Catholic papers of the trust, the going was very difficult and became more so as time went on.[43]

Against the wishes of the 'prudent' elements in the PPI Sturzo was able to insist that the decision to hold the fifth Congress of the party at Turin in April be complied with despite the mounting unease within the ruling fascist clique at the attitude he had expressed in December. Mussolini's friends were constantly pointing out to him that his PPI cabinet members were less dedicated to outright collaboration than the rest of his cabinet and with their opinion he had begun to agree although he still saw the need to retain them in the ministry.[44] Nonetheless he quickly appointed a fascist, De Stefani, as Treasury Minister when Vincenzo Tangorra died. Tangorra was an old world, academic economist whom Sturzo had not been displeased to see accept the appointment on the grounds that if PPI members were to be in the ministry at all they ought to be men loyal to the party. Tangorra's loyalty to either the regime or to the PPI was not long put to the test because he died within two months of his appointment, thus relieving him of the ignominy of any further participation in the destruction of democracy.[45]

Mussolini, however, was not as yet prepared to forego the shield of respectability which his coalition with the PPI gave him. This was especially the case in the eyes of the Church and of those foreign powers which still regarded the new government as being as democratic as previous Italian governments with the advantageous difference that it was led by a man who both wanted to do something for Italy and had the strength to carry it out. What that something was remained uncertain except in the minds of the isolated communists, the divided socialists and large numbers of PPI voters who through their local representatives had assured Sturzo of their support in an anti-collaborationist if not yet intransigently anti-fascist stand.[46] It was with this situation as a background that Sturzo remained adamant in calling for a Congress with the intention of welding the party together and clarifying its position both in the parliament and the nation.

Meanwhile the fascists wielded the stick and proffered the carrot in an attempt to divide the Catholic forces both within the Vatican and in the country at large. Priests and lay people were beaten, Catholic edifices were ruined and many of the centres belonging to the PPI or the white unions were burnt or otherwise destroyed.[47] Whether Monsignor Ernesto Pucci, a priest who on his own admission was in regular contact with both the Vatican and fascist circles, expressed the prevailing view when he later summed up one attitude to that period is uncertain. Pucci wrote that, given Mussolini was doing so much for the Church,

> it was truly no longer a case of quibbling about the value of certain acts and to malign the intentions behind them. One had to say that we were in the presence of a reformer whom Catholics themselves would never have dared to hope for; they were before that Man whom as later Pius XI had to assert Divine Providence had sent.[48]

For her part Anna Kuliscioff dared to hope that the result would be quite different. If, instead of giving in to the constant violence which was being directed against the PPI the Vatican got behind the party, 'it would not be illusory to hope for a reaction to the fascist regime which could perhaps arise outside Italy itself'.[49]

The carrot was extended to the Vatican both privately and publicly. Senator Santucci, still president of the Banco di Roma, had a house on Piazza del Gesù which could be entered either from the Piazza or from a back street. On 20 January 1923, Mussolini came in one entrance while Cardinal Gasparri used the other. The prelate and the Duce talked of the possibility of an ultimate solution to the Roman Question, they discussed the situation of the Banco di Roma and it is unlikely that Sturzo and his party were absent from their conversation. Mussolini was convinced that 'the past directors of the Bank had lost enormous sums of money through their megalomania and banking inexperience'. But he was still prepared to go ahead with the task of saving the Bank given the manifest benefit his regime would reap from this favour done to Catholic interests. Nevertheless there was a limit to his tolerance for ineptitude and as a result Santucci, to his pain, was removed a few days later from presidency of the Bank and Prince Boncompagni-Ludovisi, by now completely won to the fascist side, took his place.[50] The other person removed from the Bank's directorate was Giuseppe Vincentini, one of those who had helped the PPI in its formative days and who had always maintained good relations with it.[51] Some years later Gasparri denied having discussed his host's position in the Bank with Mussolini but it was cold comfort for the old Vatican trusty who saw too close a connection between the circumstances and who now suffered because he thought he had been betrayed by a man who had been his 'intimate friend from our earliest years'.[52] In any case the meeting made it possible for Gasparri, going out as he had come, to return to the Vatican and assure Pius that the way to a solution to the long vexed question of the Vatican in Italy had been opened.

While the introduction of the Catholic catechism was without doubt the step which the Church appreciated most in the fascist programme, the rejection of freemasonry ranked only a little behind the scholastic measure. On 13 February 1923 the fascist Grand Council declared freemasonry and fascism incompatible and proclaimed that 'for the fascist there can be only one obedience'. It was to fascism itself. This decision was taken by Mussolini and his Council to ensure the continued adherence of the nationalists who were bitterly anti masonic, but it was received with joy in the Vatican where it was proclaimed by *Osservatore Roman*o as 'an intelligent act, worthy of praise' while to *Corriere d'Italia* it was a 'courageous decision' which paved the way to a genuine renewal of the nation.[53] The reaction of *Civiltà Cattolica*, long an inflexible foe of masonry, was equally one of pleasure. It now saw more clearly the need to collaborate with the regime and invited the right wing Catholics to deal directly with Mussolini to achieve that end.[54]

Finally, Cardinal Vicenzo Vannutelli, dean of the College of Cardinals, was not slow to indicate what he thought of the 'courageous' decision. Speaking at a wedding at which Mussolini was present he saluted the man 'already acclaimed by all Italy as the reconstructor of the fate of the nation according to its religious and civic traditions'. Although *Osservatore Romano* was quick to assert that Vannutelli spoke in his own name and not that of the Holy See it would be ingenuous to suppose that he would have spoken in such terms unless aware that they would not meet with disapproval in the Vatican where no attempt was made to reject the clear imputation the cardinal's statement contained.[55] In fact the Vatican paper had praised and continued to praise Mussolini who had spoken 'with frankness' on foreign policy, whose words were 'a promising echo for the present and the future' and who generally bade fair to resolve the problems of the nation.[56]

To indicate the degree of solidarity on political affairs in the Vatican, Pius applauded the work of Gasparri and pronounced his pleasure at the 'harmony of outlook' that prevailed between himself and his Secretary of State. Some of these events must have emboldened Michele Bianchi, a Mussolini trusty, to proclaim that the Vatican knew, now that the fascists were doing so much for the Church, that the PPI served no further purpose as a result of which the clergy were being advised to abandon it. This last remark was met with the innocent rejoinder that such had always been the case as the Vatican had ever been above and beyond politics.[57] It was not easy for either of the socialist papers to comment calmly on Italian events given the harassment to which their directors were being subjected with both Serrati and Nenni arrested and the constant threat of being closed down completely. Nonetheless a writer in *La Giustizia* tried to sum up the Vatican–PPI–fascist situation on 24 March. To him the collaboration of the PPI with the fascist government could have only one end — the death of the PPI. He was sure that with the Vatican back in control 'clericalism will return completely to its old form' except it would be clerical fascism which would imply the selling out of the PPI and the reinstatement of the old bourgeois elements of the Vatican.[58] Farinacci, a member of the fascist Grand Council summed up the situation even more bluntly. 'Even though I am an atheist I recognize the necessity of the political line followed by Mussolini because with it the fascist government has emptied the Partito Popolare of its Catholic content.'[59]

In these circumstances the decision to go ahead with the Turin Congress was little less than a statement in itself that the PPI was about to make up its own mind where it stood and what its future would be. The main danger it faced was not suppression or outright extinction but absorption. The other Italian political parties did not share the problem in the same sense as the PPI because the old liberal and democratic groups had neither the party structure nor the tightly knit mass following which could be subjected to direct pressure while the parties of the left, by their declared opposition to the regime, had taken up a clear position and thus they could at least take measures to ensure their survival in the event of an attempt at suppression. The parties of the left, furthermore, were not anxious about the possibility that their supporters would be wooed away to follow the triumphal march of fascism because those amongst them who believed in socialism even in a rudimentary sense understood that fascism was not an acceptable alternative.

Within the PPI however there were many who were confused because it was apparent that the party directorate was uncertain and divided, the Church seemed already to accept if not welcome the status quo and the inner nature of fascism remained at best unrevealed. With its specious insistence on law and order while practising violence, with its lip service and legislative favours to religion while despising its essence, with its false patriotism, its economic reformism, its facade of loyalty to the king and its temporary adherence to the constitution, fascism seemed to be dedicated to much that the PPI had stood for. Finally, by allowing its members to accept cabinet posts while at the same time insisting that the party had retained its basic autonomy, serious doubts had been cast upon the intentions if not the integrity of the PPI directorate. It was a question therefore of endeavouring to resolve the situation, but it was already clear that a position in the centre of the political sphere was becoming impossible, and thus the main hope was that the party would remain united on the basic proposition of retaining its ideals and autonomy. Reports were coming through to the party directorate as well as to Mussolini that in many parts of the country, but particularly in the Veneto, the Marches and parts of the Romagna, the party branches, many members of the parish clergy and some of the bishops were emphatically anti-fascist.[60]

At the same time the right wing of the PPI, led by Mussolini's minister Cavazzoni, was determined to retain a position of loyal collaboration with the government and to this end they did all they could to obstruct the holding of the Congress. Cavazzoni expressed his views very forcibly to the Council of the party against the decision to go ahead, but he now did it before a group containing some men who no longer accepted his good faith as they had never believed in that of his Prime Minister, Mussolini.[61] In these circumstances it would be surprising if Sturzo still thought his party could maintain a centre position as there was little likelihood that the party could retain its unity given its proven and increasing tendency to fissurization. There was even less likelihood that Mussolini and the fascist Grand Council would accept a centre position from the PPI because, with that triumphalism endemic to unprincipled victors, they were not prepared to tolerate anything less than whole hearted cooperation. Nevertheless Sturzo still hoped that moderation, tolerance and good sense would prevail. He went to Turin, the homeland of Italian democracy, to find out whether others shared his hope.

Notes

1. *Avanti*, 14 November 1922. On the early period of the new regime see M. Missiroli, *Il colpo di stato* (Turin, 1924).

2. *Ordine Nuovo*, 14 November 1922.

3. *La Giustizia*, 29 October 1922, was a one-page edition. It resumed its normal format on 8 November.

4. *O.R.*, 29 October 1922.

5. Ibid., 30 October 1922.

6. Ibid., 29, 30, 31 October 1922.

7. G. Salvemini, *Stato*, pp. 266–7, gives the figures for the parliament. See also S. Jacini, *Storia*, p. 147

8. See G. Rossini (ed.), *Il delitto*, pp. 9–22; G. Spataro, *I Democratici*, pp. 61–5; N. Valeri, *G. Giolitti*, pp. 369–70 and S. Jacini, *I popolari*, p. 105.

9. *O.R.*, 1 November 1922; *Corriere d'Italia*, 1 November 1922; G. De Rosa, *Il Partito*, pp. 186–7. At Milan *L'Italia* took a fairly cautious attitude to Mussolini but it was pleased with his cabinet and thought all augured well for the future. *L'Italia*, 31 October, 1 November 1922, in B. Vigezzi (ed.), *1919–1925*, p. 575. One of the few 'liberals' who had grave reservations about the seizure of power was Luigi Salvatorelli who wrote in *La Stampa*, 1 November 1922, 'The absence of tragedy in certain moments in the life of a people can unfortunately reveal a lack of moral probity.' Cited in N. Valeri, *G. Giolitti*, p. 370.

10. G. Spataro, *I Democratici*, p. 65.

11. Senator Spataro expressed these views to me in Rome on 15 December 1974.

12. Despite its falling finances, or perhaps because of them, the Bank apparently joined with others in helping finance the March on Rome. See D. Allegra, *Come ha operato*, p. 45. This accusation against the Bank was initially made by Matteotti.

13. See G. Grilli, *La finanza vaticana in Italia* (Rome, 1961), pp. 55–6; L. Bedeschi (ed.), *La terza pagina*, p. 26; E. Santarelli, *Storia del fascismo*, 3 vols, 2nd edn (Rome, 1974), vol. 1, pp. 24–5, 356. For Crispolti's relationship with the popes of his day see F. Crispolti, *Pio IX, Leone XIII, Pio X, Benedetto XV, Pio XI. (Recordi personali)* (Milan, 1939), Crispolti was clearly an intimate of Benedict XV and Pius XI.

14. A reproduced facsimile of Mussolini's note to Tangorra dated 12 November 1922 is in Alberto De Stefani, *Baraonda bancaria* (Milan, 1960), p. 125.

15. See De Stefani, ibid. pp. 8–9.

16. F.L. Ferrari to E. Rosa S.J., 23 December 1930 in G. Rossini, *Il movimento*, pp. 17–20.

17. *O.R.*, 4, 16, 24 November 1922.

18. Mussolini in *Il popolo d'Italia*, 17 November 1922, quoted by G. Salvemini, *Stato*, p. 271.

19. Ibid., pp. 268–72; James P. Roe, *Fascism, Masonry and The Vatican in Italy* (New York, 1927), p. 3.

20. Quoted in E. Pucci, *La pace*, p. 92.

21. *New Witness*, 24 November 1922, in *Popolo Nuovo*, 10 December 1922.

22. *O.R.*, 2, 5 November 1922.

23. *La Giustizia*, 18 November 1922 and A. Kuliscioff to Turati, 25 November 1922, in *Carteggio*, vol. VI, p. 601.

24. *Corriere d'Italia*, 18 November 1922.

25. L. Sturzo, *Italy*, pp. 122–3; R. De Felici, *Mussolini il fascista*, p. 377.

26. G. Rossini (ed.), *Il delitto*, p. 24.

27. F. Medâ, 'L'Ora Che Passa' in B. Malinverni (ed.), *Civitas*, pp. 183–5.

28. G. Salvemini, *Stato*, p. 273.

29. The speech is found in L. Sturzo, *I discorsi*, pp. 217–60. Describing the speech, Lyttelton said 'Few other political leaders at the time spoke so frankly'. See A. Lyttelton, *The Seizure*, p. 121.

30 *Avanti*, 22 December 1922; *La Giustizia*, 22 December 1922. Writing in *Corriere d'Italia*, 22 December 1922, Mattei-Gentili refused to see any deeper meaning in the speech than an affirmation of loyal collaboration which, to him, was its political value.

31. *O.R.*, 22 December 1922.

32. *Acta Apostolicae Sedis*, Annus XV, vol. XIV no. 18, 27 December 1922, pp. 673–700.

33. *O.R.*, 9, 10 December 1922.

34. See G. De Rossi Dell' Arno, *Pio XI e Mussolini* (Rome, 1954), pp. 16–17.

35. *O.R.*, 28 December 1922; 6 January 1923. Giovanni Gentili was the Minister of Education who issued the new decree.

36. M. Bendiscioli, *La politica della Santa Sede (Direttive Organi Realizzazioni) 1918–1938* (Florence, 1939), pp. 76–7.

37. *Corriere d'Italia*, 6, 17 February, 6 March 1923. In the Vatican library there is a copy of Semeria's *I miei quattro papi* (Milan, 1930), with an inscription from the author to 'His Holiness Pope Pius XI — the reconciliator', dated 22/3/1930.

38. Donati to his wife, 2 November 1922. Donati said Italian history would have taken another path had Sturzo had 'the courage and strength' to take over the parliamentary group two years earlier. Quoted in G. Rossini (ed.), *Il delitto*, p. 22.

39. *L'Italia*, 28 January 1923, in B. Vigezzi (ed.), *1919–1925*, p. 575.

40. G. Spataro, *I Democratici*, p. 67. Though sons of Filippo Meda, Luigi and Gerolano did not share their father's conciliatory political position.

41. See *Corriere d'Italia*, 10, 11 February 1923 and for a letter of Meda to *L'Italia* in which he spoke of 'honest collaboration' being the order of the day for the PPI, see ibid., 2 January 1923.

42. See Donati to his wife, 14 January 1923, in G. Rossini (ed.), *Il delitto*, p. 25. For the paper in general see its own copies and L. Bedeschi (ed.), *La terza pagina*, passim.

43. Bedeschi asserts baldly that the papers of the Trust all went cleric–fascist in exchange for the salvation of the Banco di Roma. Ibid., p. 26.

44. E. Pucci, *La pace*, p. 89 and Donati to his wife, 14 January 1923, 'Mussolini recognizes that he needs us and wants our collaboration'. In G. Rossini (ed.), *Il delitto*, p. 25.

45. *Corriere d'Italia*, 23 December 1922, gives the obituary.

46. See G. Spataro, *I Democratici*, p. 67.

47. See *O.R.*, 15, 16 January 1923, 28 March 1923; *Civiltà Cattolica*, vol. 1, 3 March 1923, p. 422.

48. E. Pucci, *La pace*, p. 89.

49. A. Kuliscioff to Turati, 24 April 1923, *Carteggio*, vol. VI, pp. 12–13. On 18 January 1923 Italian Catholic Action officially asked Mussolini to ensure protection for the clergy and for its own members. No mention was made of other Italians who were being subject to fascist brutality. In the case of laity or priests who had any

association with the PPI or sympathy for it, Mussolini's assurances proved worthless. See F.L. Ferrari, *L'Azione*, p. 27.

50. See article by L. Einaudi of 5 October 1923 in vol. VII of his *Cronache*, pp. 382– and G. De Rosa, *I conservatori nazionali. Biografia di Carlo Santucci* (Brescia, 1962), p. 112.

51. G. De Rosa, *Il Partito*, pp. 203–4.

52. See Gasparri's letter of denial to Santucci in G. De Rosa, *I conservatori*, p. 105. De Rosa agrees with the denial but Mussolini made it clear that the Bank had been discussed. See G. Salvemini, *Stato*, pp. 277–8.

53. *O.R.*, 24 February 1923; *Corriere d'Italia*, 13, 15 February 1923.

54. *Civiltà Cattolica*, vol. 1, 17 February 1923, pp. 370–1.

55. See *Avanti*, 23 February 1923; *O.R.*, 24 February 1923.

56. Ibid., 25 January, 26–7 February, 23, 28 March 1923.

57. Ibid., 28 March 1923.

58. *Avanti,* 2, 3 March 1923; *La Giustizia*, 2, 24 March 1923.

59. *O.R.*, 14, 27 March 1923. I did not see this quote in *O.R.* but found it in G. Salvemini, *Stato*, p. 282. That it is in keeping with the personality of Farinacci is unquestionable.

60. See G. De Rosa, *Il Partito*, pp. 204–5.

61. Giuseppe Spataro was a member of the directorate and he told me that he had no belief in the good faith of Cavazzoni who he thought belonged only in name to the PPI. Interview, 15 December 1974. For an account of Cavazzoni's opposition to Turin see L. Cavazzoni (ed.), *Stefano Cavazzoni* (Milan, 1955), pp. 61–2.

7

THE VOICE OF THE WATCHMAN

Only fragments remain of Sturzo's correspondence in that crucial year, 1923, so that it is impossible to know his torment as he prepared for the Turin Congress. In the whole of Italy no voices proclaimed absolute conflict with the new regime except those who had never accepted the possibility of reforming society through the gradualism of parliamentary democracy. Matteotti was carefully compiling his list of fascist atrocities which were to find their appropriate, but temporary, culmination in his assassination. Turati was pondering over the letters of his beloved Anna while wondering whether flight was a more honourable solution than death, and Serrati and Nenni were experiencing the new penal system from within. For Sturzo it was a short walk from his apartment on Via della Ripetta past the ruined reminder of Rome's ancient glory, the Augusteo, and into Piazza del Popolo where the throbbing blackshirts were a warning for the present and an omen for the future. With his question 'Watchman, what of the night?' so far unanswered it was time for the little Sicilian to hold up the lamp and speak at last of the perils cloaked by the impending darkness.[1]

By the time the Congress got under way on 12 April, the PPI had already been weakened through an attempt by a group of conservatives to form a new Catholic party loyal to the fascist regime. Like the PPI this new creation, called the Unione Nazionale, professed itself independent of the Church but the fascist press hailed it as if it were stamped by ecclesiastical approval. The quick denials of both

Osservatore Romano and *Civiltà Cattolica* clouded such hopes but the fact that its founder, Marchese Carlo Ottavio Cornaggia, a former PPI deputy, was a leading Milanese layman and lifelong friend of Pius XI, served initially to throw the PPI ranks into confusion.[2] In June 1922 Cornaggia's attempt to found a right-wing Catholic party had failed, which perhaps explains official Vatican caution in regard to the Unione Nazionale which also eventually folded without success.[3] The people who made it up were themselves fascist to the extent that they were convinced ideological nationalists and held to anti-democratic ideas. As such they could scarcely expect to win much support in the PPI but they could and did tend to confuse further those Italian Catholics who were wavering in their allegiance on the political level.[4]

The other attempt to force the PPI to the right and thence into the fascist fold was shepherded by leading exponents of the collaborationist theory such as Martire, Tovini and Cesare Nava. They were determined to 'flank Mussolini's government in its work of national reconstruction' and to combat any attempt by the left wing to break the already existing ties between the party and the new regime.[5] Given the eminence of its leaders in the party, Martire, for example, was still the darling of Catholic Action in Rome, Sturzo and his allies had to attempt to thwart their efforts. Above all they had to preserve the fragile unity of the party which would have been shattered by the alienation or expulsion of the left. If that had occurred the left, led by Miglioli, would probably have gone over to the socialists. In these circumstances it was correct for *Avanti* to say that 'The popolari are at the cross roads' but it was unfair to run a cartoon showing Christ the poor man being followed into the Congress hall by a fat man smoking a cigar and carrying a portfolio marked 'Banco di Roma'.[6] The fact was that Sturzo, who had never seen himself as a minor messiah, led his anxious and confused party into the most decisive Congress of its short history.

In a curious but unmistakable sense it was rather what Sturzo failed to say at Turin than what he said that mattered. Had he anywhere praised the fascist regime, had he demanded close and firm collaboration with it, had he indicated that his party had no future without it, he would have betrayed his past, the ideals of his party and his concept of democracy. It is from this point that any understanding or criticism of Sturzo's stand at Turin must begin because Mussolini demanded all that from Sturzo and the priest knew it. The Italian historian Giorgio Galli condemned Sturzo because he did not use the word fascist in his speech but Adrian Lyttelton has redressed the balance by calling the Congress 'a triumph for Don Sturzo.'[7] It was more than enough for Sturzo to state explicitly that his party stood inflexibly 'against every type of centralizing perversion attempted in the name of the pantheistic State or of the deified Nation'; to affirm 'even after the recent political happenings' the character, spirit, substance, autonomy and finality of his party; to deny that the new regime, by its attempts to palliate the Church had emptied the PPI of its purpose; to express 'solidarity with those who knew how to suffer for an ideal and for internal peace' and to proclaim that the only possible way to collaborate was to do it standing on one's own feet rather than lying down.[8] Sturzo could leave it to Francesco Luigi Ferrari to proclaim the enmity of the PPI to the 'fascist dictatorship' and to assert with a conviction he carried to the grave that 'It is better to die free than live as slaves'.[9] From 13 April 1923 Mussolini, had he been in any doubt previously, knew exactly where Sturzo stood because he was acute enough to realize that the cold, measured terms of Sturzo were as emphatic a rejection of himself and fascism as he was likely to hear.

The Turin Congress was a success for Sturzo and the more astute political observers fully realized its anti-fascist stand. Mario Missiroli immediately applauded Sturzo and De Gasperi and said that the 'fascist concept of the State ... is the radical negation of Catholicism' while *La Giustizia* summed up the Congress as a 'continuous and compact manifestation of profound aversion to the fascist movement.'[10] By allowing collaboration on his terms to be retained Sturzo had saved the unity of the party. The right insisted on collaboration and Sturzo did not stop it while the left held out for the terms which Sturzo had himself enunciated: It was up to the fascists to abide by those terms or it would spell the end of collaboration. Thus, through his insistence on the autonomy and finality of the party Sturzo had directly laid down the gauntlet before the fascist dictatorship. Henceforth any infringement of that autonomy and finality was a proclaimed act against the still vaunted nature of Italian democracy and Sturzo was prepared to hold up his party's freedom as one yardstick of that heritage. When he declared that no amount of deals done between Church and state would deprive his party of its right to existence Sturzo warned both Pius and Mussolini that religion could not be prostituted to the service of the state nor vice versa.

Perhaps the Vatican refused to or was incapable of seeing the point, because *Osservatore Romano* seemed satisfied with the Congress and expressed pleasure at the retention of party unity, quoted at length from Sturzo and from Rodinò who had said 'We are neither fascists nor anti-fascists — we are Italians', and even referred to Gerolamo Meda who had proclaimed the absolute intransigence of the party to any attempt by the government to change the electoral laws based on proportionalism. The final comment of the paper was one upholding the old distinction between the Church and politics and regretting the use of the term 'aconfessional' because it had led to so much confusion.[11] It is possible that in the Vatican a certain degree of equanimity prevailed as to the future of the PPI because even before the Congress had begun rumours were already abroad of the imminent resignation of Sturzo.'[12] Pius XI and Cardinal Gasparri knew that the priest would bow to the dictates of religious obedience and they knew too that without him his party was finished. Meanwhile they could afford to wait and see what the response to Turin would be in the fascist ranks.

There was an immediate reaction to Sturzo's speech which was published in Mussolini's paper *Popolo d'Italia* on the following day. Entitled 'The Speech of an Enemy' it was inspired, if not actually written, by Mussolini himself. With ringing phrases it proclaimed 'Don Sturzo disowns the Empire and thus disowns the history of Catholicism, rejects the Roman and Christian empire of Constantine and denies the Sacred Empire of Dante.' The conclusion to this jingoistic claptrap was curious even it came from Mussolini: 'Don Sturzo has not got a Roman soul. He has the mentality of a pastor and of a Protestant professor like Wilson.[13] On a more practical level, however, Mussolini was faced with the immediate difficulty of what action to take in regard to the PPI membership of his cabinet. Granted its proclaimed desire to continue to collaborate with the regime, Turin had made it abundantly plain that no further reliance could be placed on Sturzo's party despite the proclamation by the right-wing leader Antonio Pestalozza that Mussolini was 'the man sent by Providence' to serve the nation, and that Sturzo's ideas had to be abandoned. Pestalozza thus foreshadowed the words of Pius XI in 1929 but, unlike the pope, Pestalozza was greeted by his hearers with several minutes of uproar and cries of 'Enough, enough'.[14] Furthermore if the fascist regime were to achieve the specious electoral stability it then considered desirable, it was necessary to change the system of elections based on proportionalism because with it in place the fascists had no hope of achieving a majority in parliament.

Mussolini had insisted that suitable changes be made in the law but it appeared certain, after Turin, that if the government voted for the abolition of proportionalism, the PPI would move a vote of no confidence in it. De Gasperi in his key motion at the Congress on collaboration with the regime had made it clear that the defence of proportionalism was a cardinal factor which would determine the PPIs attitude to the government on the grounds that without it the party would be swallowed up by the regime.[15] Hence the need for immediate action by Mussolini if he were to ensure the unity of the fascist movement and its success at the next elections. Sturzo had thus forced the Duce into a position in which he either had to choose to work with democracy in the shape of 'the only organized democratic party' in the parliament, or reject it and go down the road to totalitarianism.[16] Mussolini being what he was and with fascism bent on that course the road ahead was clear and, if Sturzo achieved nothing else at Turin, he had at least pointed out to the Italian people the direction their country was to take in the future, which was a worthy role for a 'Watchman' to assume. Not without cause Mario Missiroli wrote that it was Sturzo who had taken upon himself the task of 'defending the just, moderate and fundamental theses of democracy'.[17] But Sturzo's difficulty was that even in his own party there were so few of the resolute.

On 17 April Mussolini called the PPI members of the cabinet to meet him and he made it plain that the kind of collaboration proffered at Turin was insufficient. The parliamentary party then met but Sturzo, on the grounds that he did not want to exercise undue influence, was unwisely absent. The difference in the composition of the Congress to that of the parliamentary party in which men held and were rewarded for power was immediately apparent. Tovini moved a right-wing resolution, previously approved of by the Duce himself, which stated complete confidence in Mussolini. It was lost as it was a total denial of the Congress deliberations, but the final resolution, which made no mention of Turin, promised loyal support and hedged on proportionalism, was little better as is illustrated by the fact that Mussolini's contact and minister Cavazzoni voted for it. Sturzo was strongly opposed to the resolution but his absence was his own responsibility and it was too late to change events as Cavazzoni had immediately communicated the document to Mussolini.[18]

Jacini indicated that the only deal that could have been effective in deciding the fascist Grand Council to accept the PPI resolution was a promise by the directorate to get rid of Sturzo as secretary and to expel the prominent members of the left wing, which were decisions the party had no intention of making.[19] Mussolini presumably was loath to take decisive action as he fully realized that the presence of the PPI members in his cabinet gave him a cloak of democratic respectability but stronger council prevailed against him and he decided to 'accept' the resignations of his PPI colleagues. Paolo Mattei-Gentili deplored the fact that the Congress had ever been held and asserted that as 'Catholics and Italians' it was their duty to continue to collaborate with the regime in the future.[20]

Since its inception four years earlier the PPI had always been a central force in Italian political life irrespective of its actual role in the passing cabinets of the day. By late April 1923 it held that role no longer so that it could rely henceforth only on its own strength as a cohesive group with clear cut ideals and policies. Like the socialists and the communists it was now in a political wilderness and its previous association with the other power in Italian life across the Tiber was no longer applicable for the precise reason that the Vatican had no intention of backing a loser. Its ideals were intact but it had lost the power to have its policies even partially implemented. Its unity was shaken if not shattered and the fulcrum about which it had always pivoted in the person of Luigi Sturzo was in jeopardy. Not without reason *La Giustizia* wondered if all that the bait the fascists had offered to the Church would not now be enough to prompt the response of giving 'a little of Don Sturzo on a plate to the Viminale' where Mussolini had his headquarters.[21]

Meanwhile the fascists kept up the carrot in the form of new laws on education which were accepted in the Vatican with gratitude and the stick with beatings and doses of castor oil to priests, lay people, Catholic activists, white unionists and Popolari alike.[22] None of this was lost on Cardinal Gasparri who hastened to get out a document to the bishops in which he reiterated that the proposition that the Holy See had no connection with the PPI. He then said 'His Holiness desires all those who in any way or to any extent represent the interests of religion to pay attention to the rule of strictest prudence, avoiding even the very appearance of attitudes towards and approval of political parties.' While 'all those' embraced both priests and even those laymen with positions in Catholic Action it was apparent that the person most in Pius' mind was Sturzo. The official, fascist controlled press agency was quick to point out that by virtue of Canon 139 it was the duty of the Vatican to oblige Sturzo to resign as secretary of the PPI, otherwise it would put itself in an 'incompatible situation.'[23]

The fascist campaign against Sturzo was unsubtle, unwearied and uncouth while that of the Vatican was cautious, patient and effective. The scenario was simple enough. Sturzo had dominated the party at Turin and, despite the vacillation of its parliamentary wing, his basic determination not to allow the PPI to be swallowed up into the fascist maw had ensured its continued existence and to maintain its reserve in regard to the government. The obstacle now in the path of converting Italy into a fascist, totalitarian state was the electoral system and with visitors such as George V and his Queen ensuring Mussolini of England's 'intimate collaboration' it was necessary to make some pretence at democratic niceties.[24] In June Mussolini outlined his ideas on electoral reform which would henceforth give two thirds of the seats to any party gaining a relative majority of the vote while the other third would be awarded, generously and proportionally, to the minor parties. It was a proposition with which *Osservatore Romano* agreed and one with which Sturzo disagreed.[25]

Despite his manifest misgivings regarding Sturzo's position and behaviour Gasparri was not yet ready to bow to fascist demands and insist on his resignation. In May 1924 a series of letters passed between Carlo Barduzzi, an emissary of Gasparri, and Salvatore Contarini, secretary of the Ministry of Foreign Affairs. Gasparri apparently thought that it might be possible to work out an arrangement that would not require the 'absolute sacrifice of Don Sturzo' provided the PPI renounced its attitude to proportionalism. As a reward the PPI could then be guaranteed a 'certain number' of positions on the government electoral ticket thus ensuring their election. Ultimately it was proposed to flank the PPI with a 'Catholic party of the right' thus resolving the vexed question of Catholic attitudes to fascism and leaving the PPI to satisfy the political whims of the left-wing Catholics.[26]

For what it is worth this correspondence indicates that in the Vatican the question of Sturzo and the PPI had become of lesser moment. Father Tacchi Venturi was now in regular correspondence with Mussolini; Cardinal Vannutelli held frequent conversations with Alfredo Rocco, under-secretary of the Treasury, and Rocco told Monsignor Pucci that Mussolini intended to solve the Roman Question and that he would take steps to muzzle the press if it tried to muddy the waters beforehand. In the midst of all this it is certain that no recalcitrance on the part of the PPI would be allowed to prove an obstacle to the much longed-for reconciliation between Church and state in the peninsula which Mussolini and his fascist government seemed to be set on bringing to fruition. The regime proclaimed its faith in 'that Church which in a not far distant day could strike with an excommunication the priest Sturzo who profanes his priestly garb in the spiteful, bloodless, buffooneries of party congresses'.[27]

It did not appear that the directorate of the PPI was yet fully aware of the precarious situation in which the party now found itself for the determination was still firm not to vote for the law as outlined by Mussolini and promoted by him with threats of further blackshirt violence. On 14 June the party directorate met with the parliamentary members and Sturzo insisted that changes in the electoral law would destroy the last bulwark of democracy in the nation. This was Sturzo's last speech before the parliamentary group and everyone present followed him in his demand for an intransigent stand on the basis of the motion decided at Turin.[28] The decision of the party gave Mattei-Gentili, still editor of the powerful Roman daily, *Corriere d'Italia* which had promoted the PPI since its inception, his opportunity to resign from the directorate. By now Livio Tovini, acknowledged leader of the conservative clerical right wing had been expelled, Martire's case was under investigation and the deep fissures in the party which had only been fleetingly glimpsed in the past were becoming apparent.[29]

Sturzo knew that the warning issued by Gasparri in April was no idle threat but he continued to act on the assumption that, just as he had been allowed specifically to assume the secretaryship of the PPI by Benedict XV and by Gasparri himself, there was no reason now why general admonitions ought to apply to him any more than they had in the past. The fascist press decided it would make the issue somewhat clearer in all camps so an article was run in *Giornale d'Italia*, in which the men 'on the other side of the Tiber' were asked to ponder the likely consequences to the Church if Sturzo continued to provoke a 'revolutionary situation' and if the Catholic party was allowed to pursue its destructive tactics unchecked. *L'Osservatore Romano* came back with the time worn reminder that the Holy See was 'beyond and outside parties and political debates' but this time its bluff was called. The government organ, *Idea Nazionale*, stated bluntly that the Church could no longer deny its responsibility for the political activity of the priest, Sturzo, or the PPI in defence of proportionalism and that its 'alibi' was henceforth worthless.[30]

This admonition had its desired effect and the chosen instrument of destruction was the pen of the esteemed Monsignor Enrico Pucci, sometime ardent supporter of the PPI, writer for *Corriere d'Italia* and a constant go between from the Vatican to Italian lay and political circles. Pucci replied on 25 and 26 June with articles in the Roman daily in which he upheld the Holy See and its autonomy, defended Sturzo as a priest, reminded his readers that no absolute law was applicable in regard to priests in politics, as instanced by the priest, Seipel, Chancellor of Austria, and then proceeded to request Sturzo's resignation in order to put paid to the embarrassment of the Holy See in Italy. It was a well-directed hit because it was aimed at the one aspect of Sturzo that was likely to make him waver.

Don Luigi Sturzo remained essentially a man of the Church and, despite De Gasperi's warning that the sacking of Sturzo would enhance the opinion that the Holy See intervened directly in Italian affairs, the damage was done. Two days later Pucci pressed the point home when he declared that although he was not writing in the name of the Holy See, 'it seems ingenuous to me to suppose that I could have written, on a matter of such a delicate nature, something which was not to me clearly in accord with the mind of the Holy See'.[31] The simple men of the *La Guistizia* felt uneasy even on the fringes of this Byzantine, sombre world of intrigue, buck passing and pious platitudes. 'The truth is that he who is not right on the inside of Vatican diplomacy with all its complications doesn't understand a thing about it any longer.' The paper felt bound to refrain from further comment in order to avoid being the victim of further surprises'.[32] Sturzo himself, well versed as he was in Vatican diplomacy, knew the full impact of Pucci's intervention and said to his friends, 'If the Vatican wants to take action in my regard it has no need to make use of intermediaries to warn me.'[33]

It was scarcely a propitious moment for Donati to enter the lists but he took it upon himself to explain the position of the PPI in *Il Popolo* with a lapidary article entitled 'Citizens and believers'. He began with the assertion that the reason so many Catholics were members of the PPI was 'based on our political platform and not on any reason that is of a strictly religious nature'. To Donati it was absurd to object to the PPI because it did not concern itself with the historical relations between 'Church and State' as such matters were of interest only to those 'neo-clericals' who used democracy to safeguard their own interests. The PPI looked to 'a genuine and authentic form of democracy' and the Church allowed room for that, whereas to turn now and become followers of fascism would be mortally offensive to that sincerity and respect owed to themselves by members of the PPI both as 'citizens and as believers'.[34] Anna Kuliscioff had already arrived at the conclusion that '*Il Popolo* of Don Sturzo is exquisitely written and maintains a kind of nobility in both direction and thought',[35] but what others thought of it is less certain. Some Catholics certainly had other ideas on their desirable behaviour as 'citizens and believers' which soon became apparent.

The black nobility was composed of those old elements of papal Italy who had survived the transition to an Italian state. They came forward with a document called *Manifesto of the National Catholics* which appeared on Roman walls on 30 June and thereby entered the lists in the struggle to depose Sturzo. Signed by 43 leading Catholic laymen, all of them the pope's men, and including two princes, one duke, five marquis and 11 counts, it asserted their unconditional loyalty to the fascist regime and proclaimed their adversity to 'any undertaking which partisan spirits try to promote amongst Italian Catholics' and to 'anti-national parties which attempt to degrade and demoralize the conscience of our People'. The signatories looked especially to the clergy for their support in 'this work of redemption'.[36] It is scarcely necessary to record that *Osservatore Romano* hastened to point out that the *Manifesto* had value only as 'purely personal initiative' even though to *Avanti* both it and the Pucci letters were expressions of the innermost will of the Vatican.[37]

Richard Washburn Child, the American ambassador to Italy, with his initial foray into Italian politics went on record on the side of the strength. He spoke at a dinner on 29 June at which Mussolini, whom he praised fulsomely, was present. He said, 'During the last eight months Italy has reconciled itself in an extraordinary manner with the moral progress of the whole world by raising on high the ideals of human courage, discipline and responsibility …'[38] To this avalanche the fascists added their mite with violence and threats of violence and Mussolini warned that if the Popolari did not vote for the electoral law, he would have his henchmen occupy all the Roman parishes.

On 10 July Sturzo went into a meeting of the party directorate and resigned. To his followers and indeed to all democratic Italy it fell like a blow but it is too much to say that in all the circumstances it was a surprise. Seated in parliament Filippo Turati wrote to Anna at Milan 'The news of the resignation of Sturzo, imposed so it is said, by the Vatican... when heard in the House after two o'clock, exploded like a bomb.' Sturzo did not then reveal whether the Vatican had acted directly and told him to resign but three years later in a letter to Cardinal Bourne, Archbishop of Westminster he stated quite explicitly that his step had been taken 'at the request of the Holy See'.[39]

Although the party tried to put on a brave face, the dismissal of Sturzo was a severe loss especially at a time when its unity was severely threatened by the prospect of offering public opposition to the regime in parliament. With his customary forthrightness Francesco Luigi Ferrari tried to get the National Council of the party to force the question of Sturzo's resignation into the open by denouncing the regime in parliament as the 'violator of religious liberty' but the clear satisfaction of the Vatican, which both *Corriere d'Italia* and *Osservatore Romano* expressed at the resignation made it almost impossible to draw moral or political capital from it and, in any case, Sturzo did not want the situation made worse now that he had complied with the pressure brought to bear upon him.[40] The Roman daily, *Corriere d'Italia* under the editorship of Mattei-Gentili had from the earliest days supported the PPI fully. By 1923 it was almost completely won to the fascist cause and it wrote of 'the figure of this priest' who sacrificed himself to save the Church from the persecution caused by the 'attitude of the Popolari against electoral reform'. The Vatican paper praised Sturzo both as a priest and as a man with political sense and the implication was clear that at long last he had done the right thing at the right time.[41] In the scarcely figurative sense it could be said that the sighs of relief from both the Viminale and the Vatican were heard throughout Italy. It was indeed the right time because on the very day of Sturzo's resignation discussion began in parliament on the question of electoral 'reform' with the proposed new law taking the name of its proponent, Giacomo Acerbo, although all knew that its true framer was Benito Mussolini.[42]

Despite his resignation as secretary, the strength and firmness of Sturzo still held the party on an anti-'reform' line as had been decided at Turin.[43] As a consequence it was apparent that, provided the party held firm, Mussolini with 187 votes gathered from fascist, liberal and some democrat deputies could not win against a solid block of 207 votes which the Popolari and the opposition parties could amass together. Sturzo had been careful not to hand in his resignation at the National Council meeting until the decision had been taken to oppose the 'reform' when he felt he could do it, safe at least in the knowledge that the struggle for democracy would go on. He could even take comfort in the fact that the triumvirate elected to take on his job were Rodinò, Gronchi and Spataro who had never wavered in their adhesion to party unity and in opposition to 'reform'. In the circumstances his hopes were ill founded and it was with the bitter gall of disillusion that Spataro recorded that when the parliamentary group assembled to thank Sturzo for his life's work, Cavazzoni approached the priest and embraced him.[44]

Mussolini decided that if pure reason itself was not sufficient to lead thinking men to approve of his law then he would give them other motives to ponder on. He surrounded parliament with his fascist cadres, he published a royal decree severely limiting the freedom of the press and he made it clear that he would again unleash the reins on his blackshirts and convulse the nation in violence unless the law were passed.[45] One Italian who could never be accused of lacking in the virtue of prudence was Filippo Meda and, despite his firmness on 'reform' three months earlier, recent events indicated to him that the time was not ripe for intransigency. The party itself had wavered to the extent of promising Mussolini to vote for a watered-down version of the proposed law that would in some measure retain proportionalism but Meda knew that there was to be no meeting between the two sides in a half-way house. Despite the plea of Sturzo, which was relayed to Meda by Spataro, the old standard bearer of the democratic cause sent a letter to all the PPI deputies telling them that he was convinced the party ought to vote for the law in order to avoid 'grave harm to the country and to the party'. Meda remained absent in the cooler region of Milan while parliament struggled for its integrity in those heavy July days, but his letter was one substantial element in bringing about a decision which certainly caused harm to Italy and helped destroy the credibility of the party to which Meda had pledged his loyalty.[46]

In parliament Mussolini alternatively threatened and blandished the PPI deputies as he well knew that in their ranks alone could he hope to win votes to his side. He told them that he would not accept their form of 'Malthusian collaboration' and that it was time for them to line up with him in this 'moment in which it is possible to reconcile the Parliament with the people'. To him the proposed 'reform' was firmly based on democratic principles given that it even guaranteed a proportion of the seats to the minority parties![47] Few of his listeners were able to comprehend the fact that it was only the majority of which Mussolini thought and that majority — a fascist one — had to be given the shield of parliamentary respectability. The minorities were a problem that time and resolute action would solve. In 1919 Mussolini, then editor of the *Popolo d'Italia* had threatened to promote a march on parliament if the very law on proportional representation which he now was determined to abolish, were not passed through parliament and his posturings now moved Turati to write to Anna, who had suggested it might be time to get ready to leave the country 'Let us prepare our bags not so much to save our skins but rather to save ourselves from vomiting'.[48]

After the prudent abstention of Meda the PPI leaders were afraid to push for a completely intransigent stand against the bill because they knew that it would threaten the already weakened party unity. With Sturzo removed from his pivotal position no other figure had the strength to command the adhesion of the individual deputies. They met and 41 voted to abstain on the bill while 39 voted to oppose it. The minority accepted the decision and went to the House prepared to take the less rigid stand of abstention where, to their astonishment, they heard Cavazzoni, proponent of the abstentionist tactic, proclaim to Mussolini that he personally, and others likewise, would have voted for the bill. When the votes were taken eight members from the left, including Miglioli, voted against the bill while nine from the right, amongst whom were Cavazzoni, Mattei-Gentili and Martire, voted for it. Rather too strongly Turati wrote 'The defection of the Popolari was due especially to the betrayal of that pig Cavazzoni'.[49]

In fact Cavazzoni was only a symptom of a sickness that too often lay deep in the heart of democracy and was Italian only to the extent that it then manifested itself in Italy. It was the sickness born from pusillanimity and opportunism that so frequently made even the strong fall down before the dictator and even those who were strong in Italy now knew they were in the presence of a dictator.

That 15th day of July 1923 was a sorry one for the flickering flame of democratic Italy for it put paid to any hope that henceforth the people would be able to change their government by the normal process. One wonders what Sturzo thought soon afterwards when he read the comment of the *Times* that Mussolini could say with truth that he had saved Italy from 'a grave internal danger' and of *Osservatore Romano* which called the result of the debate 'a providential agreement between the House and the Government'. It is surely permissible to hope that he was spared reading Queen Margherita's effusion on the matter. 'Mussolini ... has saved the Nation. For him, because of the good that he has done and is doing for Italy, I have warm sympathy and maternal affection.'[50]

In one sense it can be said that the events of July had a purifying effect on the PPI in that it was at last made clear where the parliamentary deputies stood in relation to the regime. A handful of the extreme left was so disillusioned that they ceased their formal adhesion to the party without relinquishing their support of its ideals. The party itself got rid of the extreme right with the expulsion of Cavazzoni, Martire and Mattei-Gentili and the resignations of some senators including Santucci, Grosoli and Crispolti. Spataro who was himself a member of the triumvirate that, together with De Gasperi, decided on the expulsions, explained that the decision was not taken 'with a light heart' and that it was a difficult duty given 'the opposite attitude of authoritative ecclesiastical circles and the personal risk of eventual fascist persecution'.[51]

Perhaps even more importantly the Council decided to repudiate in a formal sense any connection between it and the *Corriere d'Italia*. It was significant because such a decision declared to all concerned the determination of the party to cut its shackles with the past. It was the prerogative of Mattei-Gentili to write in his editorial that he had chosen to stand up for the 'superior interests of the Church' rather than for the party he had represented in parliament. It was equally the prerogative of that party to declare that the force of the democratic ideal had to be preserved and it says something for the importance of that stand that on 31 July 1923 the Fascist Grand Council declared officially that the PPI was the 'enemy of fascism'.[52]

The aftermath of the vote on 'reformed' proportionalism and the expulsion of the right-wing elements from the PPI caused a stirring of the waters on the part of those elements in Italian Catholicism which had opted for a fascist solution to the ills of the nation. For them, had it been a clear-cut struggle between fascism and socialism, no question of conscience would ever have arisen even in a minimal sense. But the involvement of the PPI made them at least think of the implications of the fascist rise to power and as a result some justification had to be offered for their choice given that even the most innocent observer had to admit that at times it seemed apparent that the methods used by the fascists did not square entirely with the normal canons of the Christian ethic.

To the priest patriot, Father Giovanni Semeria, the very soul of fascism was shot through with nationalism and patriotism. Certainly it had been violent at times, but it had saved the country from bolshevism and, in the main, it was favourable to religion. Semeria declared, with considerable justification, that 'Priests in full communion with their Bishop are fascists, and even belong to fascist administrations' and that 'it is our Catholic duty to christianize fascism'.[53] Doctor Luigi Nicoletti was even more direct. To him no one could ever forget the violence of bolshevism and in the face of that violence the PPI was impotent because further violence was necessary to stop it. Catholics had, as a consequence, the duty to salute fascism and its leader because they had saved the country and the Church.[54] If it was any comfort to the reverend observers of the political scene the fascist organ *Popolo d'Italia* saw the situation in almost the same terms. It warned 'the fascists of all Italy' that 'today's enemy is no longer that of red subversion it is that of sturzian popolarism'.[55] In the Vatican the feeling was not identical in that its experts were by no means sure that the danger of red subversion was passed. The pro fascist prelate, Monsignor, (later cardinal) Giuseppe Pizzardo, made it clear to the directorate of the white unions that the Holy Father was acutely concerned about the left leaning inclination of the movement as well as its connection with the PPI. On both matters the directorate was advised to 'revise its position' in order to give to the Holy See the moral 'guarantees' necessary for the future'.[56]

While this struggle went on behind the scenes to deprive the PPI of its support in the unions, another was taking place to divorce the party from any base in Catholic Action. By late 1922 Pius had achieved his aim of uniting all Italian Catholic Action in the one body, directly subordinate to the hierarchy and with a central committee to control it. It comprised four main groupings of men, women, youth and university students and the president, responsible to the pope himself and appointed by him was Luigi Colombo.[57] Colombo had been a national councillor of the PPI until 1922 but by the end of that year he had come to the conclusion that the kindest fate for the party would be its immediate dissolution. This course of action he had intimated to Sturzo who, not unnaturally, had rejected the suggestion though probably aware that Colombo was not making it purely on his personal initiative.[58] The pope had made it plain repeatedly that Catholic Action was to play no political role in Italian life, and this facet of its existence was stressed again and again in 1923.[59]

Such affirmations would have been of some moral value had they not also been implied an explicit rejection of any connection with the PPI. To abandon the PPI in those circumstances when it was patently the declared enemy of the regime, was to imply, at the very least, a form of compliance with and acceptance of the fascist government. That this situation prevailed was explicit in the pages of the *Corriere d'Italia* which, from being the most consistent supporter of the PPI, switched to equally consistent support of Catholic Action and the fascist regime and in *Unità Cattolica* which had always supported Catholic Action but now added its backing to Mussolini who was told 'you are not an elegant transient on the political scene: you are a lasting element'.[60] By August 1923 the break between Catholic Action and the Partito Popolare was final when Colombo stated bluntly that Catholic Action rather than a political party was the natural arena for all those who loved Catholic principles to operate in.[61] One particular individual who had dedicated a great deal of his life to Catholic Action and who had come at last to realize that the struggle for democracy was also an element of the Christian apostolate was Father Giovanni Minzoni. He was not permitted to actuate his realization at any length.

Minzoni was parish priest of Argenta in the province of Ferrara where his activity amongst the Catholic youth was so effective that the development of fascism in the area was seriously jeopardised. He revered the memory of Murri and shared his idealism for Christian Democracy but he had kept clear of involvement with the PPI until April 1923 when he joined the party on the grounds that its harassment demanded that men of principle proclaim their solidarity with it. On the night of 23 August 1923 he was attacked by two fascist thugs and died of a fractured skull a few hours later. The man primarily responsible was Italo Balbo, chief of the National Militia, but he and his accomplices went free despite the evidence that was uncovered by *La Voce Repubblicana* and by Donati in the PPI paper, *Il Popolo*.

Minzoni died with the conviction that it was better to die than to live and conform to what he called the 'stupid servile life' imposed by fascism. Many of those who lived did not seem to mind either its stupidity or servility. His archbishop proved unable to attend the funeral service and sent a fascist priest in his stead. *Corriere d'Italia* deplored the death, but was content to await 'serenely' for a verdict on its perpetration. *L'Osservatore Romano* wrote a short account of the slaying without comment except to remark that Mussolini was saddened by it. *Civiltà Cattolica* reported the event with laconic and resigned comment. Pius himself said nothing at all while Italian Catholic Action decided to mount a campaign against verbal blasphemy in the nation. Understandably, the fascist press interpreted the silence of the Catholic organs as a sign that the ecclesiastical authorities were displeased with Minzoni for being a 'fervent' member of the PPI.[62]

A week after the affair the seventh Eucharistic Congress was celebrated at Genoa and Italy was proclaimed both 'Eucharistic and Papal'. The protomartyr of Italian Catholicism under the new regime received no mention at the Congress, but the religious event was given all possible support by the government. It was left to Ferrari to remark 'In the days of Pius X the conservative reaction created rebels, under Pius XI it creates martyrs'.[63] Count Giuseppe Dalla Torre was director of the *Osservatore Romano* in those days and he must have known from his personal experience the agony that lay open in the hearts of many of Italy's finest Catholics as they witnessed the prostitution of Christian ideals in the name of containment or expediency. Twenty years later he wrote 'Between Catholic Action and Fascism there was always an irreconcilable gulf in character, both in the moral and in the political field.'[64] In 1923 that gulf was not apparent to many, at the very least to Sturzo and the men of the PPI.

Notes

1. Giuseppe Donati writing in *Il Popolo* on 5 April 1923 made it clear that the Turin Congress would clarify the position of the PPI in regard to fascism. It was the first number of the new paper. *Osservatore Romano* was mildly derisive of it and asked whether the PPL would find it quite so simple to explain its standpoint. *O.R.*, 5 April 1923; *Avanti*, 6 April 1923, joined in the fun making from the other end of the political spectrum.

2. *Civiltà Cattolica*, vol. 2, 5 March 1923, pp. 279–81; *O.R.*, 13 April 1923, and *Corriere della Sera*, 14 April 1923.

3. E. Howard, *Il Partito*, p. 364. Cornaggia released a document inviting all those who had left the PPI, because of its refusal to collaborate with the regime, to find a refuge with him and his cosignatories. They were 55 in number and contained one prince, two marquis, three barons and 20 counts. With barbed wit Salvemini said 'with all the animals on their crests it would have been possible to put together a complete bestiary'. G. Salvemini, *Stato*, p. 284.

4. For an analysis of the right wing see R. Sgazbanti, *Ritratto politico di Giovanni Grosoli* (Rome, 1959), pp. 134–5.

5. *O.R.*, 18 April 1923.

6. *Avanti*, 12 April 1923.

7. G. Galli, *I partiti politici* (Turin, 1974), p. 224; A. Lyttelton, *The Seizure*, p. 123. That Mussolini himself feared the outcome of Turin is evident from the fact that he did all he could to persuade his PPI ministers to prevent it from being held. See E. Pucci, *La pace*, pp. 171–2.

8. L. Sturzo, *I discorsi*, pp. 311–41. For a full report of the Congress see F. Malgeri, *Gli atti*, pp. 389–548.

9. *Avanti*, 14 April 1923; F. Malgeri, *Gli atti*, pp. 430–3, gives the speech of Ferrari in full. Piero Gobetti said at the time that Ferrari was the 'new man' of the Congress and

that he typified the stand, now independent of the Vatican, of the Congress. L. Basso and L. Anderlini (eds.), *Le riviste di Piero Gobetti* (Milan, 1961), pp. 430–4.

10. *La Giustizia*, 14 April 1923.

11. M. Missiroli, *Una battaglia*, pp. 361–8; *O.R.*, 13, 14 April 1923. Filippo Meda did not attend the Congress. He wrote to his son, Gerolamo, saying that he thought the Congress could split the party and that it was thus a mistake to hold it at that moment. See G. De Rosa, *Filippo Meda*, pp. 230–1.

12. *La Giustizia*, 11 April 1923.

13. *Popolo d'Italia*, 13 April 1923.

14. Sturzo immediately got to his feet and insisted that Pestalozza be heard. He said 'Let it be recognized that he came here [to the Congress] and didn't flee, like so many others, who have taken refuge in the bosom of our adversaries.' See F. Malgeri, *Gli atti*, pp. 434–5; *Avanti*, 14 April 1923.

15. De Gasperi's motion bound the party 'to the most determined and most effective defence of proportionalism'. See F. Malgeri, *Gli atti*, p. 539.

16. M. Missiroli, *Una battaglia*, p. 364.

17. M. Missiroli, *Polemica liberale* (Bologna, 1954), p. 13. Missiroli, who had fought a duel with Mussolini in 1922, later became an acquiescent observer of the fascist regime. He eventually returned to his democratic ideals and at his death in Rome in 1974 he was widely mourned.

18. See a resumé of these events in S. Jacini, *Storia*, pp. 172–6; *Corriere d'Italia*, 17–26 April 1923; G. De Rosa, *Il Partito*, pp. 226–8. De Rosa quotes from an article in *Il Domani d'Italia*, 29 April 1923, which stated explicitly that the final motion was a 'complete renunciation of the spirit and the letter of the Congress of Turin ... Turin in its spirit was not anti-ministerial but anti-fascist ... the motion is not explicit in regard to the fascist party'.

19. S. Jacini, *Storia*, p. 175.

20. *Corriere d'Italia*, 25 April 1923. A curious document I came across in the Vatican library gave an interesting account of the whole affair. It blamed the press for giving Mussolini and the fascists a totally erroneous conception of what went on at Turin where the PPI actually 'reaffirmed its will to collaborate'. The press was then held responsible for the sacking of the PPI ministers. See *La Documentazione Cattolica*, Anno X, no. 8–9, Rome 15 May 1923, p. 277.

21. *La Giustizia*, 29 April 1923. The Palazzo Viminale in Rome was the seat of the Ministry for Home Affairs. Mussolini was Minister for both Home and Foreign Affairs.

22. *Il Popolo*, 30 April 1923.

23. *Civiltà Cattolica*, vol. 2, 19 March 1923, p. 369; G. Salvemini, *Stato*, pp. 288–9;

Codex Juris Canonici (Vatican City, 1917, 1948), pp. 38–9. Canon 139 states that a cleric 'may not assume a public office without an apostolic indult' meaning explicit papal approval which in the case of Sturzo was granted when Gasparri assented to the formation of the PPI. This warning by Mussolini has more impact when it is remembered that Gasparri was the main composer of the *Codex* in its first edition in 1917.

24. See *Corriere d'Italia*, 13 May 1923 and *O.R.*, 7, 8, 10 May 1923, for reports on the visit of the British monarch to Rome.

25. *O.R.*, 24 May 1923; *Il Popolo*, 5 June 1923; L. Sturzo, *Popolarismo*, pp. 195–209.

26. Barduzzi's letters of 6, 20, 28 May and one in early June without a precise date are found in F.M. Broglio, *Italia*, pp. 112–13.

27. Ibid., p. 114; E. Pucci, *La pace*, pp. 158–63; Emilio Settimelli in the fascist organ *L'Impero*, 15 April 1923, quoted in P. Scoppola (ed.), *Chiesa*, pp. 74–5.

28. G. De Rosa, *Il Partito*, p. 232.

29. G. Spataro, *I Democratici*, fn. 1, p. 71.

30. *Corriere d'Italia*, 18 June 1923; *O.R.*, 19 June 1923; *L'Idea Nazionale*, 20 June 1923.

31. *Corriere d'Italia*, 25, 26, 28 June 1923; *Avanti*, 28 June 1923; *Corriere della Sera*, 27 June 1923.

32. *La Giustizia*, 28 June 1923.

33. See G. Spataro, *I Democratici*, p. 74.

34. *Il Popolo*, 23 June 1923.

35. Kuliscioff to Turati, 12 May 1923, in *Carteggio*, vol. VI, pp. 19–20.

36. See the text of the *Manifesto* in P. Misciatelli, *Fascisti e cattolici* (Milan, 1924), pp. 139–41. Misciatelli, himself a marquis, signed the document. To him 'the ethical ends of Fascism coincide with those of the Catholic Church', p. 17.

37. *O.R.*, 2 July 1923; *Avanti*, 11 July 1923

38. *Corriere d'Italia*, 30 June 1923. Washburn Child later wrote an absurdly eulogistic life of the dictator entitled *My Autobiography* (London, 1936). It was allegedly written by Mussolini himself but actually put together by Child. On this see G. Megaro, *Mussolini in the Making* (London, 1938), p. 12.

39. Sturzo to Bourne, 15 June 1926, A.L.S., f. 141A, c. 9; Turati to Kuliscioff, 10 July 1923, in *Carteggio*, vol. VI, p. 67.

40. G. Spataro, *I Democratici*, p. 75, fn. 1.

41. *Corriere d'Italia*, 11 July 1923; *O.R.*, 11, 12 July 1923.

42. For the text of the law see S.W. Halperin, *Mussolini and Italian Fascism* (New

York, 1964), pp. 110–11. Acerbo, Mussolini's under-secretary of Internal Affairs, was condemned to death by the Italian High Court of Justice in 1945. The sentence was not carried out and Acerbo stood for parliament as a monarchical candidate in 1958. He was unsuccessful. See R. Zangrandi, *Il lungo viaggio attraverso il fascismo* (Milan, 1962), p. 327.

43. Sturzo wrote two articles against changes in the law in *Popolo Nuovo*, 10, 17 June 1923. Kulisciof described Sturzo as 'the most uncompromising and courageous opponent' to change and did not doubt his tenacity of purpose 'but it is yet to be seen what the PPI parliamentary party will do'. Kuliscioff to Turati, 12 June 1923, in *Carteggio*, vol. VI, pp. 41–2.

44. *Il Popolo Nuovo*, 15 July 1923; G. Spataro, *I Democratici*, p. 78.

45. *Civiltà Cattolica*, vol. 3, 4 August 1923, p. 283 and 18 August 1923, pp. 365–7.

46. Meda's letter is found in S. Jacini, *Storia*, p. 316. In fairness to Meda it must be acknowledged that none of the PPI leaders, then or later, could bring themselves to deny his integrity. Miglioli is perhaps the best example for, when his own ideological wanderings had ceased, he wrote that Meda always loved and defended the workers and the farmers. 'Looking at him we can say that a man is born a Christian democrat he doesn't become one.' G. Miglioli, *Con Roma*, p. 44. Perhaps Luigi Degli Occhi was close to the truth when he wrote in 1924, 'Meda, as an historian and a politician, is by intellectual temperament more English than Italian'. Quoted in F.L. Ferrari, *Il Domani d'Italia*, G. Dore, ed. (Rome, 1958), p. 199. Senator Spataro told me that Meda said to him regarding his letter 'I am acting on my conscience. You others can follow your own.' I said, 'He reminds me of Thomas More in reverse', and then Spataro remarked wistfully that it was Meda who, as a lawyer, went into court and defended De Gasperi at his trial in 1927. To this I said 'A little late'. Spataro agreed. Interview, Rome, 15 December 1974.

47. *Atti Parlamentari, Camera-Discussioni*, 15 July 1923, XI, p. 10667 *et seq.*

48. Turati to Kuliscioff, 15 July 1923, in *Carteggio*, vol. VI, pp. 82–4.

49. *Atti Parlamentari, Camera-Discussioni*, 15 July 1923, pp. 10676–80; Turati to Kuliscioff, 16 July 1923, in *Carteggio*, vol. VI, pp. 86–7.

50. *Times*, 2 August 1923, quoted in *O.R.*, 3 August 1923; ibid., 25 July 1923, *Popolo d'Italia*, 28 August 1923.

51. G. Spataro, *I Democratici*, p. 83. There can be little doubt that Pius XI wanted his friends, Grosoli, Santucci and Crispolti to leave the PPI. See L. Cavazzoni (ed.), *Stefano Cavazzoni* p. 71.

52. *Corriere d'Italia*, 18, 27, 28 July 1923; *Popolo Nuovo*, 22 July 1923; *Civiltà Cattolica*, vol. 3, 18 August 1923, p. 370.

53. *Corriere d'Italia*, 7 August 1923.

54. Ibid., 19 August 1923; on 28 July the same paper had scorned its rejection by the PPI with the remark 'we are before all and above all a Catholic paper'. How the sentiments of the good doctor which smack more of the Mosaic law than the New Testament can be reconciled with the profession of Christianity of *Corriere d'Italia* is a matter for speculation.

55. *Popolo d'Italia*, 3 August 1923.

56. See letter of Lamberto Giannitelli to Achille Grandi, general secretary of the white unions and also a PPI deputy. The letter is dated 9 August 1923 and his audience with Pizzardo took place that morning. The text is found in G. Pastore, *Achille Grandi e il movimento sindacale italiano del primo dopoguerra* (Rome, 1960), pp. 112–13. Salvemini later called Pizzardo 'The long arm of the fascist party in the Vatican'. See P. Alatri, *L'antifascismo*, vol. 11, p. 40. Pizzardo was created a cardinal in 1937 and became Prefect of the Congregation for Seminaries and Universities after the Second World War. See *Annuario Pontificio* (Vatican City, 1955), p. 37.

57. For an excellent account of the development of Catholic Action in the period and especially the role of the university body, see G. Marcucci Fanello, *Storia*, especially pp. 59–116.

58. See G. Spataro, *I Democratici*, p. 83, fn. 1.

59. See *O.R.*, 25 January, 22 March, 8 April, 13 April, 1 July, 8, 15 August, 4, 15, 18 October 1923.

60. *Unità Cattolica*, 19 June 1923. For *Corriere d'Italia*, see practically any issue after April 1923.

61. *O.R.*, 15 August 1923. *Corriere d'Italia*, 17 August 1923, agreed with Colombo.

62. See L. Bedeschi, *Don Minzoni* (Milan, 1973), passim; *Corriere d'Italia*, 26 August 1923; *O.R.*, 26, 27–8 August, 15 September 1923; *Civiltà Cattolica*, vol. 3, 15 September 1923, p. 556; *Popolo d'Italia*, 9 November 1923.

63. *O.R.*, 2, 17, 18 September 1923; L. Bedeschi, *Don Minzoni*, p. 121.

64. C. Dalla Torre, *Azione Cattolica e fascimo* (Rome, 1945), p. 13.

8

ENTER THE NIGHT

It is given to few men to have a sense of the present so precise that their unconscious instincts reveal the deep pattern of the future. These men are doers rather than dreamers; their involvement in life is a constant thrust that leads them inexorably to a fate that they dimly perceive, and from which there is no escape. Such a one was Roberto Farinacci. He was bred in violence, lived by violence and died through violence. Yet this chronic savage, whose strident notes shattered the peace of the city of Stradivarius for a full generation, spoke the epitaph of the movement to which he gave his turbulent being.

God knows what dreadful forebodings moved in Farinacci on the night when he stood before an enraptured crowd at the place where the Romans had laid to rest the remains of their mighty Augustus. To the descendants of those ancients, Farinacci roared 'For us there is only one form of justice — let us be judged by history.' Perceiving only the present, his audience applauded with frenzy. Both speaker and hearers had their way and history has passed its verdict. Meanwhile the present was allowed to have its fleeting day.[1]

Secure in the knowledge that the change in the electoral system, combined with the judicious use of intimidation, would result in a majority for his party, Mussolini called a general election for 6 April 1924. It was not necessary to prepare for it by the careful elaboration of a platform. The fascist movement was now consolidated in power and the steps it had already taken towards the rejuvenation of Italy's economic and social position seemed beneficial. Outside observers were impressed by all this and Cardinal William Henry O'Connell, Archbishop of Boston, was quoted in the *New York Times* on 29 February 1924 as a giving testimony to Italy's transformation: 'Italy has undergone a profound moral, economic and social transformation since Mussolini was named Prime Minister... There is order, loyalty, industrial development and cleanliness everywhere.'[2] In fact the public service had already been functioning with a reasonable semblance of efficiency before 1922 and even the railways had begun to regard a timetable as mandatory rather than merely indicative of good intentions.

Yet with his flamboyant seizure of the island of Corfu, the formal annexation of Fiume to Italy, his posturing at the Lausanne Conference and his general attempt at making Italy's presence felt in Europe, Mussolini had managed to give heart to a dispirited people and restore their image in their own eyes. That the economy was only temporarily bolstered by expedients such as pegging the lira to the dollar, that the deep divisions on a regional basis were forgotten in the enthusiasm of the moment, and that no amount of rhetoric could cover up the unrest left as a legacy of the First World War and its aftermath seemed to count for nothing as Italy settled down to its first period of political stability in eight years. So few seemed to appreciate or realize that this pottage was bought at the price of the birthright of the Risorgimento, for Italy was rapidly losing the two things for which that struggle had been endured. Democracy was dying in the embrace of dictatorship and Church was twined with state in a manner faintly reminiscent of the days of Charlemagne when another barbarian had used her for his own ends.

The PPI had prepared an appeal to the people for presentation in the event of an election and it was made public immediately the date was fixed by the government.[3] Carefully drafted by Sturzo it read like a harmless piece of party propaganda and in normal circumstances it would have had trifling significance. Yet it was direct enough to clarify the important issues at stake — the PPI, while retaining its own autonomy, was emphatically opposed to the regime. Despite the defections, the expulsions and the vacillation of Meda who refused to stand for election unless the PPI remained neutral to the government, the party was united in opposition and stood 137 candidates of whom 61 had been deputies in the previous parliament.[4] It was conceded from the start that the opposition parties had no hope of beating the government list which was made up of 356 candidates. It contained 268 fascists while the rest were camp followers who gave the fascists some semblance of respectability without posing any threat to their dominance. Amongst them appeared the names of former Popolari, Cavazzoni, Martire, Mattei-Gentili, Tovini and others whom Sturzo classified as 'clericals' and, somewhat superfluously, denied that they were 'democrats'.[5]

Despite its proclamation regarding the Church's intention to remain 'beyond and above politics', which *L'Osservatore Romano* repeated frequently in the pre-election period, it was an uneasy situation for the Vatican.[6] Sturzo's wings had been clipped, but he had not ceased to exercise his paramount position within the PPI as its founder and its inspirational spirit. His influence as leader was decisively anti-fascist and in firm opposition to those who held that ecclesiastical compliance with the fascist regime would benefit either the Church or the state. This contrasted notably with the position held in Vatican diplomatic circles where the most desirable solution was a satisfactory settlement to the Roman Question and the fascist regime had indicated that it was of the same opinion. Furthermore the temporary tranquility that fascist power had imposed upon Italy, the concessions granted to the Catholic religion, the restraint placed upon the socialist movement and the acceptance of the new regime amongst foreign powers had lulled the Vatican into a sense of complacency.

That such developments were paid for with the throttling of democracy counted little to an institution that had always proclaimed itself indifferent to the forms under which secular society organized itself and, which, in its own life insisted upon the hierarchical nature of authority and power. The concepts of Sturzo on the fundamental renewal of society had never been granted a good hearing amongst prelates who were more inclined to the view that the kingdoms of this world were given over to an adverse power. That a Minzoni had to die, that Catholic institutions had to suffer harassment were perversities with which the Church had long lived. Such things had to be borne in the hope that the future would reveal better times and, whatever else he did, Mussolini held out promise of those times.[7]

No one then claimed that the influential Jesuit priest, G. Galloni, was writing in the name of the Vatican when he contributed a piece to *L'Osservatore Romano* a week before the elections. Nonetheless it is reasonable to suppose that it would never have been published at such a time had its sentiments not been in accordance with the pope and the Secretariat of State. The ubiquitous Monsignor Pucci was now a constant emissary from the Vatican to Mussolini and his ministers and he kept insisting that he had Mussolini's word that the Roman Question would be solved and it was in this context that Father Galloni wrote his article.[8] The Jesuit began by praising Mussolini who 'has had the good sense to reject sectarianism and to turn more to religion'. He asked his readers to 'salute the noble intentions' of the dictator and to pray that 'they may endure and be efficacious' and find their fullness 'in a great act in which our fatherland and our religion embrace and say to each other "Peace be with thee"'. Quoting Pius from *Ubi arcano Dei*, Galloni concluded with 'This will be amongst the most solemn and fruitful hours'. Indeed the priest thought that it was one which Italian Catholics could hasten with their prayers.[9] *Corriere d'Italia*, secular twin of *L'Osservatore Romano* in those trying times, was more to the point. It thought that such an hour could also be hastened by the vote of Catholics.[10]

In that climate the Partito Popolare, which kept on proclaiming its adherence to democracy, Christianity, patriotism and international solidarity but remained painfully silent on the Roman Question, could not hope to win much support especially when the fascist propaganda machine warned that the Popolari were worse than the communists. When the numbers went up the PPI had attracted 645,000 votes and returned 40 members to parliament. At least they could justly claim that they were 'in every sense of the word, the chosen ones of the people' because they had been elected in the face of 'violence, illegality and terror'. The fascist list won 4,135,677 votes while the unitarian socialists obtained 418,948, the socialists 362,568 and the communists 266,415. The combined socialist representation amounted to 62 seats while the communists held 18 with eight going to the republicans and 25 to minor, democratic groups. As a result the final opposition in the parliament was composed of 135 members, while the government had 375 on its benches.[11]

Nevertheless the continued strength of the opposition parties was a source of deep irritation to Mussolini and even to the Vatican itself it was clear that they were not simply going to fade away. It was an undeniable fact that the urban proletariat in particular had shown itself disinclined to vote for the fascist regime which meant that the force of socialism was not spent. At the same time the vote for the PPI indicated that a substantial body of the Catholic masses was not easily wooed away from the party and the lower clergy, especially in country areas, had not wavered in their allegiance to the party and had done all they could to keep their people committed to the same stand.[12] To this manifestation of opposition fascism had only one reply — violence. Sackings, burnings and acts of terrorism followed the elections and they were directed in the main against PPI offices, white union organizations and in some instances against Catholic Action buildings. The acts of reprisal were especially ferocious in Lombardy where the PPI had done well in the elections and in one region alone 43 Catholic cooperatives were destroyed.[13] The pope was genuinely shocked at this renewed manifestation of fascist brutality and he sent 500,000 lire to Brianza to be distributed to the Catholic associations that had suffered. His gesture was interpreted by eager anti-fascists as a blow at the regime but to the triumphant fascists and to Mussolini himself it was only a temporary setback in the establishment of cordial relations with the Church. When it was announced two weeks later that a Cross would be set up on the Campidoglio, the *Osservatore Romano* rejoiced at this fascist act of good faith and was especially happy that it would be seen by the pilgrims during the forthcoming Holy Year in 1925.[14]

Before the opening of parliament the PPI met and elected De Gasperi as political secretary thus passing Sturzo's mantle to him.[15] Sturzo had resigned from the directorate in order to give complete freedom to De Gasperi and to remove any residual identification by either the fascists or the Church between himself and the party he had founded. He had continued his struggle to hold the party together and to have it maintain its integrity even in the face of pressure from both the fascist state and the Church itself. He had written to Rodinò pleading with the Neapolitan aristocrat and fellow founder of the PPI to use his influence with Longinotti, Merlin, Montini and the Brescian members to strengthen their resolve of outright political opposition and to refuse any moves towards coalition with the old discredited elements of Italian liberalism. Sturzo wrote 'a party that says *it is constrained to take a course of action* is a party *that disqualifies itself*', and he implied that it was better to suffer dissolution than compromise on fundamental principles.[16]

At the same time Sturzo could not go as far as the ardent idealist, Francesco Luigi Ferrari, who left the directorate in February 1924 on the grounds that it had preselected 'theorizers of convenience' who would betray 'the integral defence of democracy'. Ferrari promised Sturzo that they would remain united in the 'defence of the Christian Democratic ideal' but it grieved the priest to see the PPI lose the inspiration of one of its noblest spirits. Ferrari was badly wounded by fascist thugs in 1923 and again in November 1926 which forced him into exile in Belgium where he did his doctorate at Louvain. Italian government intervention prevented his taking a Chair at Louvain and he eked out a miserable living dying at Paris in 1933 while upholding to the last his dedication to his ideals.[17]

On 24 May 1924 the Italian parliament met for its final and brief attempt at the implementation of the democratic process. Only two elements in parliamentary life had come out strengthened by the elections of April. The fascists emerged triumphant and the communists had increased their seats by a third having drawn strength from the shattering of the left and also from the specious tolerance extended to them by the regime which had hoped thereby to foster further disunity in the socialist camp. Thus, with its powerful majority in the House and with the general acquiescence of a subdued and complaisant electorate, it was a situation in which a normal government could have been expected to get on with its work unimpeded and without the constraint of paying overmuch attention to its opposition. But this government was born of violent conflict and one thing it feared greatly was the unmasking of its guilt. The House contained at least one man whose firm resolve it was to do just that and whose name today is revered as synonymous with Italian democracy.

Giacomo Matteotti was born in 1885 and had studied law in England and Germany. Elected a socialist deputy in 1919 he had become a leading member of the breakaway Unitary Socialist party in 1922. His was a tempestuous, brittle character but his exterior hid a reserve of inflexible determination, courage and forcefulness which, since 1922, had revealed itself in a remorseless, passionate opposition to fascism. He wrote to Turati on 28 March 1924 to complain of the inertia of the socialists. 'I have no further intention of standing by idly at this funeral. I seek for life. I want a struggle against fascism.' And on 20 April 1924 he went to Brussels where he told the Congress of the Belgium Workers Party that he wasn't asking for their help in the struggle for freedom in Italy. He said 'The man who doesn't know how to regain his own liberty by his own efforts is not worthy of it'.[18]

With methodical aloofness Matteotti had watched, documented and then published the index of fascist crime in December 1923.[19] Throughout the election campaign he saw how the voters had been terrorized in those places where there was noticeable opposition to the regime and he knew that it was time to stand on the convictions of his brief manhood. Thus, when parliament sat in May, Matteotti had one purpose — to proclaim to it and to the nation that the government was marked with both invalidity and illegality. To him it ruled not on the basis of the consent of a free people but it had won its specious mandate through treachery and violence. On 30 May he rose in the chamber and spelt out the litany of fascist infamy to a chorus of imprecations and crudities from the government benches. When he asked the deputies on those benches to 'confess that no Italian voter found himself free before the ballot boxes' his words were drowned with their uproar and Farinacci cried 'Kick him out'. On resuming his seat Matteotti remarked to his comrades 'You can now prepare my funeral oration'.[20] *L'Osservatore Romano* asked the government to give the minority its rights in the parliament but the die was cast because, like another Henry II, Mussolini had already muttered his plea to be relieved of the meddlesome Matteotti.[21]

His widow later related how Matteotti had left their apartment to walk the short distance to parliament on the afternoon of 10 June 1924. She said how he had taken only ten lire with him and had left his razor behind — a clear indication that he intended to return home that night. It was an item which he would not need again, for, as he walked along the Tiber embankment where his monument now stands, he was forced into a motor car by five party thugs, stabbed to death and buried in the Roman campagna. His death was the logical, inexorable apex to the sequence of fascist outrages and his own opposition to them. When his widow and Matteotti's mother requested an audience with Pius XI in those griefstricken days following the disappearance of Giacomo it was refused. The prudent advisers in the Secretariat of State didn't want to involve the Church in any possible socialist plot concocted to throw the fascist regime into further disfavour.[22]

The murder of Matteotti was immediately accepted as a fact even though his body was not discovered until August. A wave of revulsion swept the country and for a few weeks fascism hovered on the brink of collapse. From Milan, Anna Kuliscioff summed up her own and other's feelings when she wrote to Turati on 16 June 'Poor Matteotti, had he been able to see the first signs of the reawakening of the country as a consequence of his death and martyrdom I believe he would be happy'. Ferrari called on everyone to 'Resist' and saw the murder as an 'inexorable reality' of a system that had to produce 'all the worst forms of degeneration and abomination'.[23] Nonetheless Mussolini was saved because no one with the necessary moral or legal authority was prepared to act rapidly and decisively. The King was a helpless puppet, the legal authorities were timid, compromised or impeded by the fact that Mussolini as a deputy could not be arrested, while the parliamentary opposition was divided in all things except rejection of fascism and it lacked effective leadership. Thus the people, who in large part knew now what fascism meant, vacillated and every day gained by Mussolini was a step further from his incrimination for complicity in a murder.[24]

One voice could possibly have helped to overthrow the regime but that voice remained mute. Pius XI lacked neither the courage nor the moral strength to speak. He lacked the motive because, to him and his circle of Vatican diplomatic intimates to opt for an alternative to fascism was to postpone the solution to the Roman Question, possibly throw Italy into disorder and perhaps strengthen the role of socialism in the peninsula. Thus to condemn Mussolini and his regime was to pay too high a price and while the *Corriere d'Italia* pleaded for 'Love of the fatherland' to be the overriding principle the *Osservatore Romano* hoped that justice would be done and that peace would prevail but it thought that a change in the regime would mean 'a fatal leap in the dark'.[25] Meanwhile the fatal leap was being taken that would bind Italy to its master for 20 years and lead her into the darkness of war and suffering because, short of a violent upsurgence, there was to be no chance again of overthrowing a regime that could murder a Matteotti and emerge unscathed in reputation and strengthened in power.

The grace that was on Mussolini's side was the very same grace that the opposition looked for in their plight — time. They hoped that with the passing of time the infamy of the regime would be even more clearly shown up with the revelation of the facts of the murder. But their time rested on a moral basis while Mussolini's rested on a psychological one. To all, the guilt of the regime was sufficiently clear the moment, 48 hours after the murder, that the Republican deputy Chiesa declared before the House that the Duce was an accomplice and Mussolini remained mute. That was the moral moment and every hour that passed lessened in men's minds the force of that morality. With great moral purpose but a bewildering lack of clarity the opposition deputies withdrew from the House. In effect they figuratively withrew onto the Aventine Hill thus evoking a similar episode in ancient Roman history. In practical terms they left Mussolini free to defend himself in the one forum where they could have struck him down — Parliament.[26]

In the months that followed Matteotti's death it became increasingly clear that nothing would be achieved by mere abstention from the House itself. Yet it must be acknowledged that to the men who withdrew from the fascist parliament their step was the only one that could be taken in conformity with constitutional procedure. Sforza suggested to Turati and Treves that they ought to invade Mussolini's residence and arrest him. Antonio Gramsci wanted a general strike together with the setting up of an anti-parliament while the people, now 'ordered and disciplined' and going about their daily chores gazed with wonder at such a noble gesture and quickly forgot what it was all about.[27] The only other possible solution was for the opposition parties to unite as an effective force and thus present to the country some form of feasible, constitutional alternative to the régime. Weakened but still intact their party apparatus had survived fascism since 1922 and their reaction to the crime of June 1924 had given them a unity of purpose never possible in the days when they had worked in parliament as diverse and opposing entities. Between them they could muster over a hundred deputies even if one excluded the communists who were unlikely to join in any formal alliance with other parties, but especially with their sworn enemies the socialists. The main difficulty was to overcome the barriers that prevented genuine political unity between the socialists, including the Unitary Socialists, and the PPI. Manifestly the problem was not merely political but it had moral overtones as well and it would put to the test the remark of Gasparri five years earlier when he had told Sturzo that he would prefer to see his young party unite with the socialists rather than with the old liberal forces.

The initiative was taken by the highly respected leader of the Unitary Socialists, Filippo Turati, who gave an interview in *Il Popolo* in which he said that he saw no obstacle to a form of unity between the socialists and the PPI.[28] Turati was very uneasy at the deterioration of relations between the Vatican and the PPI and it was his firm opinion that the pope himself was responsible for the hardening in attitude.[29] Nonetheless he did not think that a stage would be reached at which Pius would engage in an outright denunciation of the PPI and he did not seem to be at all aware that any talk of an alliance between the two Aventine groups might serve to press Pius towards repudiation. Thus he firmly pointed out that the socialists accepted the concept of religious freedom as a basic component of intellectual and moral freedom and as a consequence any divergence between the two standpoints was one of tactics only. De Gasperi replied a fortnight later on behalf of the PPI and he rejected any idea 'of absolute incompatability in parliamentary collaboration with the socialists'. He cited the cases of Germany, Poland and Czechoslovakia where such collaboration had proven possible. De Gasperi thought that the same applied to Italy and that the PPI ought to take the initiative and lead it.[30] Sturzo himself had taken a favourable view of collaboration. He had discussed it with Matteotti in May and then with Turati and he had written on it in *Il Popolo* without signing the article. Perhaps this was the area in which Sturzo revealed his incomprehension of the gap that existed between himself and the Vatican, between his concept of the role of Christianity in society and that held by Pius XI. It was all very well for him to lament to Petrocchi that in the Vatican his methods and political ideas were misunderstood.[31] The fact was that they were very clearly understood and as such they were emphatically rejected.

Even before Turati and De Gasperi spoke, the warning signal had been issued by the lay exponents of Vatican policy in the pages of *Corriere d'Italia*. The Aventine secession was viewed as a 'grave error' which held the country back from unity and peace and the Popolari were warned that if they united with the socialists they would merit the same judgement as the worst elements of fascism who were now held responsible for preventing the country from returning to 'civil liberty and constitutional normalcy'.[32] Turati's statement was regarded with grave concern and the question was asked whether Catholics were prepared to sacrifice everything 'to atheistic and monopolistic socialism?'. When De Gasperi replied favourably to Turati it was almost beyond the grasp of the editor of the *Corriere* how such an attitude could be adopted by a Catholic and the initial reaction was simple wonderment.[33]

Amidst a welter of recriminations, confusion and protestation the actual possibility of collaboration seemed to be taking more definite shape with constant meetings between the various elements of political theory grouped on the Aventine through July and August

1924. The regime itself was not idle and in July a set of repressive laws concerning the press was introduced which were so clearly indicative of the intention of the fascists to stifle all opposition that even *Corriere d'Italia* became alarmed despite the fact that its editor, and former PPI founder and deputy, Paolo Mattei-Gentili, was nominated undersecretary for justice in Mussolini's cabinet.[34] In its own way the Aventine was proving a moral beacon which it was impossible to ignore or extinguish short of further violence so Catholics had to be reassured that, despite the Matteotti murder and the Aventine reaction, all would be well.

Luigi Federzoni, Minister for the Interior assured the anxious Catholic masses that 'The government of Benito Mussolini has shown from the beginning that it is its precise intention to restore the freedom and prestige of the Catholic Religion in Italy' and promised that in the Holy Year of 1925 the whole world would see how well the Church was being treated.[35] A commentator noted with some relief in *L'Osservatore Romano* that the government was powerful, in power and intended to remain there and that any thought of disturbing it was fatuous. At the same time those laymen who belonged to Catholic Action were warmly praised because they kept themselves free from political action which in itself implied 'fratricidal struggles'. Meanwhile its president, Luigi Colombo, a papal appointee, refused the request of a group of young PPI members at Milan to have fascist members expelled from Catholic Action on the grounds that they supported an immoral regime. Colombo said, like Farinacci, that it would be left to 'history' to decide whether the fascists or the anti-fascists were right.[36]

Behind the scenes however a great deal of thought was being given to consolidating papal control of all Catholic lay activity in Italy. It was increasingly apparent that the appeal to Catholics to close ranks in the organizations of Catholic Action directly subject to the pope and the bishops was falling short of the desired goal. The obstacle was the continuing loyalty of large segments of the more active, better informed and generous elements of the laity to the PPI, to Sturzo himself and to the white unions. When *Il Popolo* launched an appeal for funds in the wake of the repressive press laws in July the most notable feature of the response was the number of priests who sent donations to the paper; Sturzo called one group of them 'the last hope of Italy'.[37] As *Avanti* remarked with some justice the lower segments of the clergy had remained loyal to the PPI while the higher clergy had been charmed away by Mussolini and the 'economic concessions' made to the clergy, concessions which included a higher stipend for the bishops. With poor taste, but again some accuracy, it ran a cartoon of two priests before a fascist symbol. One priest, representing the Vatican, had a copy of *L'Osservatore Romano* protruding from his pocket as he knelt before the symbol. The other stood upright holding a copy of *Il Popolo*. No one needed to be told that he represented the PPI.[38]

The vehicle chosen to spearhead the Vatican offensive was the Jesuit publication *Civiltà Cattolica*. It led off on 2 August with an article in which Matteotti was rejected as a martyr figure, a word *Il Popolo* had used of him. He was adjudged an unfortunate 'victim of the communal political delinquency' which he had helped create in 1919 with his attempts to bring about a revolution. The members of the Aventine opposition were warned that in their own way they were delinquents also in that they were acting contrary to 'the public good' and the PPI deputies were asked to listen to the warnings of the Church and to the voice of the pope.[39] There followed a series of lengthy articles in which the editor of the magazine, Father Enrico Rosa, made a number of things abundantly clear. Catholics ought henceforth to behave with circumspection and the clergy in particular were instructed on the proper attitude to take to constituted government. They were bound not to try to overthrow it by illegitimate means or even by legitimate ones unless it had become absolutely clear that such a change would lead to a better situation because 'the safety of the people ought to be for all the supreme law that must take precedence'. In the concrete circumstances it was clear to the writer that either illegitimate or legitimate means would lead to a bloody civil war and thus there could be no question of a change of government. Any alternative tactic which envisaged an alliance between the socialists and the Popolari was neither becoming, licet and certainly not opportune.

The author thought that one could not draw any parallel between the Italian situation and that in Austria and Germany where the Catholics did not help the socialists to power but merely accepted the *fait accompli* and accommodated themselves to it.[40] Furthermore there could be no parallel between the fascists and the socialists. Fascism lacked a fixed system of doctrine and, despite its excesses, it had suppressed socialist tyranny, repudiated freemasonry, reestablished order and been good to Catholics. Socialism on the other hand, even moderate socialism, was essentially opposed to Christianity, atheistic, based itself on the theory of the class war, denied private property, rejected authority, the sanctity of marriage and the family. In short, any alliance with it would be a kind of 'alliance between Christ and the Devil.' The conclusion was that there could be no doubt as to how Catholics ought henceforth behave and the clergy in particular were asked to abide by the norms established.[41]

A week later the pope sent a letter of warm congratulations to the *Civiltà Cattolica* thanking it on its most opportune 75th year for all the work it had done for the Church, the Holy See and for Catholic doctrine.[42] That same week Cavazzoni, Grosoli, Mattei-Gentili and others who had formerly been members of the PPI founded the National Italian Centre. Its purpose was to offer an alternative to Catholics who wanted to defend and give value to religious principles 'on the political level'. This was a task in which the PPI was said to have been a singular failure. The right-wing group was nationalist, anti-democratic, backed by Colombo and some segments of Catholic

Action and called by Mussolini's close associates 'an ornament of fascism'. As such it served to confuse further those Catholics who still looked upon the PPI as an expression of sound political principles.[43]

Father Giulio De Rossi sprang to the defence of De Gasperi and the PPI in his last public stand for the party to which he had given so much as director of its press office and historian of its early years.[44] He pointed out that the PPI had not been condemned for doctrinal deviation when it had collaborated with the liberals who, from the days of the Syllabus onwards, had been repudiated for their doctrines more frequently than the socialists, and he implied that what was licit in one case ought to be also licit in the other. He followed this with an article proving to his own satisfaction that collaboration with the fascists was certainly illicit.[45] Umberto Merlin, foundation member of the party and a leading Catholic figure of the Veneto stressed that, if nothing else, the hard reality of the day-to-day experience of the farmer, the worker and the small proprietor made collaboration a necessity given their persecution by the regime — a persecution they shared with their socialist brethren. *Il Popolo* itself then had the temerity to dismiss any talk of 'communist danger' to the country as mere fascist nonsense.[46] Finally Sturzo personally entered the lists with the outright affirmation that the socialists had now assumed a position of 'constitutionality, liberty and legality' which undercut the arguments of *Civiltà Cattolica* completely because in such a case there were no moral grounds to prevent collaboration.[47]

History demands that one of the most noble appeals for justice, sanity and toleration in judging the question of collaboration be recorded. It was penned in September 1924 by a man who signed himself as Gino Sergi but who was in fact Filippo Meda. Meda may have been timid, vacillating and lacking in drive but he was also an honest man with a keen intellect. To such a mind the sheer humbug that had been peddled on collaboration between the PPI and the socialists was intolerable. It was a remark of Martire that drove Meda to write an article entitled 'Vain Excuses' in his own journal *Civitas*.[48] Martire had argued that so long as the Popolari affirmed their right to collaborate with the socialists they also had to extend the same right to Catholics who wanted to collaborate with the fascists. Then Martire went on: 'The right to assert this compatability [with socialism or with fascism] carries with it the duty to prove it and, at that, in relation to the supreme interests of the Church and the Country.' Meda replied with a classical distinction which begged the question, but was effective. He said that Italian Catholics didn't need any proof of the compatability of collaboration with the socialists because such was as yet only an hypothesis and, if the time came to put it into practice, it would have to be seen in the concrete reality of the conditions, the objectives and the persons with whom it was proposed to collaborate. Then Meda took Martire's argument by its essence and rattled the dry bones of hypocrisy and cant it contained.

> But what about you clerical fascists, you are not dealing in hypotheses at all and the Catholics of Italy want to know what motivates you? They have no right to ask you why you are not democrats, why you abandoned, freely or otherwise, the party which you had stood for while it was comfortable to do so... they have no right even to ask you why you aren't against fascism: all that is merely negative and of your refusal to act no one, except God, can demand an account... But it is entirely positive for the Christian people of our country — the people of our villages and of our mountains, martyred and persecuted by their present rulers... governed often by the cudgel and the revolver, driven from their clubs and cooperatives, impeded from voting or forced by threats to vote for those whom they do not want — to ask you to account for this intolerable situation. They now ask it of you because you, who one day called yourselves their friends and whose confidence you asked and were given, are the same ones who now give weight to, give credit to and proclaim such a system as worthy of favour... because it is in conformity with the supreme interests of the Church and the Nation.

De Gasperi, Sturzo, De Rossi, Meda and the 'Christian people' of Italy had to wait a week for a reply and they were given it by a much more authoritative source than Martire. Pius himself decided that it was time to clarify the situation beyond any shadow of doubt. He took the opportunity to address a group of university students who were well known for their continued adhesion to the PPI. The pope reiterated in slightly less precise terms the arguments against collaboration used by *Civiltà Cattolica* and especially rejected any collaboration which would 'pave the way for and allow to come to power' a party which he did not name but which, in the context, clearly meant the socialist. In ringing tones he spoke of 'spirits that cannot but lead to disastrous consequences for the public good'. To him Italy, because of the 'historical, political and religious' differences between it and other countries could not take them as a model in this vital matter.[49] To the *Corriere d'Italia* on the following day the case was simple. '*Roma locuta est, causa finita est*' but *Il Popolo* vainly and valiantly tried to swing the argument back the other way and assert that all had to examine their consciences and implied that the point could be made equally well in regard to collaboration with the fascists.[50] There were several further exchanges until finally Dalla Torre insisted that conscience did not enter into it except in so far as obeying the pope was concerned, and that the pope was explicitly condemning any form of collaboration with the socialists.[51]

Once collaboration had been rendered impossible from the side of the PPI, and granted that the socialists may themselves ultimately have baulked at it given their own divisions, the future of the Aventine opposition and that of the PPI was decided. Without unity of action the Aventine was a noble protest that had sooner or later to pass into history as precisely that. Sturzo was quick to realize that such was the case and he immediately bent his efforts to try to persuade the opposition to return to the Chamber.[52] But it was difficult for men who had taken their stand on a moral principle to return to that forum in which it was already apparent that the only law was that of force. It was all very well for Giolitti to scorn the Aventine protestors saying they were 'Decent people who get together in their family circle to exchange speeches which few people bother to read' but those protestors were entitled to assert that they, by their affirmation of a 'question of morality', had to go down as men who had upheld the truth.[53] On that basis the battle of the Aventine was not lost; it was merely postponed.

Once the PPI was effectively blocked from collaboration with the only other cohesive force in opposition it was doomed to wither away and the papal discourse was the *coup d'grace* that ensured its demise as a party. It still claimed to be an aconfessional party with the freedom to make its own decisions but it also claimed to be obedient to the papacy in moral matters and Pius had taken care to make collaboration with the socialists a moral matter. If a date can be fixed for the true birth of the PPI it is that when Cardinal Gasparri told Sturzo in December 1918 that he would place no obstacle in the way of its foundation. Equally its day of death can be fixed as 9 September 1924 when Pius XI made it clear that it could no longer function as an autonomous body of Catholics in Italian political life. On the trade union level the same situation prevailed because the white unions had made it abundantly clear that they also could not collaborate with the fascist regime and, once they had lost their political expression through the nullification of the PPI, their own end was in sight.[54]

Notwithstanding all this, a certain amount of tidying up had to be done. Sturzo was still an irritant both to the Vatican and to the fascist state and it did not seem likely that he would voluntarily relinquish his role as a major anti-fascist force in Italy. In July 1924 he went for a few days rest at the ancient abbey of Montecassino but Spataro and Vincenzo Mangano persuaded him to flee the monastery when word got around that the fascists of Cassino had sworn not to let him escape with his life.[55] He had already decided that his place was alongside 'the humble, the suffering and the persecuted in the cause of morality and justice' but it was equally clear that he would not be allowed to remain in that position with impunity. In August he went to Grado where the local fascists decided to 'teach him a lesson' but he again escaped unharmed. On his return to Rome in September Farinacci raved in print about 'the foul priest of Caltagirone', 'this reject of our race, this creature whose Italian birth makes us ashamed' and asked the Vatican to suspend him from his priestly ministry.[56] His apartment on Via Principessa Clotilde was broken into on the night of 12 September by a group of fascists intent, as Mussolini had specified, on his 'material suppression' but he had already taken refuge in the home of Prince Rufo Ruffo della Scaletta.[57]

One avenue of public activity remained open to Sturzo and that was in his capacity as a writer. His book *Popolarismo e Fascismo* had been published in January 1924 and he had continued to write for *Il Popolo* culminating with his article on collaboration on 6 September which had helped provoke Pius' reaction and which the *Osservatore Romano* had cited specifically to indicate that it was not merely an academic matter on which the pope had spoken but a very real danger.[58] The time had come to silence Sturzo completely so Gasparri sent a letter to the bishops telling them to put a stop to the political activity of their priests and in particular to their writing for papers connected with political parties.[59]

As a priest this was the death knell to Sturzo's activity in Italy because he had to obey the directive of ecclesiastical authority. Thinking back on this episode 50 years later Senator Spataro insisted that Sturzo realized that the Vatican was constantly threatened because of his own position and that 'the cassock weighed heavily on his shoulders'. Sturzo had said that the sight of the blackshirts oppressed him, not because of physical fear but because of what they meant to Italian democracy, that he felt more and more isolated from his friends and that the decision to support the regime taken by Santucci and others 'grieved him deeply'. As a result he had no option but to lay down his pen.[60]

For Sturzo there remained one final step — exile. The decision to leave Italy was not taken by Sturzo but by Gasparri with the approval, if not at the suggestion of Pius XI. Sturzo's brother Mario had been bishop of Piazza Armerina in Sicily since 1913 and he received a very harsh letter from Gasparri. He was informed that it was 'the desire, nay the command of the Holy Father' that Luigi Sturzo leave Italy forthwith and that 'if you want to, communicate this yourself to your brother, otherwise other means will be found to do so'.[61] This explains the curious letters in the Sturzo correspondence which he wrote to Monsignor Pizzardo on 28 September to tell him that he wanted to leave Italy to study abroad, and another three weeks later in which he told his brother that he was going to London 'at the wish of the well known person' who was clearly recognizable to Mario as Cardinal Gasparri.[62] Furnished with a Vatican diplomatic passport which he did not request, Sturzo left Rome on 25 October 1924 for what he and others thought would be a brief exile.[63] Twenty one years later, in October 1945, Sturzo thought that the day of his return was at hand. The Vatican thought otherwise because within its walls there remained 'hostility' to his return and the motives were still political.[64] On 6 September 1946 the 'Watchman' came home, this time for good. The ranks of those who had fought by his side had been thinned by death but amongst those who met him stood the little Roman lawyer Giuseppe Spataro who remained true to the end.

Back in Italy the long agony of dictatorship unfolded as Mussolini and his fascist regime tightened its grip on the whole apparatus of the state. The PPI survived for a time and held its last Congress in Rome in June 1925 where De Gasperi proved a worthy leader of the party but by December *Il Popolo* had been closed down by the government and there was no money left to keep a party structure in existence. De Gasperi begged for a word of comfort from Sturzo and Gronchi wrote to him 'I feel that I am alone: alone and sad'.[65] The word came but it was not of comfort and it was not from Sturzo whose name was soon forgotten except by those who had known and revered him.[66] It came from the man for whose accession to power Pius XI was initially so grateful. On the same day on which the Italian fascist parliament declared that all the 123 men who remained on the Aventine had forfeited their seats, it reintroduced the death penalty. The date was 9 November 1926 and the gesture was symbolic of a regime that left death as its historical legacy. Luigi Sturzo would have rejoiced that on that same day the motive given for the dissolution of his beloved party was that 'it engaged in activity contrary to the national order of the State'.[67] It was a good cause to which he had devoted both his manhood and his priesthood.

It is fitting to conclude this narrative with the words of three men who have figured largely in its pages. In many ways their words are an explanation or an apologia for the positions they took up in the 1920s. As such they serve to illustrate the fact that any man who faces the reality of his human existence demands the respect of those who come to narrate or to read his story. Not long before his death in 1939, when socialism was a mere memory in Italy and when fascism was triumphant in a semi-pantheistic state, when the joyfulness of conciliation between Church and state had turned to bitterness in the conflicts between Mussolini and Pius, the old pope said,[68]

> Late, too late in my life I have discovered that religion is threatened from more than one side; it is threatened from the other side also. For what remains of my life I will consecrate it to helping my children to share my discovery with me.

From his lonely exile in Paris, Francesco Luigi Ferrari addressed an appeal to the clergy of Italy which was distributed clandestinely. Entitled 'Justice and Liberty' it read in part,[69]

> Obedience and respect mean neither servility nor adulation. The Church of Christ is not and ought never to be a court where honours are reserved for him who best adapts himself to flattering the prince and where the one purpose of life is wealth

and promotion. Obedience and trust must be accompanied by the kind of Christian sincerity which leads a man to tell his superiors the truth and nothing but the truth.

Giuseppe Stragliati was one of the few former members of the PPI who remained by Sturzo's side in exile. He was in Paris when Ferrari died and he wrote later to Sturzo in anguish. His sorrow was not so much for the loss of that ardent spirit, but more because he felt compelled to tell Sturzo that his own spirit had suffered a loss. He told the priest that, while he remained a Christian, he no longer believed in the Church because 'Christ has absolutely nothing whatever to do with that outfit'. From London Sturzo replied,

> If we believe in the Church it is not because of the merits of Pius XI or of any other pope, nor will we leave it because of their unworthiness. We believe in the Church because Jesus Christ himself founded it.[70]

Notes

1. Any reader with a further interest in Farinacci can consult H. Fornaci, *Mussolini's Gadfly: Roberto Farinacci* (Nashville, 1971). On 28 April 1945 he was shot by partisans who, presumably, were unaware that he had helped to depose Mussolini in 1943.

2. As early as May 1923 De Stefani claimed that the economic situation had been 'radically bettered' and by 1924 the government asserted that it was well on the way to balancing the budget. See A. De Stefani, *L'opera finanziaria del governo fascista* (Rome, 1923), p. 35. For O'Connell see P. Nazzareno, 'L'attegiamento della stampa cattolica-moderata americana verso il Fascismo prima e dopo la Conciliazione' in G. Rossini (ed.), *Modernismo*, p. 55. On the role of industry in the rise of fascism all the other studies are summed up in the cryptic remark of RIS in 'Gli industriali e il regime' in B. Malinverni (ed.), *Civitas*, p. 245, 'fascism was financed before and after its rise by the fat purses of big industry. History will reveal this story.' RIS was writing in 1924.

3. The text is in *Popolo Nuovo*, 30 January 1924.

4. Ibid., 1 March 1924.

5. *Il Popolo*, 9 February 1924 quoting Sturzo who had been interviewed by *La Stampa*.

Martire later became a firm opponent of the regime. He was expelled from parliament and sent into exile. See F. Magri, *La Democrazia*, vol. 2, pp. 31–4.

6. *O.R.*, 24 January, 7, 10, 11–12, 21 February 1924. On 8 February 1924 *O.R.* reminded its readers that good Catholics had to act for 'the greater good of society and the country' but that they must not forget that such good was 'inseparable from morality and the Catholic religion... which is the premise and foundation of every other good'.

7. C.F. Weiss, 'Corporatism and the Italian Catholic Movement', PhD thesis, Yale 1955, pp. 107–8, defended Pius XI's abandonment of the PPI. To him it 'did not imply any value judgment on the Church's part, but was based on empirical influences which might have been drawn by the most democratic minded of Popes'. While it is difficult to object to the logic of this statement it is as well to bear in mind that Pius XI was not a democrat in any sense and that the source of those 'influences' was a fascist government constantly engaged in violence and gross deception.

8. E. Pucci, *La pace*, pp. 158–63.

9. *O.R.*, 31 March 1924. When Mussolini took another step in his religious pilgrimage on 28 December 1925 he did it comforted with the sentiments of Father Tacchi Venturi, S.J., who assured him that such an act would bring 'particular consolation to the Holy Father' and that God's blessing would comfort him 'under the weight of the immense labours undertaken for the fatherland and for religion'. His step was the celebration of a church marriage with his wife. See R. De Felice, *Mussolini il revoluzionario*, p. 80.

10. *Corriere d'Italia*, 27 March 1923.

11. *Popolo Nuovo*, 15 April 1924; *Avanti*, 11 April 1924.

12. P. Alatri, *L'antifascismo*, vol. 2, p. 40. Alatri quoted from Salvemini who said that Pius XI would have been even more strongly in favour of the regime had he thought the lower clergy would have supported him. Ibid.

13. See *Il Popolo*, 10, 11, 12, 13, 15 April 1924.

14. *O.R.*, 2 May 1924.

15. *Il Popolo*, 21 May 1924.

16. Sturzo to Rodinò, Rome, 6 and 7 March 1924. A.L.S., f. 94, c. 91 and f. 94, c. 92. Giorgio Montini was the father of Pope Paul VI. He remained a loyal member of the PPI until the end.

17. See the Declaration of Ferrari to the Party Directorate, Rome, 16 February 1924, and Ferrari to Sturzo, Rome, 17 February 1924, A.L.S., f. 94, c. 55 and f. 94, c. 57. On the role of the Italian exiles in the fascist era see A. Garosci, *Storia dei fuorisciti* (Bari, 1953).

18. A Schiavi, *La vita e l'opera di Giacomo Matteotti* (Rome, 1957), pp. 117–18, 124–5. See also G. Matteotti, *Scritti e discorsi*, intro. A.G. Casanova (Parma, 1974),

and P. Permali, *Lezioni sul antifascismo* (Bari, 1960), esp. F. Schiavetti, 'Il delitto Matteotti e l'Aventino', pp. 68–81.

19. G. Matteotti, *Un anno di fascismo* (Rome, 1923). The document still had value 10 years later. When the regime was inducing children in 1934 to join its youth movement Spataro gave it to his nine-year-old son to read. Spataro told Sturzo proudly that the boy 'spontaneously' refused to join the organization. Spataro to Sturzo, Aix les Bains, May 1934, A.L.S., f. 78A, c. 27.

20. *La Giustizia*, 31 May 1924; *Avanti*, 31 May 1924; G. Arfè, *Storia*, p. 363.

21. *O.R.*, 4 June 1924. Gronchi spoke in the name of the PPI and although he did not use the same terms as Matteotti he was sufficiently outspoken on the government's illegal methods to arouse the ire of the fascists. *Atti Parlamentari Camera*, 4 June 1924, vol. 1, pp. 144–55.

22. *O.R.*, 18, 25 June 1924 and E. Beyens, *Quatre ans à Rome 1921–1926* (Paris, 1934), pp. 235–6. Beyens was the Belgian ambassador to the Vatican and an intimate of Gasparri who told him that the pope had asked Gasparri to see them, to give them the pope's blessings and a rosary each.

23. Kulisciof to Turati, 16 June 1924, *Carteggio*, vol. VI, p. 206; F.L. Ferrari in *Il Domani d'Italia*, 29 June 1924.

24. It is probable that Mussolini was not directly involved in the murder but it is certain that its perpetrators feared no reprisal by him. It is absurd to suggest that his statesmanlike qualities prevented his complicity. See S. Maurano, *Ricordi di un giornalista fascista* (Milan, 1973), p. 31. For an excellent summary and a balanced view of the murder and its aftermath see A. Lyttelton, *The Seizure*, pp. 239–44.

25. *Corriere d'Italia*, 14 June 1924; *O.R.*, 16–17, 25 June 1924. The American Jesuits in their review *America* saw in the murder of Matteotti a greater motive to defend Mussolini who had 'to stabilize law and order'. See P. Nazzareno 'L'atteggiamento' in G. Rossini (ed.), *Modernismo*, p. 59.

26. The opposition simply refused to enter the Chamber without physically withdrawing from the parliament building itself.

27. C. Sforza, *L'Italia*, p. 131; Mario Montagnana in P. Alatri, *L'antifascismo*, col. 1, p. 116; F. Guarneri, *Battaglie*, p. 104.

28. *Il Popolo*, 1 July 1924.

29. Turati to Kulisciof, 26 June 1924, in *Carteggio*, vol. VI, pp. 233–4.

30. See *Popolo Nuovo*, 15–30 July 1924, and *Corriere d'Italia*, 17 July 1924.

31. Sturzo to Petrocchi, 13 August 1924, in G. Petrocchi, *Don Luigi*, p. 21.

32. *Corriere d'Italia*, 22, 28 June 1924.

33. Ibid., 17, 18 July 1924.

34. Ibid., 4, 9 July 1924. Mattei-Gentili was given responsibility for matters relating to religion. See *Relazione e schemi di disegni di legge* (Rome, 1925).

35. *O.R.*, 21–22 July 1924. That the Vatican was much preoccupied about the image Italy would present to visitors from the Catholic world during 1925 is constantly in evidence in *O.R*, throughout the latter half of 1924. F.L. Ferrari summed up in pungent words the role of the Holy Year in the Vatican denunciation of the PPI. According to him the Vatican felt that the PPI's opposition to the regime would 'disturb the tranquillity of the Holy Year' and that it opted to uphold the regime in order to ensure 'the appearance of internal tranquillity'. Thus Pius thanked the regime at the end of the Holy Year for all it had done to keep order. See F.L. Ferrari, *L'Azione*, p. 150.

36. *O.R.*, 24 July, 15 August 1924; Colombo is quoted in *L'Italia*, 17 January 1925.

37. *Il Popolo*, 27 July 1924.

38. *Avanti*, 30 September, 2 October 1924; in early 1924 Gramsci saw the real problem of the PPI as that of keeping intact its mass following, forgetting its past reformism and engaging in a decisive anti-fascist struggle. A. Gramsci, *La costruzione del partito comunista, 1923–1926* (Turin, 1971), p. 12.

39. *Civiltà Cattolica*, vol. 3, 2 August 1924, pp. 193–206.

40. Even the Catholic Centrum in Germany took the view that fascism was a good thing because it spelt the end of the forces of Italian liberalism and that Pius did right in preventing the establishment of links between the PPI and the socialists. In Germany Catholics were delighted at the progress made under Mussolini towards a solution to the Roman Question and thought the work of Don Sturzo was a mere 'pile of ruins'. See K.E. Lönne, 'Il fascismo italiano nel giudizio del cattolicesimo politico della Repubblica di Weimar' in G. Rossini (ed.), *Modernismo*, pp. 33, 36.

41. *Civiltà Cattolica*, vol. 3, 16 August 1924, pp. 303–6.

42. *OR.*, 14 August 1924. There were other views of the work of *Civiltà Cattolica* and Don Andrea Baraldi, parish priest of Saccolongo in the diocese of Padua, summed them up on 1 June 1925 in a letter to Father Rosa. He said that Mussolini had 'bought' both Rosa and his Journal and that it would be a good thing to suppress the Jesuits forthwith because both they and the pope were fascists. See quote in A. Fiocchi, *P. Enrico Rosa S.J.*, p. 190. The sad irony of the affair was that Rosa had been for years a firm friend of the PPI and took up his new stand in obedience to the pope.

43. See *Corriere d'Italia*, 14 August 1924. The new body had its headquarters in the central office of the newspaper. On the Centro see A. Carapeile, *Il Centro Nazionale Italiano. Origini scopo e attivita* (Rome, 1928), and R. Sgarbanti, *Ritratto*, pp. 155–62, 188–99. The founders of the Centro affirmed that, in their view, fascism drew 'its main inspiration from the Catholic religious faith'. They hoped that because of their stand they would one day 'have the honour to be remembered by whoever speaks of Italy in the first quarter of the twentieth century'. See 'Il Centro Nazionale' in B.

Malinverni (ed.), *Civitas*, pp. 293–303.

44. See F. Magri, *Atti*, pp. 686–7. De Rossi died in 1925.

45. *Popolo Nuovo*, 15, 30 August 1924; De Rossi was not quite as blunt as Igino Giordani who summed up the moral problem neatly by saying that the PPI could collaborate with a murderer but 'with a Marxist — no'. I. Giordani, *Rivolta cattolica*, p. 220. To Giordani 'The Church is a mother: not a concubine'. Ibid., p. 166.

46. *Il Popolo*, 31 August, 4 September 1924.

47. Ibid., 6 September 1924.

48. G. Sergi, 'Le Vane Scuse' in B. Malinverni (ed.), *Civitas*, pp. 237–43. Spataro says that one of the pseudonyms under which Meda wrote was Gino Sergi. See G. Spataro, *I Democratici*, fn. 1, p. 93.

49. *O.R.*, 10 September 1924.

50. *Corriere d'Italia*, 11 September 1924; *Il Popolo*, 11 February 1924.

51. *OR.*, 12, 14, 17 September 1924.

52. See G. Rossini, *Il movimento*, p. 169.

53. Giolitti to Corradini, 14 April 1925, in G. De Rosa, *Giolitti*, p. 25; see also *La Questione morale dopo le risultanze dell'istruttoria De Bono presso l'Alta Corte di Giustizia* (Rome, 1925), p. 12, and S. Colarizi, I *democratici all'opposizione. Giovanni Amendola e l'unione nazionale (1922–1926)* (Bologna, 1973).

54. L.R. Sanserverino, *Il movimento sindicale cristiano dal 1850 al 1939* (Rome, 1950), states that between the Christian social movement and fascism collaboration was impossible and that by July 1924 'the freedom of the union movement was, in practice, suppressed' (pp. 367–9).

55. This account of Sturzo's last few months in Italy is based on the reminiscenses of his close companion of those days, Giuseppe Spataro, in his *I Democratici*, pp. 111–14, his interview with me in Rome, 15 December 1974 and the letters in A.L.S. See also F. Piva and F. Malgeri, *Vita*, pp. 287–94.

56. Farinacci is quoted in G. Spataro, *I Democratici*, p. 113.

57. Nitti wrote to Sturzo from his own exile in Zurich on 24 December 1924 to tell him that Mussolini had made this statement about himself and Sturzo in 1923. Nitti also remarked 'I am happy that you are not in Italy [where there is] such vileness, such debasement of human dignity.' He also thought that fascism would come to an end 'presto'. A.L.S., f. 160A, c. 50.

58. *O.R.*, 17 September 1924.

59. See text in *Civiltà Cattolica*, vol. 4, 18 October 1924, pp. 167–9.

60. At this point in our interview on 15 December 1974 I remarked 'Unlike Fathers Pucci and Semeria'. Spataro smiled and was silent.

61. See G. De Rosa, 'Luigi Sturzo nella storia d'Italia', in *Cronache Parlimentari Siciliane*, November 1971, p. 1447.

62. Sturzo to Pizzardo, Rome, 28 September 1924, A.L.S., f. 140A, c. 1; Sturzo to Mario Sturzo, Rome, 18 October 1924, ibid., f. 117A, c. 19.

63. Sturzo to Salvemini, London, 3 February 1937, A.L.S., f. 17A, c. 7; Rufo Ruffo della Scaletta to Sturzo, Posillipo, 16 December 1924, ibid., f. 1115A, c. 87. The prince thought that Mussolini would soon fall and that the day of Sturzo's return was close. De Gasperi thought also that the absence would be brief and told Sturzo 'I and all the others have needed you badly'. De Gasperi to Sturzo, November 1924, ibid., f. 111A, c. 2. The greater part of this letter is in code. In fact Sturzo remained in exile until 1946.

64. Scelba to Sturzo, 11 April 1946, ibid., f. 196A, c. 419.

65. De Gasperi to Sturzo, Rome, 29 December 1925, ibid., f. 165A, c. 230. Gronchi to Sturzo, Milan, 19 January 1926, ibid., f. 165A, c. 206. Donati, editor of *Il Popolo*, was forced to flee to Paris in June 1925 where he died on 17 August 1931. Mussolini would not allow his wife to leave Italy to be present at his deathbed. On Donati see L. Bedeschi, *Giuseppe Donati* (Rome, 1959), and G. Donati, *Scritti politici*, intro., and notes by G. Rossini, 2 vols (Rome, 1956).

66. When Monsignor G. Galbiati, successor to Pius XI in the Ambrosian library wrote the life of the pope in 1939 Sturzo's name was not mentioned, but Mussolini was called 'the providential Man of colossal energy'. See G. Galbiati, *Papa Pio XI* (Milan, 1939), p. 224 and *passim*.

67. G. Spataro, *I Democratici*, p. 167. Many of those whose names were listed on that day as having 'lost their mandate' are worthy of remembrance. Among them were De Gasperi, Gramsci, Grandi, Gronchi, Jacini, Longinotti, Montini, Turati and Rodinò. See *O.R.*, 11 November 1926.

68. See C. Sforza, *L'Italia*, p. 148.

69. F.L. Ferrari, *L'Azione*, pp. 187–99.

70. G. Stragliati to Sturzo, Paris, 27 April 1933, A.L.S., f. 31A, c. 24; Sturzo to Stragliati, London, 4 March 1938, ibid., f. 95A, c. 41.

BIBLIOGRAPHY

A Note on Sources

The immense riches of Italian historical writing since 1945 make the task of the research worker both practical and pleasurable. Italian historians have published most of the relevant primary source material so that for the most part it is now possible to work from readily available sources. In this connection Professors De Rosa, Malgeri and Piva placed the Sturzo correspondence at my disposal and their knowledge of it facilitated my own work. Although I was unable to use Vatican archival material which was not then available on my period, I endeavoured to fill the gap by a thorough use of *Osservatore Romano*, *Civiltà Cattolica* and the hitherto little used Roman daily, *Corriere d'Italia*. I found the latter especially useful as it gave an insight into the mentality of the Catholic group who switched their support from the Partito Popolare to fascism after 1922. The translastions in this work are mine.

Books, Theses and Periodical Articles

Acta Apostolicae Sedis, vols 10–818, Rome, 1918–1926.

Agòcs, S., 'Christian Democracy and Social Modernism in Italy during the Papacy of Pius X', *Church History*, vol. 42, no. 1, March 1973.

Alatri, P., *L'antifascismo italiano*, 2 vols, Rome, 1971.

— *Le origini del fascismo*, 2nd edn, Novara, 1963.

Alessandrini, F., 'Un pontificato', *Studium*, vol. 6, June 1954.

Allegra, D., *Come ha operato il Vaticano nel corso del regime fascista a sostegno della reazione*, Rome, 1954.

Ambrosini, G., *Partiti politici e gruppi parlamentari dopo la proporzionale*, Florence, 1921.

Ambrosini, L., *Fra Galdino alla cerca per la coscienza politica dei popolari*, Milan 1920.

Ambrosino, V., 'Le Parti Populaire Italien', Univ. of Paris DES thesis, 1965.

Ambrosoli, L., 'Problemi della storia del Partito Popolare Italiano', *Rivista storica del socialismo*, October–December 1958.

Amendola, G., *La democrazia italiana contro il fascismo 1922–1924*, Naples, 1960.

Andreotti, G., *De Gasperi e il suo tempo*, 2nd edn, Verona, 1964.

Annuario pontificio per l'anno 1955, Vatican City, 1955.

Aquarono, A., *L'organizzazione dello stato totalitario*, Turin, 1965.

Aquilante, F., *Il Patto Gentilioni. Gli eletti coi voti dei cattolici alla XXIV legislatura*, Rome, 1914.

Are, G., *Economia e politica nell'italia liberale, 1890–1915*, Bologna, 1974.

Arfé, G., *Storia del socialismo italiano, 1892–1921*, Turin, 1965.

Arrò, A., *Il Partito Popolare e la Questione Romana*, Turin, 1919.

Aspetti della cultura cattolica nell'età di Leone XIII, ed. G. Rossini, Rome, 1961.

Gli atti dei congressi del Partito Popolare Italiano, ed. F. Malgeri, Brescia, 1969.

Atti del convengo di studio tenuto a Spoleto nei giorni 7–8–9 Settembre 1962, ed. G. Rossini, Rome, 1963.

Atti del convengo su 'I cattolici e la politica estera in Italia', Milan, 1966.

Atti Parlamentari, Camera dei Deputati, Discussioni, 1919–1921, vols I–X, 1921–3; vols I–IX, 1924–8; vols I–IX, Rome, 1920–9.

Atti Parlamentari, Camera dei Senatori Discussioni, 1919–1921, vols I–IV; 1921–3, vols I–V; 1924–7, vols I–IV, Rome, 1920–9.

Aubert, R., *Le Pontificat de Pie IX (1846–1878), Histoire de L'Eglise*, vol. 21, ed. A. Fliche and V. Martin, Paris, 1952.

Baldini, F., 'I discorsi programmatici del Partito Popolare Italiano', unpublished doctoral thesis, Istituto Luigi Sturzo, Rome, 1959–60.

Il Banco di Roma, ed. L. Splendore, Rome, 1913.

Banco di Roma, *Dall'impero di Roma all'impero fascista*, Rome, 1940.

— *Relazione del consiglio d'amministrazione e dei sindicati*, Rome, 1891.

Bandini, M., *Cento anni di storia agraria italiana*, Rome, 1963.

Barletta, M.A., 'L'Osservatore Romano ed il PPI', unpublished doctoral thesis, Istituto Luigi Sturzo, Rome, 1959–60.

Barzini, L., *The Italians*, New York, 1964.

Bedeschi, L., *I cattolici disubbidienti*, Rome, 1959.

— *La corrispondenza inedita fra Sturzo e Murri 1898–1906*, Bologna, 1972;

— *Dal movimento di Murri all'appello di Sturzo*, Milan, 1969.

— *Don Minzoni. Il prete ucciso dai fascisti*, Milan, 1973.

— *L'Emilia ammazza i preti*, Bologna, 1951.

— *Giuseppe Donati*, Rome, 1959.

— *I pionieri della D.C. Modernismo cattolico 1896–1906*, Milan, 1966.

— *Le origini della Gioventù Cattolica*, Rocca San Casciano, 1959.

— *Obbedientissimo in Cristo ... Lettere di don Primo Mazzolari al suo vescovo 1917–1959*, Vicenza, 1964.

Bellia, S., *Chiesa e stato nel pensiero di L. Sturzo*, Rome, 1956.

Bendiscioli, M., *Antifascismo e resistenza, Impostazioni storiografiche*, Rome, 1964.

— *La politica della Santa Sede (Direttivi–Organi–Realizzazioni) 1918–1938*, Florence, 1939.

Bendetto XV, i cattolici e la prima guerra mondiale, ed. G. Rossini, Rome, 1965.

Berselli, A., *L'opinione pubblica inglese e l'avvento del fascism 1919–1925*, Milan, 1971.

Bertoli, B., *Le origini del movimento cattolico a Venezia*, Brescia, 1965.

Beyers, B.E., *Quatre ans à Rome 1921–1926*, Paris, 1934.

Biagio, G., *Il Mezzogiorno dopo la guerra*, Naples, 1918.

Bierbaum, M., *Biografia de S.S. el Papa Pio XI*, Barcelona, 1924.

Bilmeyer, K. and Tuechle, H., *Storia della chiesa*, 4 vols, Italian ed., Brescia, 1969.

Binchy, D.A., *Church and State in Fascist Italy*, London, 1941.

Boggiani, P., *I due anni dell'episcopato genovese del Cardinale Pio Boggiani: Atti pastorali*, Acquapendente, 1922.

Bonomi, I., *Dal socialismo al fascismo*, Rome, 1924.

— *La politica italiana da Porta Pia a Vittorio Veneto 1870–1918*, 3rd edn, Turin, 1966.

— *La politica italiana dopo Vittorio Veneto*, Turin, 1953.

Brezzi, C., *Cristiani sociali e intransigenti, L'opera de Medolago Albani fino alla 'Rerum Novarum'*, Rome, 1971.

Brogio, F.M., *Italia e Santa Sede dalle Grande Guerra alla Conciliazione — Aspetti politici e giuridici*, Bari, 1966.

Buonaiuti, C.M., *Non Expedit. Storia di una politica, 1866–1919*, Milan, 1971.

Buonaiuti, E., *Pellegrino di Roma. La generazione dell'esodo*, Rome, 1945.

Cammett, J.M., *Antonio Gramsci and the Origins of Italian Communism*, Stanford, 1967.

Camp, R.L., *The Papal Ideology of Social Reform: a Study in Historical Development 1878–1967*, Leyden, 1968.

Candeloro, G., *Il movimento cattolico in Italia*, Rome, 1953.

— *L'Azione Cattolica in Italia*, Rome, 1945.

Cantono, A., *Il programma del 'Partito Popolare Italiano'*, Turin, 1919.

Caponigri, A.R., 'Don Luigi Sturzo', *Review of Politics*, vol. 14, 1952.

Cappelli, G., *La prima sinistra cattolica in Toscana*, Rome, 1962.

Caputo, C., 'L'enigma popolare', *Studi cattolici*, no. 132, February 1972.

Carapelle, A., *Il centro nazionale italiano. Origini, scopo e attività*, Rome, 1928.

— *Il cardinale Pietro Gasparri*, pref. A. Piolanti, Rome, 1960.

Caretti, S., *La rivoluzione russa e il socialismo italiano*, Pisa, 1974.

Carter, B.C., *Italy Speaks*, pref. L. Sturzo, London, 1947.

Casacca, N., *Il Papa e l'Italia*, Bologna, 1919.

Cassels, A., *Mussolini's Early Diplomacy*, Princeton, 1970.

Castelli, C., *Il Vaticano nei tentacoli del fascismo. La storia ignorata di una lotta sotterranea*, Rome, 1946.

— *La chiesa e il fascismo*, Rome, 1951.

Castronovo, V., *La stampa italiana dall'unità al fascismo*, Bad, 1973.

Catalano, F., *L'Italia dalla dittatura alla democrazia 1918–1948*, Milan, 1962.

— *Potere economico e fascismo. La crisi del dopoguerra 1919–1921*, Milan, 1964.

— *Storia dei partiti politici italiani*, Turin, 1965.

Cervelli, I., *I cattolici dall'unita alla fondazione del Partito Popolare*, Bologna, 1969.

Chabod, F., *L'Italia contemporanea, 1919–1948*, 4th edn, Turin, 1961.

Che cosa è il fascismo fascista? no. 1 of *I quaderni della cooperazione*, Rome, 1927.

Chiesa e stato attraverso i secoli, eds S.Z. Ehlen and J.B. Morrall, Italian trans, Milan, 1958.

Chiesa e stato nel pensiero di L. Sturzo, ed. F. Della Rocca, Rome, 1956.

Civardi, L., *Cenni storici dell'Azione Cattolica Italiana, 1865–1931*, Pavia, 1933.

— *Manuale di Azione Cattolica*, 2 vols, Pavia, 1926.

'Civitas'. *Antologia degli scritti più significativi apparsi dal 1919 al 1925 sulla rivista Civitas fondata e diretta da Filippo Meda*, ed. B. Malinverni, Rome, 1963.

Clough, S.B., *The Economic History of Modern Italy*, New York, 1961.

Codex Iuris Canonici with preface by Card. P. Gasparri, Vatican City, 1917.

Colarizi, Simona, *Dopoguerra e fascismo in Puglia, 1922–1926*

I democratici all'opposizione. Giovanni Amendola e l'unione nazionale 1922–1926, Bologna, 1973.

Il colloquio di un secolo fra cattolici e socialisti 1864–1965, ed. I. Giordani, Rome, 1966.

Il comportamento elettorale in Italia, ed. G. Galli, Bologna, 1968.

Congresso regionale Lombardo della società della Gioventù Cattolica Italiana, Brescia, 1923.

Corner, P.R., *Fascism in Ferrara*, Oxford, 1974.

Cortesi, L., *Le origini del Partito Comunista Italiano. Il PSI dalla Guerra di Libia alla scissione di Livorno*, Bari, 1972.

Crispolti, F., 'I confessioni di un clerico–fascista', *Vita sociale*, no. 23, September–December 1966.

— 'Il Partito Popolare Italiano', *Nuova antologia*, 16 February 1919.

— *Pio IX, Leone XIII, Pio X, Benedetto XV, Pio XI (Ricordi personali)*, Milan, 1939.

D'Alessandro, A., 'Il Banco di Roma e la guerra di Libia', *Storia e politica*, no. VII, July–September 1968.

Dalla Torre, G., *Azione Cattolica e Fascismo*, Rome, 1945.

— *I cattolici e la vita pubblica italiana*, 2 vols, Rome, 1962.

— 'Sul solco politico di un grande pontificato', *Vita e pensiero*, October 1957.

D'Ambrosio, F., *Bibliografia sturziana*, Naples, 1961.

Davidson, A., 'The Italian Communist Party 1921–1924: An Inner Party Dispute', *A.N.U. Historical Journal*, vol. 1, no. 1, October 1964.

De Felice, R., *Il fascismo. Le interpretazioni dei contemporanei e degli storici*, Bari, 1970.

— *Mussolini il duce. Gli anni del consenso 1929–1936*, Turin, 1974.

— *Mussolini Il rivoluzionario 1883–1920*, Turin, 1965.

— *Mussolini il fascista. La conquista del potere 1921–1925*, Turin, 1966.

— *La penultima ventura*, ed. Milan, 1974.

De Gasperi, A., *I cattolici dall'opposizione al governo*, Bari, 1955.

Del Bo, D., *Italian Catholicism in Crisis*, Milwaukee, 1957.

Del Giudice, V., and Renieri, A., *I massimi problemi del Partito Popolare innanzi al Congresso Nazionale di Napoli (8–10 Aprile 1920)*, Naples, 1920.

Del Giudice, V., *La Questione Romana ed i rapporti tra stato e chiesa fino alla conciliazione*, Rome, 1947.

Il delitto Matteotti tra Il Viminale e l'Aventino, ed. G. Rossini, Bologna, 1966.

Delle Donne, G., 'Reviste e dibattito politico', *Nuova antologia*, vol. 552, no. 109, 1974.

Delzell, C., *Mussolini's enemies. The Italian Anti-Fascist Resistance*, Princeton, 1961.

De Mattei, R., *Il problema della democrazia dopo l'Unità*, Rome, 1934.

De Rosa, G., 'L'Azione Cattolica e Il "Regime" nella prospettiva di F.L. Ferrari', *Humanitas*, no. 5, May 1958.

— *I conservatori nazionali. Biografia di Carlo Santucci*, Brescia, 1962.

— *La crisi dello stato liberale in Italia*, Rome, 1955.

— *Filippo Meda e l'età liberale*, Florence, 1959.

Bibliography

— *Giolitti e il fascismo. In alcune sue lettere inedite*, (with appendix, *Venti anni di politica nelle carte di Camillo Corradini*), Rome, 1957.

— 'Una lettera inedita del Cardinale Gasparri sul Partito Popolare', *Analisi e prospettivi*, no. 1, January–February 1959.

— 'Luigi Sturzo nella storia d'Italia', *Cronache Parlamentari Siciliane*, November 1971.

— *Il movimento cattolico in Italia dalla Restaurazione all'età giolittiana*, 2nd edn, Bari, 1972.

— *I partiti politici in Italia*, Bergamo, 1972.

— *Il Partito Popolare Italiano*, 2nd edn, Bari, 1972.

— *Rufo Ruffo della Scaletta e Luigi Sturzo*, Rome, 1961.

— *L'Utopia politica di Luigi Sturzo*, Brescia, 1972.

De Rossi, G., *Il Partito Popolare Italiano nella XXVI legislatura*, Rome, 1923.

— *Il primo anno de vita del Partito Popolare Italiano dalle origini al Congresso di Napoli*, Rome, 1920.

De Rossi Dell'Arno, G., *Pio XI e Mussolini*, Rome, 1954.

De Stefani, A., *Baraonda bancaria*, Milan, 1960.

— *L'opera finanziaria del governo fascista*, Rome, 1923.

Diggins, J.P., *Mussolini and Fascism. The View from America*, Princeton, 1972.

Dizionario dei termini politici, ed. G. Calchi Novate, Milan, 1972.

La Documentazione Cattolica, anno X, no. 8–9, 15 May 1923.

Donati, G., *Scritti politici*, with introductory notes by G. Rossini, 2 vols, Rome, 1965.

— *1919–1925 Dopoguerra e fascismo. Politica a stampa in Italia*, ed. B. Vigezzi, Bari, 1965.

Dore, G., *Dieci anni di lotta politica 1915–1925*, Città di Castello, 1947.

Due Risorgimenti: Pagine di storia italiana 1796–1947, eds L. Pasqualini and M. Saccente, Bologna, 1965.

L'economia italiana dal 1861 al 1961. Studi nel primo centenario dell'Unità d'Italia, ed. A. Fanfani, Milan, 1961.

Einaudi, M., and Goguel, F., *Christian Democracy in Italy and France*, Notre

Dame, 1952.

Einaudi, L., *Cronache economiche e politiche di un trentennio (1893–1925)*, 7 vols, Turin, 1961–5.

Le encicliche sociali dei papi da Pio IX a Pio XII, ed. I. Giordani, Rome, 1956.

Engel-Janosi, F., *Vom Chaos zur Katastrophe*, Wien München, 1971.

Fanelli, F., *Don Sturzo e il Partito Popolare Italiano*, Gubbio, 1923.

Fappani, A., *Guido Miglioli e il movimento contadino*, Rome, 1964.

Fascism: An anthology, ed. N. Greene, New York, 1968.

Federzoni, L., *Paradossi di ieri*, Milan, 1926.

Ferrara, M., *Luigi Sturzo*, Rome, 1925.

Ferrari, F. L., *Il Domani d'Italia*, ed. G. Dore, Rome, 1958.

— *L'Azione Cattolica e il regime*, Florence, 1957.

— *Le règime fasciste italien*, Paris, 1928.

Ferrero, G., *Da Fiume a Roma. Storia di quattro anni, 1919–1923*, Milan, 1923.

— *Le dittature in Italia. Depretis–Crispi–Giolitti–Mussolini*, Milan, 1924.

Filippo Turati attraverso le lettere di corrispondenti, 1880–1925, ed. A. Schiavi, Bari, 1947.

Finer, H., *Mussolini's Italy*, London, 1935.

Fiocchi, A., P. *Enrico Rosa S.J scrittore della Civiltà Cattolica 1870–1938. Il suo pensiero nelle controversie religiose e politiche del suo tempo*, Rome, 1957.

Fiori, G., *Vita di Antonio Gramsci*, Bari, 1974.

Fogarty, M.P., *Christian Democracy in Western Europe, 1820–1953*, London, 1957.

Fornari, H., *Mussolini's Gadfly: Roberto Farinacci*, Nashville, 1971.

A Free Church in a Free State?: The Catholic Church, Italy, Germany, France, 1864–1914, ed. E.C. Helmeich, Boston, 1964.

Galati, V.G., *La Democrazia Cristiana*, Milan, 1958.

— *Religione e politica. Popolari Liberali e Fascisti nella lotta politica del 1919–1924*, first published Turin, 1925, republished and edited by F. Malgeri, Brescia, 1966.

Galbiati, G., *Papa Pio XI*, Milan, 1939.

Galli, G., *I partiti politici*, Turin, 1974.

— *Storia del Partito Comunista Italiano*, 2 vols, Milan, 1958.

Gallo, M., *Mussolini's Italy. Twenty years of the Fascist era*, New York, 1973.

Gambasin, A., *Il movimento sociale nell'Opera dei Congressi 1874–1904*, Rome, 1958.

Gammaldi, A, 'II pensiero politico di Alcide De Gaspari e il programma della Democrazia Cristiana', unpublished doctoral thesis, Univ. of Rome, 1972–3.

Ganapini, L., *Il nazionalismo cattolico. I cattolici e la politica estera in Italia dal 1871 al 1914*, Bari, 1970.

Garosci, A., *Storia dei fuorusciti*, Bari, 1953.

Gaspari, C., *Opera tratta dagli scritti di Gaspari Colosimo 1916–1919*, Pompei, 1959.

Gaudenti, A.C., *Luigi Sturzo. Il Pensiero e le opere*, Rome, 1945.

Gemelli, A. and Olgiati, F., *Il programma del Partito Popolare Italiano come non è e come dovrebbe essere*, Milan, 1919.

Ghisalberti, C., *Storia costituzionale d'Italia 1849–1945*, Bari, 1974.

Ginnari, B., *Il Mezzogiorno dopo la guerra*, Naples, 1918.

Giolitti, G., *Discorsi extraparlamentari*, ed. N. Valeri, Turin, 1952.

— *Discorsi parlamentari*, 4 vols, Rome, 1953–6.

— *Memorie della mia vita*, 3rd edn, Milan, 1945.

Giordani, I., *Pionieri della Democrazia Cristiana*, Rome, 1945.

— *Rivolta cattolica*, Turin, 1925.

Giovannini, C., *Politica e religione nel pensiero della Lega Democratica Nazionale, 1905–1915*, Rome, 1968.

Gobetti, P., *La rivoluzione liberale. Saggio sulla lotta politica in Italia*, Turin, 1948.

Graham, R.A., *Vatican Diplomacy: A Study of the Church and State on the International Plane*, Princeton, 1959.

Gramsci, A., *La costruzione del Partito Comunista 1923–1926*, Turin, 1971.

— *Note sul Machiavelli. Sulla politica e sullo stato moderno*, Turin, 1949.

— *Il Risorgimento*, Rome, 1971.

Gregor, A.J., *The Ideology of Fascism: The Rationale of Totalitarianism*, New York, 1969.

Grieco, R., 'Le ripercussioni della rivoluzione russa in Italia', *Stato Operaio*, no. 1, November–December 1927.

Grilli, G., *Grande capitale, destra cattolica. Trent anni di vita politica italiana*, Florence, 1959.

— *La finanza vaticana in Italia*, Rome, 1961.

Gualerzi, G., *La politica estera dei popolari*, Rome, 1959.

Guarneri, E., *Battaglie economiche tra le due grandi guerre*, Milan, 1953.

Guasco, M., *Romolo Murri e il modernismo*, Rome, 1968.

Gui, L., *Il Partito Popolare Italiano e i patti agrari*, Rome, 1956.

Hales, E.E.Y, *The Catholic Church in the Modern World: A Journey from the French Revolution to the Present*, New York, 1960.

Halperin, S.W., *Mussolini and Italian Fascism*, New York, 1964.

— *The Separation of Church and State in Italian Thought from Cavour to Mussolini*, Chicago, 1937.

Hamilton, A., *The Appeal of Fascism*, New York, 1973.

Howard, E.P, *Il Partito Popolare Italiano*, Florence, 1957.

Italian Fascisms from Pareto to Gentile, ed. A. Lyttelton, London, 1973.

Italy from the Risorgimento to Fascism: An Enquiry into the Origins of the Totalitarian State, ed. A.W. Salomone, New York, 1971.

Jacini, S., *I popolari*, Milan, 1923.

— *Il regime fascista*, Milan, 1947.

— *Storia del Partito Popolare*, Milan, 1951.

Jemolo, A.C., *Chiesa e stato in Italia negli ultimi cento anni*, Turin, 1948.

Kirkpatrick, I., *Mussolini. A Study in Power*, New York, 1964.

Kothen, R.S.J., *L'enseignement social de L'eglise*, Louvain, 1949.

Labriola, A., *La dittatura della borghesia e la decadenza della società capitalistica*, Naples, 1924.

La lotta politica in Italia dall'unità al 1925, ed. N. Valeri, Florence, 1945.

Luigi Sturzo nella storia d'Italia: Atti del convegno internazionale di studi promosso dall'Assemblea Regionale Siciliana (Palermo–Caltagirone, 26–28 Novembre 1971), 2 vols, Rome, 1973.

Lussu, E., *Marcia su Roma e dintorni*, 2nd edn, Rome, 1945.

Luzzatto, G., *L'economia italiana del 1861 al 1894*, Milan, 1963.

Lyttelton, A., *The Seizure of Power. Fascism in Italy 1919–1929*, London, 1973.

Mack Smith, D., *Italy. A Modern History*, Ann Arbor, 1959.

Magister, Sandro, *La politica vaticana e l'Italia 1943-1978*, Rome, 1979

Magri, F., *L'Azione Cattolica in Italia*, Milan, 1953.

— *La Democrazia Cristiana in Italia*, 2 vols, Milan, 1954–5.

— *Nuove questioni di storia contemporanea*, Milan, 1968.

— *Un pioniere dell'Azione Cattolica Cristiana — Angelo Mauri 1873–1936*, Milan, 1956.

Malgeri, F., *La guerra libica, 1911–1912*, Rome, 1970.

Malvezzi, N., *Pio XI nei suoi scritti*, Milan, 1923.

Mangano, V., *La crisi della pace. Da Genova all'Aja*, Rome, 1922.

— *Il pensiero sociale e politica di Leone XIII*, Rome, 1931.

Marcucci-Fanello, G., *Don Minzoni*, Bari, 1974.

— *Don Pini*, Modena, 1972.

— 'G. Miglioli e il problema contadino', *Storia e politica*, October–December, 1968.

— *Storia della F.U.C.I.*, Rome, 1971.

Marini, G., *Storia del potere in Italia 1848–1967*, Florence, 1967.

Martini, A., *Studi sulla Questione Romana e la conciliazione*, Rome, 1963.

Martinolli, G., *La concezione politica di Luigi Sturzo*, Trieste, 1971.

Martire, E., *Filippo Crispolti. Note biografiche*, Milan, 1943.

Mastellone, S., *Uno scritto poco conosciuto di Franceso Luigi Ferrari*, Florence, 1969.

Matteotti, G., *Scritti e discorsi*, Parma, 1974.

— *Un anno di fascismo*, Rome, 1923.

Maurano, S., *Ricordi di un giornalista fascista*, Milan, 1973.

Maurilo, G., *Romolo Murri e il modernismo*, Rome, 1968.

Meda, F., *Pensiero ed azione. Conferenze e discorsi*, Milan, 1921.

— *Scritti scelti*, ed. G. Dore, Rome, 1959.

Megaro, G., *Mussolini in the Making*, London, 1938.

Melograni, P., *Gli industriali e Mussolini. Rapporti tra Confindustria e fascismo dal 1919 al 1929*, Milan, 1972.

— *Storia politica della Grande Guerra 1915–1918*, Bari, 1969.

Miglioli, G., *Con Roma e con Mosca. Quarant'anni di battaglie*, Cremona, 1945.

Misciatelli, P., *Fascisti e cattolici*, Milan, 1924.

Missiroli, M., *Una battaglia perduta*, Milan, 1924.

— *Il colpo di stato*, Turin, 1924.

— *Il fascismo e la crisi italiana*, Bologna, 1921.

— *L'Italia d'oggi*, Bologna, 1932

— *Polemica liberale*, Bologna, 1954.

Modernismo, fascismo, comunismo. Aspetti e figure della cultura e della politica dei cattolici nel '900, ed. G. Rossini, Bologna, 1972.

Mollat, C., *La Question Romaine de Pie VI à Pie XI*, Paris, 1932.

Molony, John, *A New Age of the Human Person*, ed., Melbourne, 1963

— *The Roman Mould of the Australian Catholic Church*, Melbourne, 1969.

— *The Worker Question: A new historical perspective on Rerum Novarum*, Melbourne and Dublin, 1991

— *By Wendouree*, Ballan, 2010.

Mongiardo, G., *Il pensiero sociale dell chiesa*, 2 vols, Vatican City, 1973.

Montanelli, I., *L'Italia di Giolitti*, Milan, 1974.

Monteleone, R., *Lettere al re*, Rome, 1973.

Moro, A., *Luigi Sturzo*, Rome, 1959.

Morrison, K.F., *The Investiture Controversy*, Chicago, 1971.

Mosca, G., *Il tramonto dello stato liberale*, Catania, 1971.

Il movimento cattolico bergamasco 1913–1921, Bergamo, 1921.

Murri, R., *Battaglie d'oggi*, 4 vols, Rome, 1903–4.

— *La Democrazia Cristiana Italiana*, Rome, n.d. probably 1945.

— *Dalla Democrazia Cristiana al Partito Popolare Italiano*, Florence, 1920.

Mussolini, B., *My Autobiography*, trans. R.W. Child, London, 1928.

— *Omnia opera*, eds E. and D. Susmel, 35 vols, Florence, 1951–63.

Un Nemico dei lavoratori: Il comunismo, no. 4 of *I quaderni delle cooperazioni*, Rome, 1927.

Nenni, P., *Storia di quattro anni 1919–1922*, Milan, 1946.

Nolte, E., *Three Faces of Fascism*, London, 1965.

Il Nord nella storia d'Italia, ed. L. Cafagna, Bari, 1962.

Il nuovo codice penale, intro S. Cicala, Rome, 1931.

Il nuovo codice di procedura penale, intro S. Cicala, Rome, 1931.

Olmi, E., *Alcide De Gasperi*, G. De Rosa historical consultant, television series R.A.I. Channel 1, 22, 29 October and 5 November 1974.

Omodeo, A., *L'eta del Risorgimento*, Naples, 1931.

Orlando, V.E., *Memorie, 1915–1919*, ed. R. Mosca, Milan, 1960.

— *I miei rapporti di governo con la Santa Sede*, 2nd edn, Milan, 1942.

Ottaviani, A., *Institutiones iuris publici ecclesiastici*, 2nd edn, Rome, 1936.

Pacelli, F., *Diario della Conciliazione*, Vatican City, 1959.

Il Papa e il fascismo, Federazione Giovanile Comunista Italiana, Rome, 1931.

The Papal Encyclicals in Their Historical Context, ed. A. Fremantle, New York, 1956.

Passerin, E., 'Recenti studi sull'Azione Cattolica in Italia tra Ottocento e Novecento', *Stadium*, no. 4, April 1954 and no. 5, May 1954.

Pastore, G., *Achille Grande e il movimento sindicale italiano del primo dopoguerra*, Rome, 1960.

Un Patto di Pace tra Popolari e Fascisti, Arezzo, 1925.

Pecora, G., *Don Davide Albertario. Campione del giornalismo cattolico*, Turin, 1934.

Permali, P., *Lezioni sull'antifascismo*, Bari, 1960.

Perticole, G., *La politica italiana nell'ultimo trentennio*, 3 vols, Rome, 1945.

Petrocchi, G., *Collaborazionismo e ricostruzione popolare*, Rome, 1923.

— *Don Luigi Sturzo. Note e ricordi*, Rome, 1945.

Pio XI nel trentesimo della morte 1939–1969. Raccolta di studi e di memorie, Milan, 1969.

Piva, F. and Malgeri, F., *Vita di Luigi Sturzo*, Rome, 1972.

Poulantzas, N., *Fascism and Dictatorship: The Third International and the problem of Fascism*, London, 1974.

Pucci, E., *La pace del Laterano*, 2nd edn, Florence, 1929.

La questione morale dopo le risultanze dell'istruttoria De Bono presso l'Alta Corte di Giustizia. Documento pubblicato a cura delle opposizioni seccesionisti, Rome, 1925.

Repaci., A., *La marcia su Rome*, 1st ed., 2 vols, Rome, 1963, new ed., 1 vol., Milan, 1972.

Relazioni e schemi di disegni di legge, Rome, 1928.

Le riviste di Piero Gobetti, eds L. Basso and L. Anderlini, Milan, 1961.

Rhodes, A., *The Vatican in the Age of the Dictators 1922–1945*, London, 1973.

Ritter von Lama, F., *Papst und Kurie in ihrer Politik nach dem Weltkrieg*, Bayern, 1925.

Rizzo, F., *Luigi Sturzo e la questione meridionale*, Rome, 1957.

The Roman Question: Extracts from the Despatches of Odo Russell from Rome 1858–1870, ed. N. Blackiston, London, 1972.

Roe, J.P., *Fascism, Masonry and the Vatican in Italy*, New York, 1927.

Romeo, R., *Breve storia della grande industria in Italia*, 3rd edn, Florence, 1967.

Rosa, F., *I partiti politici e 'L'Azione Cattolica' in Italia*, Rome, 1925.

Rosboch, F., *La politica finanziaria fascista*, Rome, 1924.

Rosengarten, F., *The Italian Anti-Fascist Press, 1919–1945*, Cleveland, 1968.

Rossi, Elena Aga, *Dal Partito Popolare alla Democrazia Christiana*, Rocca di San Casciano, 1969.

Rossi, Ernesto., *Il manganello e l'aspersorio, La collusione fra il Vaticano e il regime fascista nel Ventennio*, Florence, 1958.

Rossi, M.G., *Francesco Luigi Ferrari. Dalle leghe bianche al Partito Popolare*, Rome, 1965.

— *Il movimento cattolico bergamasco 1913–1921*, Bergamo, 1921,

— 'Movimento cattolico e capitale finanziaro: appunti sulla genesi del blocco clerico-moderato', *Studi storici XII*, no. 2, 1972.

Rossini, G., *De Gaspari e il fascismo*, Rome, 1974.

— *Il movimento cattolico nel periodo fascista. Momenti e problemi*, Rome, 1966.

Roveri, A., *Le origini del fascismo a Ferrara: 1918–1921*, Milan, 1974.

Ruffini, F., *Relazione tra stato e chiesa. Lineamenti storici e sistematici*, Bologna, 1974.

Rumor, M., *Omaggio a Luigi Sturzo*, Rome, 1964.

Sabbatucci, G., *I combattenti nel primo dopoguerra*, Ban, 1974.

Saggi sul Partito Popolare Italiano, Rome, 1969.

Salomone, A.W., *Italy in the Giolittian Era: Italian Democracy in the Making, 1900–1914*, Philadelphia, 1945.

Salvatorelli, L., *Pio XI e la sua eredità pontificale*, Turin, 1939.

— *La politica della Santa Sede dopo la guerra*, Milan, 1937.

— *Storia d'Italia nel periodo fascista*, Turin, 1956.

Salvemini, G., *Clericali e laici*, Florence, 1957.

— *Come siamo andati in Libia*, Florence, 1912.

— *L'Italia vista dall'America*, ed. E. Tagliacozzo, Milan, 1969.

— *Le origini del fascismo in Italia*, Milan, 1961.

— *Il Partito Popolare e la questione romana*, Florence, 1922.

— *Stato e chiesa in Italia*, ed. E. Conti, Milan, 1968.

— *Under the Axe of Fascism*, London, 1936.

Sanseverini, L.R., *Il movimento sindicale cristiano dal 1850 al 1939*, Rome, 1950.

Santarelli, E., *Il socialismo anarchico in Italia*, 2nd edn, Milan, 1973.

— *Storia del fascismo*, 3 vols, Rome, 1967–74.

Sarti, R., *Fascism and the Industrial Leadership in Italy 1919–1940. A Study in the Expansion of Private Power Under Fascism*, Berkeley, 1971.

Scalia, C., *L'etica nella scienza economica*, Rome, 1924.

Schiavi, A., *La vita e l'opera di Giacomo Matteotti*, Rome, 1957.

Scoppola, P., *La chiesa e il fascismo: Documenti e interpretazioni*, Bari, 1971.

— *Chiesa e stato nella storia d'Italia*, Bari, 1967.

— *Coscienza religiosa e democrazia nell'Italia contemporanea*, Bologna, 1966.

— *Crisi modernisti e rinnovamento cattolico in Italia*, Bologna, 1961.

— *Dal neoguelfismo alla Democrazia Cristiana. Antologia di documenti*, Rome, 1963.

— *La democrazia nel pensiero cattolico del novecento*, Turin, 1972.

— 'Il modernismo politico in Italia: Lega Democratica Nazionale', *Rivista storica italiana*, no. 69, 1957.

— 'Per una valutazione del popolarismo', *Quaderni di cultura e storica sociale*, no. 5, May 1953.

Scritti di sociologia e politica in onore di Luigi Sturzo, ed. Istituto Luigi Sturzo, 3 vols, Bologna, 1953.

Secchia, P., *L'azione svolta dal partito comunista in Italia durante il fascismo 1926–1932. Ricordi, documenti inediti e testimonianze*, Milan, 1970.

Secco Suardo, D., *I cattolici intransigenti. Studio di una psicologia e di una mentalità*, Rome, 1962.

— *Da Leone XIII a Pio X*, Rome, 1967.

Semeria, G., *I miei quattro papi*, Milan, 1930.

Seton-Watson, C., *Italy from Liberalism to Fascism, 1870–1928*, London, 1967.

Sforza, C., *L'Italia dal 1914 al 1944 quale io la vidi*, Rome, 1944.

— *Realtà politiche e formule economiche*, Rome, 1923.

Sgarbanti, R., *Ritratto politiche di Giovanni Grosoli*, Rome, 1959.

Silvestri, C., *Turati l'ha detto*, Milan, 1946.

Siniscalchi, AM., *Il fallimento del Partito Popolare*, Naples, 1923.

Il socialismo nella storia d'Italia. Storia documentaria dal Risorgimento alla Repubblica, ed. G. Manacorda, Paris, 1966.

Soderini, E., *Il pontificato di Leone XIII*, 3 vols, Milan, 1932–3.

Sotgiu, G., *L'Italia di Giolitti, (Testi, documenti)*, Cagliari, 1972.

Spadolini, G., *Giolitti e i cattolici 1901–1914*, Florence, 1960.

— *L'opposizione cattolica da Porta Pia al '98*, 3rd edn, Florence, 1955.

Spataro, G., *I Democratici Cristiani dalla dittatura alla repubblica*, Verona, 1968.

Spriano, P., *L'occupazione delle fabbriche. Settembre 1920*. Turin, 1964.

— *Storia del Partito Comunista Italiano*, 3 vols, Turin, 1967.

Stato e chiesa, ed. V. Gorresio, Bari, 1957.

Stefano Cavazzoni, ed. L. Cavazzoni, Milan, 1955.

Stella, P., *Il prete di Caltagirone. Don Luigi Sturzo*, Catania, 1971.

Sturzo, L., 'Christian Democracy in Italy', *The Commonweal*, 28 January 1944.

— *Church and State*, 2 vols, Notre Dame, 1962.

— *Democrazia e democratici*, Rome, n.d. circa 1950.

— *I discorsi politici*, Rome, 1951.

— *Figure del movimento Cristiano–sociale in Italia*, ed. Radio Italiana, n.d. circa 1950.

— *L'Italia di domani*, London, 1943.

— *Italy and Fascismo*, trans. Barbara Carter, London, 1926.

— *La Croce di Costantino*, ed. G. De Rosa, Rome, 1958.

— *Lettere ai Democratici Cristiani*, Rome, 1947.

— *Lotta di classe come legge di progresso*, Milan, 1902.

— *Il Partito Popolare Italiano*, 3 vols, Bologna, 1956.

— *Popolarismo e fascismo*, Turin, 1925.

— *Saggi e discorsi politici e sociali*, ed. C. Vincenzio, Rome, 1973.

Il Sud nella storia d 'Italia, ed. R. Villari, Ban, 1961.

Taliani, F.M., *Vita del Cardinale Gasparri segretario di Stato e povero prete*, Milan, 1939.

Talluri, B., 'La Civiltâ Cattolica e il fascismo 1922–1924', *Studi senesi*, vol. LXXVII (III Serie, XIV), Fasc. 2, 1965 and vol. LXXVII (Serie, XV), Fasc. 2, 1966.

Tannenbaum, E.R., *The Fascist Experience: Italian Society and Culture, 1922–1945*, New York, 1972.

Tasca, A., *I primi dieci anni del PCI*, Bari, 1971.

— *Nascita e avvento del fascismo*, Florence, 1950.

La terza pagina de Il Popolo 1923–1925 (Cattolici democratici e clerico-fascisti), ed. L. Bedeschi, Rome, 1973.

Togliatti, P., *Momenti della storia d'Italia*, 2nd edn, Rome, 1973.

Toniolo, G., *La Democrazia Cristiana*, Rome, 1900.

— *Opera omnia*, 16 vols, Vatican City, 1947–53.

Torregrossa, I., *Perchè sono democratico cristiano*, Rome, 1900.

Trimarchi, G., *La formazione del pensiero meridionalista di Luigi Sturzo*, Brescia, 1965.

Turati, F., and Kuliscioff, A., *Carteggio*, ed. A. Schiavi, vol. V, *Dopoguerra e fascismo (1919–1922)*, vol. VI, *Il delitto Matteotti e l'Aventino (1923–1925)*, Turin, 1953, 1959.

de T'Serclaes, C., *Le Pape Lèon XIII*, 3 vols, Paris, 1894.

Valente, G., *Aspetti e momenti dell'azione sociale dei cattolici in Italia 1892–1926*, ed. F. Malgeri, Rome, 1968.

Valeri, N., *Da Giolitti a Mussolini: momenti della crisi del liberalismo*, Florence, 1956.

— *Giovanni Giolitti*, Turin, 1971.

'Il Vaticano e Il fascismo', *Nuova antologia*, no. 109, vol. 522, 1974.

Vaussard., M., *Histoire de l'Italie contemporaire 1870–1946*, Paris, 1950.

— *Il pensiero politico e sociale di Luigi Sturzo*, Brescia, 1966.

Vercesi, E., *Il movimento cattolico in Italia 1870–1922*, Florence, 1923.

— *Il Vaticano, l'Italia e la guerra*, Milan, 1928.

Viana, M., *La monarchia e il fascismo*, Rome, 1951.

Vidler, A.R., *The Church in an Age of Revolution. 1789 to the present day*, London, 1961.

Vigezzi, B., *L'Italia di fronte alla prima guerra mondiale*, vol. 1, *L'Italia neutrale*, Milan, 1966.

Vigorelli, G., *Gronchi: Battaglie d'oggi e di ieri*, Florence, 1956.

Vistalli, F., *Benedetto XV*, Rome, 1928.

Vito, F., *Comunismo e cattolicesimo*, Milan, 1945.

Vittore, C., *Il socialismo. Suo valore teoretico e pratico*, Turin, 1900.

Vivarelli, R., *Il dopoguerra in Italia e l'avvento del fascismo (1918–1922)*, vol. 1, *Dalla fine della guerra all'impresa di Fiume*, Naples, 1967.

Vöchting, F., *La questione meridionale*, Naples, 1955.

Webster, R.A., *Christian Democracy in Italy 1860–1960*, London, 1961.

Weiss, C.F., 'Corporatism and the Italian Catholic Movement', Univ. of Yale, D. Phil. thesis, 1955.

Whyte, A.J., *The Evolution of Modern Italy*, Oxford, 1944.
Zangrandi, R., *Il lungo viaggio attraverso il fascismo*, Milan, 1962.
Zoppi, S., *Romolo Murri e la prima democrazia cristiana*, Florence, 1968.

Newspapers and Journals

Avanti
Civiltà Cattolica
Corriere della Sera
Corriere d'Italia
Domani d'Italia
Giornale d'Italia
La Giustizia
Idea Nazionale
Il Messaggero
Il Mondo
Ordine Nuovo
L'Osservatore Romano
Paese Sera
Popolo d'Italia
Il Popolo Nuovo
Il Popolo
Stato Operaio
L'Unità
Unità Cattolica
Voce Repubblicana

Periodicals

Analisi e prospettivi
A.N.U. Historical Journal
Church History
Humanitas
Nuova Antologia
Quaderni di cultura e storia sociale
Review of Politics
Rivista storica italiana
Rivista storica del socialismo
Storia e politica
Studi cattolici
Studi senesi
Studi storici
Studium
Vita e pensiero
Vita sociale

INDEX

Acerbo, Giacomo 142, 206, 216n
Adenauer, Konrad 6, 8, 119
Albertario, Davide 20, 41n
Amendola, Giovanni 162, 167n, 179, 245n
Angeli, Prof. 786, 136n
Aosta, Duke of 162
Aquinas, Thomas 23, 24, 71
Arezzo, Emanuele 45n

Badoglio, General Pietro 162
Balbo, Italo 138n, 212
Barduzzi, Carlo 200, 215n
Barrès, Maurice 97
Benedict XV xiii, 9, 36, 45n, 57, 65, 80n, 81n, 83, 141, 163n, 171, 190n, 202
Bertini, Giovanni 60
Bertone, Giovanni Battista 117, 137n
Bianchi, Michele 187
Bissolati, L. 154
Boggiani, Cardinal 99, 150, 165n
Boncompagni Ludovisi, F., 73, 185
Bonomelli, Bishop Geremia 15
Bonomi, Ivanoe 105n, 115, 119, 121, 122, 128, 129, 132, 134, 136n, 141, 145, 148, 154, 164, 165n
Bordiga, Amadeo 102
Buonaiuti, Ernesto 38n, 42n

Canaletti Gaudenti, Alberto 182
Candeloro, G 32, 42n, 43n, 44n
Cardijn, J. 26, 42n, 103
Cavazzoni, Stefano 49, 76n, 119, 120, 123, 137n, 144, 164n, 1725, 174, 188, 1925n, 198, 206, 208, 209, 216n, 221, 233.
Cerretti, Bonaventura 65
Child, Richard Washburn 204, 215n
Churchill, Winston 156
Ciano, Galeazzo 142
Cingolani, Mario 93
Colajanni, Napoleone 17
Colombo, Luigi 93, 211, 217n, 231, 233, 244n

Contarini, Salvatore 200
Cornaggio, Marchese Carlo Ottavio 194
Corradini, Camilo 159, 245n
Crispi, Francesco 20
Crispolti, Fiippo 84, 88, 105n, 106n, 190n, 209

Dalla Torre, Count Giuseppe 161, 171, 179, 212, 217n, 236
Dalser, Ida 154
D'Annunzio, Gabriele 36, 83, 115, 136n
D'Aragona, Ludovico 101
De Felice, Renzo 136n, 155, 165n, 167n, 243n
De Gasperi, Alcide 4, 6, 8, 62, 93, 107n, 119, 120, 133, 137n, 154, 164, 172, 182, 195, 203, 209, 214n, 216, 224, 229, 230, 234, 236, 239, 246n
Del Giudice, Vincenzo 91
De Nicola, Enrico 118, 134
De Rosa, Gabriele 107, 109n, 129, 136n, 138n, 139n, 164n, 165n, 166n, 167n, 189n, 192n, 214n, 215n, 245n, 246n, 247
De Rossi, Giulio 59, 77n, 112, 113, 119, 191n, 234, 236, 245n
De Stefani, Alberto 174, 183, 190n, 241n
Donati, Giuseppe 176, 177, 182, 183, 191n, 203, 212, 213n, 246n

Fanelli, Francesco 71, 81n, 167n
Farinacci, Roberto 116, 187, 192n, 219, 226, 231, 238, 241n, 245n
Federzoni, Luigi 231
Ferrara, Mario 55, 78n
Ferrari, Cardinal Carlo 98
Ferrari, Francesco Luigi 146, 164n, 166n, 167n, 174, 176, 182, 190n, 195, 205, 212, 213n, 216n, 224, 225, 227, 240, 241, 242n, 243n, 244n, 246n

Galli, Giorgio 1195, 213n
Galloni, G. 222

Gasparri, Cardinal Pietro xii, xiii, 9, 10, 49, 50, 53, 57, 71, 77n, 80n, 81n, 86, 88, 89, 93, 96, 97, 120, 123, 127, 129, 139n, 141-143, 150, 160, 163n, 164n, 171, 175, 179, 185, 186, 192n, 196, 199, 200, 202, 215n, 229, 237-239, 243

Gasti, G. 155, 156, 166n

Gemelli, Agostino 57, 61, 62, 69, 79n, 80n, 129

Gentiloni, Ottorino 33, 34, 35, 44n

George V, (England) 200

Giolitti, Giovanni 27, 28, 31, 34, 35, 44n, 45n, 78n, 87, 100-102, 114-118, 121, 123, 125, 129, 131-135, 136n, 137n, 139n, 144, 150, 159, 165n, 167n, 175, 189n, 237, 245n

Giordani, Igino 38n, 59, 245n

Gramsci, Antonio 40n, 228, 244n, 246n

Gronchi, Giovanni 4, 103, 206, 229, 243, 246n

Grosoli, Giovanni 24, 25, 58, 93, 209, 213n, 216n, 233

Guidi, Rachele 154

Harmel, Leon 23

Helleputte, J. 23

Howard, Edith Pratt 81n, 106n, 165n, 166n, 213n

Jacini, Stefano 4, 59, 72, 142, 160, 172

Jemolo, Arturo Carlo 74, 81n

John XXIII, Pope xiii, 12, 167n

Kulisicoff, Anna 135, 139n, 164n, 184, 190n, 204, 215n, 216n, 227, 243n

La Rosa, Luigi xi, xiv

Leo XIII, Pope 1, 7, 15, 17, 18, 21, 23, 32, 33, 39n, 56, 60, 64, 68

Longinotti, Giovanni Maria 33, 60, 224, 246n

Lussu, Emilio, 146, 164n, 167n

Lyttelton, Adrian 136n, 195, 213n, 243n,

Mangano, Vincenzo, 39n, 237

Margherita, Queen 208

Marolli, Luigi 94

Martire, Egilberto 74, 93, 105n, 108n, 158, 194, 202, 208, 209, 221, 234, 235, 236, 242n

Matteotti, Giacomo xii, 84, 115, 122, 128, 144, 158, 165n, 167n, 190n, 193, 225-228, 230-232 232, 242n, 243n

Mauri, Angelo 85, 105n, 164n

Meda, Filippo 25, 33, 37, 44n, 51, 78n, 79n, 91, 93, 95, 98, 100, 108n, 109n, 114, 119, 120, 134, 136n, 138n, 142, 144, 148, 149, 164n, 165n, 173, 178, 183, 206, 207, 214, 216n, 221, 234, 245n

Meda, Gerolamo 182, 196

Medolago Albani, Stanislao 20, 25, 40n, 42n

Merlin, Umberto 224, 234

Miglioli, Guido 36, 45n, 51, 60, 67, 69, 79n, 80n, 86, 91-93, 107n, 115, 116, 123, 125, 136n, 176, 182, 194, 208, 216n

Minzoni, Giovanni 211, 212, 217n, 222

Missiroli, Mario 451, 77n, 137n, 139n, 165n, 195, 198, 214n

Modigliani, Giuseppe Emanuele 122, 144

Monterisi, Nicola 12

Montini, Giorgio 224, 242n

Murri, Romolo 17, 19-26, 29-31, 40n, 42n, 43n, 44n, 47, 55, 56, 61, 78n, 79n, 172, 177, 182, 212

Mussolini, Benito xii, xiii, 1, 2, 3, 7, 31, 36, 38, 76, 77n, 78n, 86, 104, 125-127, 136n, 138n, 142, 145, 147, 149-153, 155, 156, 158, 161-162, 164n, 165n, 166n, 169-179, 181-188, 189, 192n, 194-201, 204, 206-208, 211, 212, 213n, 214n, 215n, 216n, 219, 220, 222, 223

Mussolini, Edda 154

Nava, Cesare 154, 194

Nenni, Pietro 151, 165n, 169, 187, 193

Nicoletti, Dr Luigi 210

Nitti, Francesco Saverio xi, xiv, 60, 70, 73, 74, 80n, 81n, 83, 87, 90, 93, 95, 96, 97

O'Connell, Cardinal 177, 179, 180, 184

Olgiati, Francesco 61, 62, 69, 80n

Orlando, Vittorio Emanuele 65, 93, 134, 148
Osio, Arturo 90

Pacelli, Ernesto 33
Pacelli, Eugenio 12
Paganuzzi, G. B. 21, 24, 70, 80n, 125, 126, 138n
Palermi, Paul 161
Pericoli Paolo, 93
Pestalozza, Antonio 197, 214
Petrocchi, Giuseppe 138n, 230, 243
Pignatelli, Prince Michele 129
Pius IX 10, 13, 15, 39n, 64, 163n
Piux X 24, 29, 35, 36, 42n, 44n, 65, 212
Pius XI xi, xiii, 1, 7, 145, 149, 150, 156, 158, 163n, 170, 178, 179, 180, 184, 190n, 191n, 194, 196, 197, 212, 216n, 227, 230, 237, 239, 240, 241, 242n, 246n
Pius XII 12, 33
Pizzardo, Monsignor Giuseppe, 210, 217n, 239, 246n
Pozzi, Arrigo 98, 108n
Pucci, Monsignor Ernesto 126, 163, 184, 191n, 201-204, 213n, 222, 245n

Ratti, Achille 129, 141, 142, 143, 161, 163n
Rocco, Alfredo 201
Rodino, Giullo 60, 119, 128, 164n, 196, 206, 224, 242n, 246n
Roncalli, Angelo 12, 167
Rosa, Enrico 55, 65n, 108n, 174, 178, 232, 244n
Rughi, Father 125

Salandra, Antonio 35, 36, 135
Salvemini, Gaetano 35, 45n, 53, 64, 75, 77n, 81n, 106n, 138n, 164n, 166n, 213n, 217n, 241n, 246n
Sangnier, Marc 24
Santucci, Carlo 50, 73, 88, 93, 157, 174, 179, 183, 185, 192n, 209, 238
Sarto, Cardinal 24
Seipel, Monsignor Ignaz 88, 202
Semaria, Giovanni 66, 182, 210, 245n
Sergi, Gino 234

Serrati, Giacinto 145, 187, 193
Sforza, Carlo 88, 159, 228
Soderini, Edoardo 33, 166n
Spataro, Giuseppe xii, 4, 107, 108n, 144, 148, 164n, 166n, 173, 182, 191, 192n, 206, 207, 209, 216n, 237-239, 243n, 245n, 246n
Stragliati, Giuseppe 241
Suarez, F. 71
Suhard, Emanuel 12

Tacchi Venturi, Pietro 201, 242n
Tangorra, Vincenzo 172, 174, 183, 190n
Tedeschi, Giacomo Radini 12
Tittoni, Tommaso 27
Togliatti, Palmiro 76n, 87
Tovini, Livio 136n, 194, 198, 202, 221
Toniolo, Giuseppe 20, 41n
Treves, Claudio 66, 90, 101, 102, 150, 158, 165n, 228
Turati Filippo 85, 101, 102, 109n, 114, 135, 143, 145, 146, 147, 150, 151, 158, 165n, 177, 191n, 205, 207, 208, 22-230

Vacirca, Vincenzo 86
Valente, Giambattista 103
Valeri, Nino 133, 136n
Vannutelli, Cardinal 186, 201
Vigorelli, Remo 68
Vittorio Emanuele III, 2, 36, 162, 167n

Wilson, Woodrow 52, 66, 197

Zanetti, Francesco 63

www.ingramcontent.com/pod-product-compliance
Ingram Content Group UK Ltd.
Pitfield, Milton Keynes, MK11 3LW, UK
UKHW041415180426
11947UKWH00007B/139